S

W9-AQN-392

DATE DUE

May 4	

BRODART, CO.   Cat. No. 23-221

STONY THE ROAD

ALSO BY HENRY LOUIS GATES, JR.

WRITTEN BY:

Figures in Black: Words, Signs, and the Racial Self

The Signifying Monkey: A Theory of Afro-American Literary Criticism

Loose Canons: Notes on the Culture Wars

Colored People: A Memoir

The Future of the Race, with Cornel West

Thirteen Ways of Looking at a Black Man

Wonders of the African World

*The Trials of Phillis Wheatley: America's First Black Poet and
Her Encounters with the Founding Fathers*

In Search of Our Roots

Tradition and the Black Atlantic: Critical Theory in the African Diaspora

Life Upon These Shores

Black in Latin America

The African Americans: Many Rivers to Cross, with Donald Yacovone

And Still I Rise: Black America since MLK, with Kevin M. Burke

100 Amazing Facts about the Negro

Dark Sky Rising: Reconstruction and the Dawn of Jim Crow, with Tonya Bolden

EDITED BY:

The Norton Anthology of African American Literature, with Nellie Y. McKay

Africana: The Encyclopedia of the African and African American Experience,
with Kwame Anthony Appiah

The Image of the Black in Western Art, with David Bindman

The New Negro: Readings on Race, Representation, and African American Culture, 1892–1938,
with Gene Andrew Jarrett

African American National Biography, with Evelyn Brooks Higginbotham

Dictionary of African Biography, with Emmanuel K. Akyeampong

Dictionary of Caribbean and Afro-Latin American Biography, with Franklin W. Knight

The Annotated African American Folktales, with Maria Tatar

STONY
THE ROAD

Reconstruction,
White Supremacy,
and the Rise of
Jim Crow

HENRY LOUIS GATES, JR.

PENGUIN PRESS
NEW YORK
2019

PENGUIN PRESS
An imprint of Penguin Random House LLC
penguinrandomhouse.com

Copyright © 2019 by Henry Louis Gates, Jr.
Penguin supports copyright. Copyright fuels creativity, encourages diverse voices,
promotes free speech, and creates a vibrant culture. Thank you for buying an
authorized edition of this book and for complying with copyright laws by not
reproducing, scanning, or distributing any part of it in any form without
permission. You are supporting writers and allowing Penguin to
continue to publish books for every reader.

Section on the European roots of the Harlem Renaissance as seen through the eyes
of Victoria Earle Matthews and Picasso's impact on black artists from *The African
Americans: Many Rivers to Cross* by Henry Louis Gates, Jr., and Donald Yacovone,
published by Hay House, Inc., Carlsbad, California, 2013. Used by permission
of the publisher. (This text appears in different form in this book.)

Illustration credits appear on pages 295–296.

LIBRARY OF CONGRESS CATALOGING-IN-PUBLICATION DATA
Names: Gates, Henry Louis, Jr., author.
Title: Stony the road : Reconstruction, white supremacy, and the rise of Jim Crow /
Henry Louis Gates, Jr.
Description: New York : Penguin Press, 2019. |
Includes bibliographical reference and index.
Identifiers: LCCN 2018056211 (print) | LCCN 2019000788 (ebook) |
ISBN 9780525559542 (ebook) | ISBN 9780525559535 (hardcover)
Subjects: LCSH: African Americans--Segregation--History. |
Reconstruction (U.S. history, 1865-1877) | African Americans--History--1863-1877. |
African Americans--History--1877-1964. | White supremacy movements--United
States--History. | Racism in popular culture--United States--History. |
Visual communication--Social aspects--United States--History. |
United States--Race relations--History--19th century. |
United States--Race relations--History--20th century.
Classification: LCC E185.61 (ebook) | LCC E185.61 .G253 2019 (print) |
DDC 973/.0496073--dc23
LC record available at https://lccn.loc.gov/2018056211

Printed in the United States of America
1 3 5 7 9 10 8 6 4 2

Designed by Amanda Dewey

Dedicated to
The Mother Emanuel Nine

In memory of

*The Reverend Clementa Pinckney, South Carolina state senator
and senior pastor of Mother Emanuel AME Church,
and his fellow worshippers,
The Reverend Sharonda Coleman-Singleton
Cynthia Hurd
Susie Jackson
Ethel Lee Lance
The Reverend DePayne Middleton-Doctor
Tywanza Sanders
The Reverend Daniel Lee Simmons, Sr.
Myra Thompson*

*Martyrs to White Supremacy
Charleston, South Carolina
June 17, 2015*

CONTENTS

The holders of twenty hundred million dollars' worth of property in human chattels procured the means of influencing press, pulpit, and politician, and through these instrumentalities they belittled our virtues and magnified our vices, and have made us odious in the eyes of the world. Slavery had the power at one time to make and unmake Presidents, to construe the law, dictate the policy, set the fashion in national manners and customs, interpret the Bible, and control the church; and, naturally enough, the old masters set themselves up as much too high as they set the manhood of the negro too low. Out of the depths of slavery has come this prejudice and this color line. It is broad enough and black enough to explain all the malign influences which assail the newly emancipated millions today.

In reply to this argument it will perhaps be said that the negro has no slavery now to contend with, and that having been free during the last sixteen years, he ought by this time to have contradicted the degrading qualities which slavery formerly ascribed to him. All very true as to the letter, but utterly false as to the spirit. Slavery is indeed gone, but its shadow still lingers over the country and poisons more or less the moral atmosphere of all sections of the republic.

The office of the color line is a very plain and subordinate one. It simply advertises the objects of oppression, insult, and persecution. It is not the maddening liquor, but the black letters on the sign telling the world where it may be had. . . . The color is innocent enough, but things with which it is coupled make it hated. Slavery, ignorance, stupidity, servility, poverty, dependence, are undesirable conditions. When these shall cease to be coupled with color, there will be no color line drawn.

—FREDERICK DOUGLASS, "The Color Line,"
North American Review, June 1881

The most magnificent drama in the last thousand years of human history is the transportation of ten million human beings out of the dark beauty of their mother continent into the new-found Eldorado of the West. They descended into Hell; and in the third century they arose from the dead, in the finest effort to achieve democracy for the working millions which this world had ever seen. It was a tragedy that beggared the Greek; it was an upheaval of humanity like the Reformation and the French Revolution. Yet we are blind and led by the blind. We discern in it no part of our labor movement; no part of our industrial triumph; no part of our religious experience. Before the dumb eyes of ten generations of ten million children, it is made mockery of and spit upon; a degradation of the eternal mother; a sneer at human effort; with aspiration and art deliberately and elaborately distorted. And why? Because in a day when the human mind aspired to a science of human action, a history and psychology of the mighty effort of the mightiest century, we fell under the leadership of those who would compromise with truth in the past in order to make peace in the present and guide policy in the future.

—W. E. B. DU BOIS, *Black Reconstruction in America*, 1935

PREFACE

The writing of this book was occasioned by a documentary film series that I was producing for PBS concerning the period after the Civil War known as Reconstruction (1865–1877)—when the United States, at least in theory, attempted to come to terms with its original sin of slavery—and the period known as Redemption immediately following, when the gains of Reconstruction were systematically erased and the country witnessed the rise of a white supremacist ideology that, we might say, went rogue, an ideology that would long outlast the circumstances of its origin. I define the Redemption era as starting in 1877, when the last of the former Confederate states were reclaimed by Southern Democrats, and reaching its zenith in horror—the highest point of the lowest low—with the screening by President Woodrow Wilson at the White House in 1915 of D. W. Griffith's *The Birth of a Nation.* The film was an unapologetic, blistering attack on what the Redemptionist Griffith saw as the appalling tragedy that Reconstruction had been, represented through a dazzlingly effective marshaling of racial pornography in the emerging language of the motion picture.

These were years of only the most nominal freedom for most African Americans, and successive generations of black people would attempt to stem the tide of racism that was engulfing many of the gains of equal rights and equal protections made under the Thirteenth, Fourteenth, and Fifteenth Amendments through the concept of a New Negro, a phenomenon that began in 1894 and culminated in 1925, with the birth of the Harlem Renaissance. Accordingly, this book is an intellectual and cultural history of black agency and the resistance to and institutionalization of white supremacy.

In a sense, the kernel of the idea for this film and book was formed at Yale University during the 1969–1970 academic year, my very own *annus mirabilis*, when I was a sophomore studying the wonders of African American history. The yearlong survey course, whose syllabus began in 1619 and the first of its kind I'd ever taken, ended abruptly in mid-April, when the university voted to engage in a "moratorium" on classes in sympathy (and solidarity) with the Black Panther leader Bobby Seale, who was on trial in New Haven as part of the New Haven Nine. The doors to the classroom hadn't been closed, however, before I encountered for the first time the period known as Reconstruction, the years following the Civil War that witnessed the election or appointment, officially, of approximately two thousand black officeholders, "from sheriffs to senators," as the historian Eric Foner puts it.[1] Neither this period nor these admirable men who took their seats in the halls of Congress such a short time after slavery had ended had been part of any American history course I had taken in high school. Our class, taught by the Pulitzer Prize–winning historian William S. McFeely, was assigned two books that have shaped my understanding of Reconstruction since: W. E. B. Du Bois's *Black Reconstruction in America* (1935) and Rayford W. Logan's *The Betrayal of the Negro: From Rutherford B. Hayes to Woodrow Wilson* (1965). (Both Du Bois and Logan, incidentally, earned their PhD degrees in history from Harvard.) Whereas Du Bois records and celebrates the many achievements that black people made in the all-too-brief decade or so that usually defines the period, Logan deftly chronicles the racist reaction to Reconstruction during Redemption (a term that, before this course, had been unknown to me and that still today verges on the obscure and unfamiliar to most), when the former Confederate states "redeemed" themselves at the expense of black rights, especially the right of black men to vote. In other words, I learned about Reconstruction and its odious alter ego, as it were, in back-to-back assigned readings in our class. I have connected Reconstruction with Redemption ever since, as the apex and nadir, as Logan termed it, of the African American experience. I have long wanted to make a documentary series about it, and to write about it.

That same academic year, I took a seminar in the history department with David Griffith on the period known as the Harlem Renaissance, which I would later learn was sometimes also called the New Negro Renaissance. I was fascinated by the concept of a "New Negro" and wrote a paper in which I attempted to trace its origin. (I didn't get very far!) But I also tried my best to examine the irony of feeling forced to claim a condition of "newness" that inevitably entailed a criticism and rejection of the old. There couldn't exist a New Negro without some sort of condemnation of the Old Negro. Who was this Old Negro? And how did we spot a new one? I would return to the subject of the New Negro several times as my career as a professor of African American literature evolved, first in an essay for the journal *Representations*, and then more fully in a book that I coedited with a fellow literary scholar, Gene Jarrett, which included many essays published about the concept of a New Negro between 1894 and the end of the Harlem Renaissance. Since that book was published, I've found even more essays and iterations of the concept of a New Negro and have updated my thoughts about the evolution of this curious idea here, establishing firmly that the New Negro was born as a response to the dynamic Southern orator and *Atlanta Constitution* editor Henry Grady's Redemptionist claim, first articulated in 1874 in an essay in his paper, of the birth of a "New South," and as an elaboration of the African American journalist and historian George Washington Williams's mandate exactly ten years later, in 1884: "We want, we demand leaders, first of all, who are not ashamed of the race." One decade later, in 1894, the New Negro was born, christened by a white man but quickly adopted and embraced by successive generations of the African American cultural elite.

In this book, I attempt to show that the New Negro was the black community's effort to roll back Redemption, which was itself a rollback to Reconstruction, and to do so by coining a metaphor, of all things, and then by seeking to embody that metaphor. The period between 1894 and 1925 that saw a succession of redefinitions and reconfigurations of the trope of the New Negro reveals black agency at its most creative and, perhaps, its most dispirited, when an all-out assault on black rights and black bodies by white supremacist ideology expressed itself in a plethora of forms and forced the backs of African American leaders to the proverbial wall. Desperate times call for desperate measures, and redefining who and what a "Negro" is was the black intellectual's inventive, if sometimes ironic, response. The discourse of the New Negro is endlessly fascinating to me, and I've tried to share my fascination in the penultimate chapter of this book.

If we ask ourselves why black people would feel the need to invent a New Negro in the decade in which Jim Crow segregation was rising, the answer is perhaps because the onslaught on the Old Negro had been so brutally effective. On one level, this book is a close reading of the history of the use of this imagery in the larger war to kill Reconstruction and any thought of realizing the promise of the Fourteenth Amendment's Equal Protection Clause (not to mention the Fifteenth Amendment's voting rights protections). Simultaneously, this book tells the history of the use of imagery embodying the counternarrative by black people themselves in civic and cultural self-defense. I want to explicate the sharp differences between Jim Crow imagery—varied, pervasive, and devastating—and the artistic weapons African Americans themselves deployed in response, not only through successive iterations of a New Negro, but also in literature, photography, musical composition, theatrical performance, painting, sculpture, and women's club movements, among other cultural and social forms. In doing so, another dichotomy emerged even within African American discourse between the stereotyped and debased "Old Negro" (rural, Southern, impoverished, illiterate, premodern, "uncivilized," even "unwashed") and the New Negro (increasingly urban and urbane, modern, educated, cultured, international, professional, well attired and well appointed, "clean," both literally and figuratively). This dichotomy sometimes took the most basic, elemental forms, as Booker T. Washington exemplified when he preached the "gospel of the toothbrush" to the first generation of freed slaves, actively admonishing them to employ a toothbrush, a bar of soap, and all manner of hygiene products.

The historical backdrop to this war of imagery is the story of Reconstruction and the rise of Jim Crow segregation: the enormous promise of emancipation, the revolution of Reconstruction (national rebirth, birthright citizenship, the franchise, black institution building, and perhaps the most promising and most threatening development of all, the sudden expression of black political power), and its tragic unraveling at the hands of a recalcitrant South and an ever more indifferent North. At the nadir—the political, economic, social, and legal hardening around segregation—violence, disenfranchisement, and lynching coincided with a scientific, cultural, intellectual, and artistic hardening of antiblack racist concepts of "race." That process of dehumanization triggered a resistance movement to the counterrevolution that had taken down Reconstruction among a rising generation of the black elite that then laid the foundation for the civil rights revolution to come in the twentieth century, starting with Ida B. Wells's campaign against lynching in 1892, W. E. B. Du Bois's Niagara Movement in 1905, then the birth of the NAACP four years later, and culminating in the civil rights movement led by Martin Luther King, Jr., and others, which reached its zenith with the passage of the Civil Rights Act of 1964 and the Voting Rights Act of 1965.

The title of this book is taken from the second verse of James Weldon Johnson's canonical poem "Lift Every Voice and Sing." Today we know it best as the Negro National Anthem—the NAACP declared it so in the post–World War I years—but it had its origins in a segregated school in Johnson's hometown of Jacksonville, Florida. Johnson wrote the poem to commemorate the ninety-first birthday of Abraham Lincoln, itself commemorated by a visit to the school by Booker

T. Washington, for whom the students performed the poem (set to music by the poet's brother, John Rosamond Johnson) for the first time, on February 12, 1900. How appropriate that Johnson, a Victorian sage, a brilliant polymath, and one of the proverbial "deans" of the coming Harlem Renaissance, wrote it in honor of Booker T. Washington, for some the very first embodiment of the New Negro.

Because the poem constitutes the lyrics to this anthem, it is undoubtedly the most popular poem—at least its first verse—ever written by an African American poet. Read closely and you'll see its second verse is a lesson in black history, a meditation on the history of the Negro from Reconstruction through Redemption to the birth of a New Negro at the turn of the century. Its second verse begins with reflections on slavery:

> *Stony the road we trod,*
> *Bitter the chast'ning rod,*
> *Felt in the days when hope unborn had died.*

These lines record the anguish of Redemption:

> *We have come over a way that with tears has been watered.*
> *We have come, treading our path through the blood of the slaughtered.*

And these lines, out of sequence, look to the birth of a new era, the era of the New Negro, at the dawning of the twentieth century:

> *Yet with a steady beat, have not our weary feet,*
> *Come to the place for which our fathers sighed?*

> *Out from the gloomy past, till now we stand at last*
> *Where the white gleam of our bright star is cast.*[2]

Many of us know precious little about Reconstruction, a period filled with such great hope and expectations for the freedwomen and freedmen, but one that was far too short to ensure a successful transition from slavery to freedom, from bondage to free labor, for the almost four million black human beings who found themselves in perpetual slavery on the eve of the Civil War. What confounds me is how much longer the rollback of Reconstruction was than Reconstruction itself; how dogged was the determination of the "Redeemed South" to obliterate any trace of the marvelous gains made by the freedpeople, especially the prodigious number of black men who exercised the right to vote and the emergence of a black political leadership class within just a few years of emancipation. Moreover, the painfully long period following Reconstruction saw the explosion of white supremacist ideology across a baffling array of media and through an extraordinary variety of forms, from print to art. The visual essays punctuating each chapter present an illustrative sampling of these images, some designed to warp the mind toward white supremacist beliefs, while others counteract the mendacity and visual distortions of white supremacy with images made of, by, and for black artists, intellectuals, and citizens. These images, deployed through time in the push and pull of revolution and reaction, were themselves weapons in the battle over the status of African Americans in post-slavery America, and some continue to be manufactured to this day. I offer them to readers here without comment in an effort to avoid detracting from the power they possess. They speak for themselves.

Although, as I've mentioned, I have been interested in Reconstruction and its unfortunate aftermath since I was an undergraduate, and I have been teaching works by black authors from the second half of the nineteenth century for decades, the urgency of making a film about the period first struck me, curiously enough, in 2008, during an interview with Chris Rock for my PBS series *African American Lives 2*, in which we traced the ancestry of several well-known African Americans. When I told Chris that his great-great-grandfather Julius Caesar Tingman had served in the US Colored Troops during the Civil War, enrolling on March 7, 1865, a little more than a month after the Confederates evacuated from Charleston, South Carolina, he was brought to tears. But there was more: I then explained to Chris that seven years later, while still a young man in his mid-twenties, this same ancestor was elected to the South Carolina House of Representatives as part of that state's Reconstruction government. Chris was flabbergasted, his pride in his ancestor rivaled only by gratitude that Julius's story had been revealed at last. "It's sad that all this stuff was kind of buried and that I went through a whole childhood and most of my adulthood not knowing," Chris said. "How in the world could I not know this?" I realized then that even descendants of black heroes of Reconstruction had lost the memory of their ancestors' heroic achievements. I decided that I would try to do something about that. The result is our PBS series and this book.

What seems clear to me today is that it was in this period that white supremacist ideology, especially as it was transmuted into powerful new forms of media, poisoned the American imagination in ways that have long outlasted the circumstances of its origin. You might say that anti-black racism once helped fuel an economic system, and that black crude was pumped and freighted around the world. Now, more than a century and a half since the end of slavery in the United States, it drifts like a toxic oil slick as the supertanker lists into the sea. When Dylann Roof murdered the Reverend Clementa Pinckney and the eight other innocents in Mother Emanuel AME Church in Charleston, South Carolina, on June 17, 2015, he didn't need to have read any of the history recounted in this book; it had, unfortunately, long become part of our country's cultural DNA and, it seems, imprinted on his own. I have written this book both to celebrate the triumphs of African Americans following the Civil War and to explain how the forces of white supremacy did their best to undermine those triumphs in all the years since, through to the present.

Henry Louis Gates, Jr.
West Tisbury, Massachusetts
July 29, 2018

STONY THE ROAD

One

ANTISLAVERY/
ANTISLAVE

The only place the American historian could find for the colored man was in the background of a cotton-field, or the foreground of a canebrake or a rice swamp, to adorn the pages of geography, and teach the rising generations of civilized and Christianized America the true position of the generous Negro. . . . But a change has come over the spirit of their dreams. . . . [O]ld things are passing away, and eventually old prejudices must follow. The revolution has begun, and time alone must decide where it is to end.

—C. P. S., "The Crisis," *Pacific Appeal* 24, September 13, 1862

I actually think the great evil of American slavery wasn't involuntary servitude and forced labor. The true evil of American slavery was the narrative we created to justify it. They made up this ideology of white supremacy that cannot be reconciled with our Constitution, that cannot be reconciled with a commitment to fair and just treatment of all people. They made it up so they could feel comfortable while enslaving other people. . . . [S]lavery didn't end in 1865; it just evolved. . . . The North won the Civil War, but the South won the narrative war.

—BRYAN STEVENSON, *Vox* magazine interview, May 2017

The hope engendered by the triumphant election of Barack Obama as the first black president of the United States called to mind other exhilarating historical moments for African Americans, especially during the Civil War and Reconstruction, including the signing of the Emancipation Proclamation on January 1, 1863, the ratification of the Thirteenth Amendment on December 6, 1865 (which legally abolished slavery), and the passage of the Reconstruction Acts, which inspired a collective sense of optimism among formerly enslaved African Americans, "a millennial sense of living at the dawn of a new era," in the words of Eric Foner.[1] At the dawn of a new era in the next millennium, President Obama's election, unthinkable even a decade before and unprecedented in its potential implications for ameliorating race relations, led some commentators to speculate about an "end of race and racism" narrative. Among the many writers who embraced this optimistic idea was the novelist and philosopher Charles R. Johnson, who argued even in the summer before Obama was elected, "It is no longer the case that the essence of black American life is racial victimization and disenfranchisement, a curse and a condemnation, a destiny based on color in which the meaning of one's life is thinghood, created even before one is born."[2] Regardless of the outcome, Johnson argued, the brilliance and poise that Obama displayed during his campaign alone would spur the country to "transcend parochialism, tribalism, and that most pernicious of fictions—race."[3] Obama had written far more cautiously in *The Audacity of Hope* two years before his election that "such prejudices" were "subject to refutation."[4] Johnson may have been one of the first writers to embrace this idea, but he was far from alone. Claims about the dawn of "a post-racial America" led the Harvard sociologist Lawrence D. Bobo to reflect upon the several different manifestations of this phenomenon in a searching critique published in 2011.[5] Looking back roughly two years after Donald J. Trump's election, the idea that one black person's occupancy of the White House—and a presidency as successful as his—could have augured the end of race and racism seems both naïve and ahistorical.

Obama's election, to my enormous surprise, revived an old metaphor with a long and curious history in African American letters, that of a New Negro, a "new" kind of black person. For example, Johnson aptly characterized the Obamas' many strengths in this way: "Eloquent and elegant, charismatic and holding [degrees] from Harvard Law, always comfortable in [their] skin, [Barack] and Michelle are also avatars of a new black America."[6] The professor and political historian Ronald Williams made the link between Obama and the metaphor of the New Negro explicit in a perceptive essay titled "The New Negro in African American Politics."[7] Invoking the metaphor of the New Negro to account for the extraordinary feat that Barack Obama achieved unwittingly connected the Obama presidency to the optimism and expectations—and severe disappointments—of the rise and fall of Reconstruction, in the aftermath of which the metaphor itself was first coined as a complex defensive mechanism that black people employed to fight back against racial segregation. This book is about that optimism and those expectations, the painful manner in which they crumbled, and the creative manner in which African Americans sought to counter Jim Crow segregation as it systematically rolled back the dramatic, once unimaginable gains that they had achieved in the decade or so following the end of the Civil War.

We might think of the New Negro as Black America's first superhero. It was, as we shall see, the shrewd and canny, if complicated, black response to the claim of the birth of a "New South," a phrase coined by the charismatic white supremacist journalist Henry Grady as early as 1874, but then popularized in a widely commented-upon speech he delivered to a New York audience twelve years later in 1886. The declaration of the existence of a New South only a decade after the end of Reconstruction was warmly embraced by key interests in the North and signaled the triumph of the South's "Redemption." Grady's metaphor was intended to demonstrate to the North, in seductive, easily digestible language that the South—though it had nothing for which to apologize, and most certainly not the institution of slavery—had reinvented itself following the war and had now achieved "the perfect democracy," precisely as it was aggressively dismantling the advances in rights that black people had enjoyed during Reconstruction. That's how Grady packaged it anyway. Redemption, as the civil rights attorney Bryan Stevenson points out, essentially imposed a system of neo-enslavement on the South's agricultural workers, who were the recently freed African Americans and their children.

Grady's clever declaration of the birth of a New South unfolded as part of what we might say amounted to a terrorist campaign against the freedmen and freedwomen, waged not only through physical violence and intimidation, but also through a massive wave of propaganda hell-bent on permanently devaluing the freedpeople's very humanity—often referred to in scientific literature of this period as "the nature of the Negro"[8]—on defining who, and what, a black person actually "was," within or, alarmingly, outside of the human community. This propaganda war was so brutally effective that it demanded a response from black people themselves in all available media. One such response was the declaration of the advent of a so-called New Negro, a postwar phenomenon that stood as evidence that the disparaging claims about the Negro's beastlike "nature" were horribly mistaken. So powerful was the trope of the New Negro that one is tempted to say that it has turned out to be, ironically, one of the most lasting legacies of the long Reconstruction era. Indeed, the philosopher and critic Alain Locke, who appropriated the term in 1925 for his own purposes at the apex of the Harlem Renaissance, would later argue that every generation of African Americans needed to renew itself through successive "New Negro Movements."[9]

Why the reconstitution of a supposedly New Negro? It became a necessity, it was argued, because the image of the Old Negro had been so devastatingly deconstructed by the "redeemed" South in the rollback of Reconstruction. This process calls to mind the alt-right–fueled rollback of policies pivotal to President Obama's legacy under the counterrevolution being led by his successor, President Donald J. Trump.[10] Who could have predicted that the election of the first black president would become a focal point for triggering a dramatic rise in the public expression of some of the oldest, nastiest, and most vulgar white supremacist animus about black people? That reactionary rancor extended a tradition that had begun with the defense of slavery long before the Civil War and continued throughout it—indeed, the 1864 presidential election was full of fearmongering over the supposed racial "amalgamation" that would follow if Lincoln won another term—taking on new and equally energetic forms of venality well into the twentieth century. This desperate effort to reassert white supremacy and decimate the gains in black equality promised by Reconstruction led to the effective disenfranchisement of black male voters in the former Confederate states and the imposition of "separate but equal" as the law of the land. While white supremacist ideologies never disappeared, I think that many of us, viewing Obama's election as the culmination of the successes of the civil rights movement, had convinced ourselves that the more excessive forms of white supremacy had gone deep underground, or at least lay dormant. But because these beliefs continue to manifest themselves so very openly today in the wake of the end of the two terms of the first black president, it is useful to retrace their history as well as the manner in which black people and their allies so nobly fought back against them through a variety of strategies ranging from political action to symbolic gestures at the level of representation, such as the invention of the concept of a New Negro. In that sense, when hopeful commentators hailed the election of the first black president by employing this metaphor, they unintentionally reconnected Black America, full circle, to an earlier period when the fight against white supremacy was literally a life-and-death struggle.

A LOOK AT RECONSTRUCTION

The eruption of the expression of white supremacist ideology in what increasingly appears to be a determined attempt to roll back the very phenomenon of a black presidency is just one reason that the rise and fall of Reconstruction and the surge of white supremacy in the former Confederate states following the end of the Civil War are especially relevant subjects for Americans to reflect upon at this moment in the history of our democracy. In fact, I'd venture that few American historical periods are more relevant to understanding our contemporary racial politics than Reconstruction. Think of the fundamental questions that the study of the period forces us to consider: Who is entitled to citizenship? Who should have the right to vote? What is the government's responsibility in dealing with terrorism? What is the relationship between political and economic democracy? These are all Reconstruction questions. Reconstruction—when the country intended to institutionalize for its black citizens what President Lincoln had called "a new birth of freedom"—saw the passage of the country's first civil rights laws and the amending of the Constitution, forming the basis of the rights revolution of the modern era that continues to this day, most recently in the ruling that established the right to marry without discrimination based on gender or sexual preference.[11]

One of the most shocking things to realize about Reconstruction is how painfully short it was, compared to the dreadfully long duration of slavery. Though scholars differ on when Reconstruction began—whether in 1861 or 1863 or 1865—it was clearly on the road to ending by the Panic of 1873, the first "Great Depression" in post–Civil War America, and suffered a devastating political blow just four years later, with the Compromise of 1877, which, in the most stripped down of terms, secured the election of Republican Rutherford B. Hayes by giving him the electoral votes of Democratic South Carolina and Louisiana in exchange for a promise to withdraw the remaining federal troops from those statehouses. Regardless of its brevity, Reconstruction remains one of the most pivotal eras in the history of race relations in American history—and probably the most misunderstood.

When the Civil War began in 1861, Reconstruction was really a process question: If and when the Union was saved, how would the eleven states that had seceded to form the Confederacy be reabsorbed? On that the US Constitution was silent. Improvisation would prove unavoidable.

As the rebellion dragged on and the war hardened, the definition of Reconstruction changed. There could be no "reconstructing" the Union as it had been. With the aim of the struggle eventually expanding from saving the Union alone to saving it by emancipating the Confederacy's slaves (and with the arming of those brave black men among them willing to fight and die for the cause), Reconstruction took on a double meaning: both of readmitting the conquered Confederate states to the Union and of granting freedom, citizenship, and a bundle of political, civil, and economic rights to African Americans—both those free *before* the war and those freed *by* it. Reconstruction, in this sense, meant repairing what the war had broken apart while simultaneously attempting to uproot the old slave system and the ideology underpinning it that had rationalized the process of making property of men a "black and white" issue. As the historian David Blight says, Reconstruction at once called for both "healing" and "justice," and those competing ends would not only remain in tension throughout the period; they would also prolong an enormous amount of racial violence until Reconstruction itself was overthrown.[12]

The process of Reconstruction involved nothing less than the monumental effort to create a biracial democracy out of the wreckage of the rebellion. Though that effort ultimately was thwarted, Reconstruction saw the passage of a vast array of legislation aimed at transforming the status of the formerly enslaved, beginning with Congress's passage of the Civil Rights Act of 1866, the nation's first federal civil rights law. The ratification of the Thirteenth, Fourteenth, and Fifteenth Amendments in 1865, 1868, and 1870, respectively, permanently altered the status of African Americans under the US Constitution. And, after seizing control of Reconstruction policy from President Andrew Johnson, who had called for a speedy readmission of the former Rebel states (as they hastily set about imposing a series of harsh "Black Codes" on the freedmen and freedwomen almost as soon as the war ended), Congress, between March 1867 and March 1868, passed four successive Military Reconstruction Acts that carved the defeated Southern states (save Tennessee) into five military districts and required them to hold elections for new constitutional conventions, which wouldn't be deemed legitimate unless black men were given the vote. They also had to ratify the Fourteenth Amendment, which, among other things, established birthright citizenship and prohibited any state from "abridg[ing] the privileges or immunities of citizens of the United States," "depriv[ing] any person of life, liberty, or property, without due process of law," or "deny[ing] to any person within its jurisdiction the equal protection of the laws."

During the longer Reconstruction era, including the Redemption period that followed it, an estimated two thousand black men served in office at every level of government, including two US senators and twenty congressmen, from Hiram Revels (Republican from Mississippi), who took office in the Senate on February 25, 1870, and Joseph Rainey (Republican from South Carolina), who joined the House on December 12 of that same year; to George Henry White (Republican from North Carolina), who took office in the US House of Representatives on March 4, 1897, and left office on March 3, 1901.

White was the last African American to serve in either house of Congress until Oscar Stanton De Priest, a Republican from Chicago, took office in the House on March 4, 1929, in the midst of the New Negro movement. His election reflected Chicago's changing demographics resulting from the influx of black people from the former Confederate states during the Great Migration. In other words, the black people who had been impoverished by the South's agricultural economy and disenfranchised by white supremacist state constitutions and legislation not only migrated to cities in the North for work, but voted when they did so, effectively fighting back from their new homes against the dismantling of their rights in their old homes. The South would wait even longer to see the return of black representation post-Reconstruction. It wasn't until 1972 that Georgia and Texas elected Andrew Young and Barbara Jordan, respectively, to the US House of Representatives. For North Carolina, it would be another twenty years from this milestone, with the electoral victory of Eva Clayton in 1992.

With the aid of the Freedmen's Bureau, created shortly before the Civil War's end, on March 3, 1865, to assist former slaves in matters relating to education, health, contracts and legal dealings, and often elusive land ownership, African Americans reconstituted families torn apart by the slave system, exercised their right to marry, and navigated the transition to the contract-based free labor system. They pursued land for farming, and, even when that promise was betrayed, they persevered, building businesses, churches, schools, and other legacy institutions. They attained literacy, educated their children, and created art, literature, and other cultural forms to express the African American experience, including singing

"The First Colored Senator and Representatives,"
lithograph, Currier & Ives, New York, 1872.

the spirituals that bonded them to generations of their ancestors for whom freedom was, in the words of Langston Hughes, the ultimate "dream deferred."[13]

In the broadest terms, Reconstruction was a revolutionary time in American life—a time of national renewal extended out from four years of Civil War, death, and destruction that narrowed the gap between the country's ideals and laws and advanced racial progress. Yet it was also a turbulent and brutally violent period, one marked by rapid economic change and new forms of white resistance that included everything from organized paramilitary assaults and political assassination to night rides and domestic terror.

Over time, the federal military occupation that enabled the nation's bold experiment in what could be called biracial democracy lost support among the cost-conscious and war-weary parts of the political and economic leadership in the North. The Panic of 1873 and the economic depression that followed it further sapped the civic will and led many voters to cast blame on the party in charge in Washington since the Civil War: the Republican Party, without whom Reconstruction would have been a dream without a policy or a prayer. Year after year, election after election, the counterrevolution led by white Southern Democrats only intensified until their crusade to "redeem" the former Confederate states knocked down every last domino. By 1877, Redemption governments enveloped the South in what was euphemistically described as "home rule" (as opposed to the federal military occupation, which Southerners had derided as "bayonet rule"). Eventually these governments paved the way for a spate of Jim Crow segregation laws and the wholesale disenfranchisement of black voters at the end of the nineteenth century that would bring the African American people to what Rayford Logan called "the nadir"—the rock-bottom lowest point in American race relations—during which time, Logan argued, African Americans suffered a "continued decline, in recognition of [their] political and legal rights."[14] Moreover, he continued, in the last decade of the nineteenth century, "the South launched a counterattack that further curtailed the already diminished rights of the Negro,"[15] a counterattack perhaps best exemplified—certainly most dramatically exemplified—in the film *The Birth of a Nation*, with its depictions of ignorant, unqualified, venal black elected officials whose most ardent desire seems to have been to rape white women. Images like this would dominate, both consciously and unconsciously, the popular image of Reconstruction for most Americans until the necessary process of revision began in earnest with W. E. B. Du Bois's *Black Reconstruction in America* in 1935. The book would take its place as a canonical work in the long struggle by historians to recapture Reconstruction from Redemption's apologists, a process realized by Eric Foner's monumental study, *Reconstruction: America's Unfinished Revolution, 1863–1877*, published more than half a century later, in 1988. This process of revision continues in remarkable detail and subtlety to this day.[16]

Reconstruction revealed a fact that had been true but not always acknowledged even before the Civil War: that it was entirely possible for many in the country, even some abolitionists, to detest slavery to the extent that they would be willing to die for its abolition, yet at the same time to detest the enslaved and the formerly enslaved with equal passion. As Frederick Douglass said, "Opposing slavery and hating its victims has become a very common form of abolitionism."[17] Being an advocate of the abolition of slavery was not the same thing as being a proponent of the fundamental equality of black and white people, or the unity of the human species (as we shall see in chapter 2 of this book), to say nothing of equal citizenship rights and equal protection under the law. A dismaying example is Abraham Lincoln himself, hailed by so many African Americans, after the Emancipation Proclamation, as our Moses. Learning that Abraham Lincoln, who undoubtedly deplored slavery, reportedly used the N-word can be every bit as jarring for some black people as learning that there's no Santa Claus.[18] Similarly, Lincoln's ambivalent attitudes about race and the colonization of freed black people either in South America or back to Africa can be difficult to reconcile. Lincoln's views, however, were in the process of evolving positively as the Union headed to victory over the Confederacy, in part because of his relationship with Frederick Douglass, and in part because of the crucial role that the heroism of the black soldiers of the US Colored Troops played in the Union's victory; in fact, by 1864, Lincoln was referring to them as his "black warriors."[19]

The distinction between supporting the abolition of slavery and supporting—indeed, even *believing in*—equal rights for the formerly enslaved emerged well before the Civil War. The *New York Times*, just two days following the signing of the Emancipation Proclamation, noted one of the concerns arising from slavery's abolition: "If the Proclamation makes the slaves actually free, there will come the further duty of making them work. . . . All this opens a vast and most difficult subject."[20] A political cartoon printed soon after the abolition of slavery in the British Empire in 1833 had raised the same concern.

The odd notion that an enslaved black person would work and that a free black person would not was only one example of a deeper racist

"An Emancipated Negro," George Cruikshank, lithograph, 1833.

ideology that emerged in debates over abolition and the future of free black citizens. ("Whence comes the assertion that the 'nigger won't work'?" an Alabama freedman asked, ironically noting, "We used to support ourselves and our masters too when we were slaves and I reckon we can take care of ourselves now.")[21] In fact, the well-known Boston abolitionist Wendell Phillips (whose written endorsement of Frederick Douglass appeared in his original 1845 slave narrative) no doubt spoke for many when he publicly worried about this aspect of the Emancipation Proclamation, concerned that it "frees the slave and ignores the negro."[22]

Phillips had reason to be anxious. Consider the case of Andrew Johnson, then the military governor of Tennessee. Johnson declared his support for the abolition of slavery at the end of 1863, but, as Eric Foner writes, "his conversion . . . was based less on concern for the slave than hatred of the Confederacy and of the slaveholders he believed had dragged poor whites unwillingly into rebellion. As he remarked to General Palmer, 'Damn the Negroes, I am fighting those traitorous aristocrats, their masters.'"

By war's end, the connection between being antislavery and antislave would become patently apparent. "Slavery is dead," the *Cincinnati Enquirer* proclaimed when the war concluded; but "the negro is not, [and] there is the misfortune." Foner notes that at the Maryland Constitutional Convention during the middle of the Civil War, delegates celebrated a "free and regenerated" Maryland; "however, little concern was evinced for the fate of the former slaves. Many delegates," Foner adds, "felt compelled to deny that voting for abolition implied 'any sympathy with *negro equality*.'" A Maryland Unionist remarked, after the constitution won narrow approval in a referendum held in the fall of 1864: "There has been no expression, at least in this community, of regard for the negro—for human rights." As the diarist and self-described gentleman from Philadelphia Sidney George Fisher stated bluntly: "It seems our fate never to get rid of the Negro question. No sooner have we abolished slavery than a party, which seems [to] be growing in power, proposes Negro suffrage, so that the problem—What shall we do with the Negro?—seems as far from being settled as ever. In fact it is *incapable* of any solution that will satisfy both North and South."[23] Despite the presence of antiblack racism in the North, many white Northerners were willing to accept black legal and political equality as very few in the South were. That included, in a few Northern states, the right to vote.[24]

It is important to remember that there were those in the North, such as Charles Sumner and Thaddeus Stevens, who were both antislavery and, as it were, "pro-slave," without whom Reconstruction would never have happened. Of course, there were many who were neither. White supremacist beliefs certainly predated the Civil War and Reconstruction, in both the North and the South. Frederick Douglass frequently excoriated Northern racism as a sort of evil twin of proslavery sentiment in the South, and he suffered a considerable amount of jeering, harassment, and even physical abuse during abolitionist rallies at which he was a speaker. In fact, he once wrote, he "could not remember to have made a single antislavery tour [during which he had] not been assailed by this mean spirit of caste."[25] In "Prejudice against Color," an essay that he published on June 13, 1850, in his paper the *North Star*, he provided a definition of "prejudice" that could easily have been one of white supremacy as well: "Prejudice against color does not exist in this country," he began ironically. "The feeling (or whatever it is) which we call prejudice, is no less than a *murderous, hell-born hatred* of every virtue which may adorn the character of a black man."[26] The roots of antiblack racism extend much further back beyond the nineteenth century, of course; but it's fair to say that white supremacist ideology, which evolved to justify the enslavement of black human beings, assumed new forms and changed in tune and timbre almost as soon as the Civil War ended and freedmen and freedwomen began to assert their rights, especially the right of black males to register and vote in 1867. Charting how white supremacy evolved during Reconstruction and Redemption is crucial to understanding in what forms it continues to manifest itself today.

In other words, the Civil War ended slavery, but it didn't end antiblack racism. Proslavery rhetoric and white supremacist ideology had naturally marched arm in arm. But when the South lost the Civil War—at a staggering cost in blood and treasure—white supremacist ideologies continued, unbridled and disengaged from the institution of slavery.

One could make the case that, with the emergence of black male suffrage in 1867 in the Southern states, where black male voters were either a majority or close to a majority, antiblack racist discourse only intensified, because it was forced to do so, in what amounted to a rhetorical and martial terrorist campaign to reestablish white supremacy as the unofficial law of the land. This movement used as its weapons, in addition to lynching, mutilation, rape, beatings, and mayhem, a surfeit of verbal and visual imagery to debase the popular image of the Negro in every way that it could. Meanwhile, antiblack racism in the North, even among those who had opposed slavery, continued to grow in some quarters, as the reactionary forces against Reconstruction in the South increased in strength. Clearly the North was a safer place for a black person to be living, but the region was never free of antiblack racism.

The difference between being antislavery and, as it were, pro-Negro (or even neutral about racial difference and the fiction of racial essences) manifested itself dramatically during the Civil War and especially after the signing of the Emancipation Proclamation. But the French traveler and writer Alexis de Tocqueville had raised the issue as early as 1835. "I am obliged to confess that I do not regard the abolition of slavery as a means of warding off the struggle of the two races in the Southern states," he wrote in *Democracy in America*. "The Negroes may long remain slaves without complaining; but if they are once raised to the level of freemen, they will soon revolt at being deprived of almost all their civil rights; and as they cannot become the equals of the whites, they will speedily show themselves as enemies." Tocqueville went on to say that "I can discover only two modes of action for the white inhabitants of [the South]: namely, either to emancipate the Negroes and to intermingle with them, or, remaining isolated from them, to keep them in slavery as long as possible." Obviously, those Southern "white inhabitants" chose the latter, never entertaining even the possibility of the former.

But there was a third path that Tocqueville apparently didn't imagine: the emancipation of the slaves, followed by their virtually complete subjugation after they were "emancipated," which is precisely what happened to the free Negro in the Redeemed South, culminating in the institutionalization of Jim Crow. Call it quasi-freedom or quasi-slavery: a state of being trapped in a nether zone, between a state of being and nothingness, painted as unworthy of citizenship rights granted prematurely by contemporaries eager to justify the implementation of neo-slavery, and perhaps not surprisingly by early historians of Reconstruction whose work was used to justify Jim Crow.[27] (Even Tocqueville himself had predicted, quite problematically, "If liberty be refused to the Negroes of the South, they will in the end forcibly seize it for themselves; if it is given, they will before long abuse it," which is precisely how the exercise of black political power would be denigrated by journalists and scholars alike.)

Deep-seated antiblack racism was the challenge that black people faced after their emancipation from slavery and during Reconstruction. And its elimination, we know painfully, did not occur, for a complex of reasons: because of the stubborn history and momentum of white supremacy; because of the Redeemed South's political economy, especially the continuing importance of the production of and profit from commodities such as cotton; because of the signal role of cheap black labor in the economy; and because of the need to neutralize, if not erase, the startling manifestation of black political power beginning in 1867, virtually as soon as black men were allowed to register and vote. Redemption was a war to emasculate the early manifestations of what we might think of as "Black Power," as it expressed itself both politically and, to a much lesser extent, economically in the glory years of Reconstruction. The proverbial genie had to be put back in the bottle, and the Redeemed South went about that process with unmatched passion and vengeance.

A SECOND SLAVERY

American slavery was the perfect fusion of race and class. And when it ended formally, as a legal institution, after the tragic wartime sacrifice of an almost inconceivable 750,000 lives, ways had to be found to reinvent and maintain the exploitation of black labor to sustain the modes of production on which the South's profits were based. Postwar, cotton's role in the American economy was only growing. Sven Beckert points out, "Global cotton consumption doubled from 1860 to 1890, and then by 1920 doubled once more." Nothing was more important to the South following the war than maintaining the profit margin on cotton production. As Beckert shows in ample detail: "It took a multiyear struggle on plantations, in local courthouses, in state capitols, and in Washington to determine the outlines of a new system of labor in the cotton-growing regions of the United States. That struggle began the moment the fighting ended, when plantation owners, utterly ruined by the economic and political effects of defeat in war, sought to restore a plantation world as close to slavery as possible." Despite the fact that "contracts had to be made and wages paid . . . life was to go on as before."[28]

The cultural and economic historian Gene Dattel's account of what happened next is telling. "After the Civil War," Dattel writes, "America discovered with relief that cotton could indeed be grown without slave labor."[29] White landowners replaced slavery with sharecropping, which proved a most devastating combination with Jim Crow segregation. Between exploitation of his or her labor by the sharecropping system and unscrupulous storekeepers and landlords, "the former slave inevitably ran a greater and greater debt, living in virtual debt peonage," writes Pete Daniel, the accomplished historian of the American South.[30] Poor whites found themselves ensnared in sharecropping as well, but the owners of cotton land grew richer than ever. Dattel tells us, "[D]espite the destruction of the conflict, the South would produce exponentially more cotton than before the war."[31]

This system of neo-slavery, which emerged in parallel to the politics of the Reconstruction era, was justified by what we might think of as an all-encompassing, suffocating white supremacist discourse, which had a logic, a history, and a momentum of its own, one whose peculiar mode of reasoning and argumentation, with its own symbols and signs, would carry on long after slavery, Reconstruction, and Redemption ended. I often wonder if Frederick Douglass and his fellow abolitionists could have imagined the extent to which this antiblack racist discourse would remain very much alive in American society a century and a half after the end of the Civil War.

"A WAR OF IDEAS"

Key players at the end of the Civil War on both sides were keenly aware that a second set of battles loomed as part of a different kind of war, one of propaganda, images, and ideas that would determine the status of freedwomen and freedmen in the culture, politics, and economy of the South. As Edward A. Pollard, a member of the wartime editorial staff of the *Richmond Examiner*, noted just one year after the end of the war in his hugely influential polemic *The Lost Cause: A New Southern History of the War of the Confederates*, "All that is left the South is 'the war of ideas.'"[32]

The Lost Cause myth that Pollard promoted developed along two overlapping lines. First, its advocates argued, the Civil War was not an act of treason but rather a revolt against an overreaching federal government, in which the Confederates lost but fought with courage and honor. In this sense, they viewed the Civil War as similar to the American Revolution, with Robert E. Lee as George Washington in a gray uniform. Second, slavery did not cause the war, and even though many (but not all) Lost Cause advocates ultimately accepted slavery's demise, they did not link it to racial equality. Indeed, on the contrary, the Lost Cause was fundamentally based on white supremacy. Two postwar books make this clear: Pollard's aforementioned *The Lost Cause* and the former Confederate president Jefferson Davis's *The Rise and Fall of the Confederate Government* (1881). Pollard argued that "She [the former Confederacy] must submit faithfully and truly to what the war has properly decided. But the war properly decided only what was put in issue: the restoration of the Union and the excision of slavery; and to these two conditions the South submits. But the war did not decide Negro equality." Looking back sixteen years after the war's end, Davis argued that heroic Southerners were only trying to fend off the North's "unlimited despotic power" and that slavery "was in no wise the cause of the conflict, but only an incident." Slavery, in fact, had a positive benefit, he maintained, as the enslaved were "trained in the gentle arts of peace and order and civilization; they increased from a few unprofitable savages to millions of efficient Christian laborers."[33]

Perhaps no one was better equipped to fight back against these arguments in this war of ideas than Frederick Douglass. A master of self-fashioning and self-invention, of the manipulation of signs and symbols for political ends, Douglass established his own subjectivity—and by extension that of "the Negro," whom he, as an exemplar, was defined as "representing"—in at least two ways: rhetorically, by revising his own story about the shaping of himself over three autobiographies, and visually, by sitting for photographs, both because he seemed rather to have liked images of himself, and also as a political strategy, to counter the plethora of negative visual stereotypes of black people as subhuman that played a key part in justifying slavery and black second-class citizenship.

Well before the Civil War, Douglass, who published his first autobiography in 1845, when he was still a fugitive slave, understood that a pivotal battleground in what would become a war of representation, lasting through Reconstruction and Redemption, over the redefinition of freedwomen and freedmen from chattel slaves into human beings—from ostensible "objects" into subjects, from property into citizens—would be waged at the level of the symbolic, its weapons verbal and visual images of black people. Writing in 1878, a year after the Compromise of 1877 choked off political Reconstruction, Douglass perceptively observed that the Civil War had been "a war of ideas, a battle of principles, . . . a war between the old and new, slavery and freedom, barbarism and civilization"; a war, moreover, "between men of thought as well as action, and in dead earnest for something beyond the battlefield." The recent rebellion, Douglass mused from the distance of just over a decade, had been fought on two fronts: as an ideological or a metaphysical war that had manifested itself in the deadliest of manners, through the devastating toll of the deaths of three-quarters of a million people, sacrificed to destroy or protect a perverted way of life. In this sense, Frederick Douglass and Edward Pollard were reading their times retrospectively through the same lens, albeit through distinctly different sets of eyes.

Pollard, like Douglass, was something of a strategic genius in this war of symbols and interpretation, launching a preemptive volley through the definition of terms almost as soon as the Thirteenth Amendment had been ratified. One of the key arguments in *The Lost Cause* was that it was of the utmost importance to redefine the terms of the causes of the war itself, by making a case for the nature of the "work" black people had been required to perform before the war: "The occasion of that conflict was what the Yankees called—by one of their convenient libels in political nomenclature—slavery; but what was in fact nothing more than a system of Negro servitude in the South . . . one of the mildest and most beneficent systems of servitude in the world."[34] What for Pollard had been a mild form of servitude had for Douglass been one of the world's most heinous perversions: the enslavement of almost four million human beings by the eve of a war fought to end this immorality. As Douglass had put it in an editorial published in his newspaper, *Douglass' Monthly*, in November 1862, "Verily the work does not end with the abolition of slavery, but only begins." Even Douglass could have no idea of how difficult a task that "work" would be in the decades to come. In fact, the end of the war had been a time of unparalleled optimism for Douglass, for his fellow abolitionists, and indeed for the entire black community.

Before assessing the accomplishments of the decade or so during which Reconstruction policy attempted to redress almost two and a half centuries of Anglo-American slavery, it is useful to revisit the sheer excitement and optimism that African Americans expressed at its demise. Our awareness of the assault on emerging black rights and the debacle to come only makes these sentiments more poignant.

Eric Foner describes the upbeat, exhilarated mood of black people in the South in the months just before the war ended: "On February 18, 1865, Union forces entered Charleston, among them the black 54th Massachusetts Infantry singing 'John Brown's Body.' Five weeks later the city witnessed a 'grand jubilee' of freedom, a vast outpouring of celebration and pride by the city's black community." Four thousand African Americans held a parade and celebrated a mock funeral for slavery. On April 14, just after Appomattox, Northern abolitionists, ministers, and political leaders flew the American flag over Fort Sumter. Foner writes that "the most affecting moment came when a black man stepped forward with his two small daughters to thank William Lloyd Garrison for his long labors on behalf of the slaves. . . . One white army officer was moved to tears by the raising of the standard 'that now for the first time is the black man's as well as the white man's flag.'"[35]

Following the war and the ratification of the Thirteenth Amendment, this initial sense of optimism, a sense of virtually unlimited possibility, only grew. A focus on the right to vote, the right to a free, public education, and the right to own land were the next campaigns in the quest for equal rights, for the elimination of barriers to social elevation, and for the equal protection of the law. For three days in October 1865, the National Equal Rights League held its first annual convention. John Mercer Langston—a lawyer, an educator, an abolitionist, and an office-holder who would go on to establish the law school at Howard University, serve as consul-general to Haiti, and win a contentious election in Virginia for a seat in the US House of Representatives—was the organization's president.[36] At the convention, only months after the Civil War's end, African Americans expressed hope for the future in the form of the right to cast their votes:

Mr. [J. Henry] Harris, of North Carolina, said that he was glad of the opportunity extended him of standing before such an audience as confronted him. He thanked God that as an American citizen, as a negro, and as a man, he had lived to see the American flag floating over territory which Government has declared forever free. The gentleman made allusion to his experience in Canada, Oberlin, and other parts of Ohio, as warranting him in endorsing an oft repeated assertion of President Langston's, that "white men are white men" the world over. And he felt that the elevation of the Negro depends upon his own right arm. . . .

J[ohn] D. Richards offered the following Resolution, which was adopted:

Resolved, That in the reconstruction of the Southern States, justice demands that the Elective franchise be extended to men of color in those States, and if the Government fail to do so, it will prove recreant to every principle of honesty and good faith. That as colored men have fought to defend and perpetuate the unity of this Government, and maintain its liberties, every principle of honor demands that they should be placed on a footing with other citizens.[37]

A state convention of freedpeople in Alabama defined what freedom meant to African Americans: "We claim exactly *the same rights, privileges and immunities as are enjoyed by white men*—we ask nothing more and will be content with nothing less. . . . The law no longer knows white nor black, but simply men, and consequently we are entitled to ride in public conveyances, hold office, sit on juries and do everything else which we have in the past been prevented from doing solely on the ground of color."[38]

By 1867, the role of education and the need for more teachers throughout the South, especially black teachers, had become patently apparent, especially with all of the expectations brought by the three Reconstruction Acts, passed on March 2, March 23, and July 19, which, building on the Civil Rights Act of 1866, wrestled the momentum for black rights away from the resistance of the executive branch and toward an enlightened, non-racist society. With an illiteracy rate of some 90 percent by most estimates, the need of the black community (the size of the population of Canada, or the state of New York) for access to a basic education could not be gainsaid. Sarah Louise "Sallie" Daffin, an African American woman from Philadelphia who taught in an American Missionary School in Arlington, Virginia, reported how freedpeople were embracing the merits of education and urged black churches to play a role in meeting this enormous demand:

> At this time we can perceive indications of the importance of the colored people themselves taking hold of the work, and endeavoring to assist in removing the great stumbling block of ignorance out of the way, that Christianity and Education may be firmly rooted on a soil where once slavery and its accompanying legions of crime and woe held precedence.
>
> Our colored churches should be aroused to a proper sense of their duty, and send forth their own teachers into the fields of the South. *The great need is colored teachers.* Not those who can only boast of education—but we want those whose moral and religious reputations will bear any test that will be likely to meet them at every point.[39]

In April 1867, African Americans in Augusta, Georgia, celebrated the passage of the first two Reconstruction Acts, which they hoped, at last, would begin to counter the resistance of President Andrew Johnson and the Old South's *ancien régime* to freeing the "freed" from the state of limbo in which they had been suspended since the ratification of the Thirteenth Amendment: free, but not citizens, and not possessing the right to vote. Lewis Carter, a Congregational preacher, exclaimed, "That old ship, the institution of slavery is dead, and I am glad of it. Shall I employ its captain or its manager to bear me through the ocean again? [Cheers, and voice No! No!]. Is it because I am angry with the captain? No. It is because I have lost confidence in him. . . . How can we, as a people, support those that have vowed to enslave us."[40]

By midsummer, expressions of the passion for education had only grown in intensity. On July 27, 1867, Robert G. Fitzgerald, an African American born free in Delaware, who had served in the Union army and navy and now taught in Virginia, recorded in his diary how passionately freedpeople had taken to education: "They tell me before Mr. Lincoln made them free they had nothing to work for, to look up to, now they have everything, and will, by God's help, make the best of it."[41] And a few days later, on August 3, 1867, Burnet Houston, emboldened by the momentum generated by the Reconstruction Acts, declared to his former master, George S. Houston (who would go on to be the Democratic governor of Alabama), "I have all the rights that you or any other man has, and I shall not suffer them abridged."[42]

Black people had become keenly aware, in the two years since the end of the war, that there existed an inextricable linkage between economic advancement and political rights. As one plantation owner put it, according to Steven Hahn, an expert on the history of slavery and emancipation, "You never saw a people more excited on the subject of politics than are the negroes of the south. They are perfectly wild."[43] A newspaper article on August 7, 1867, quoted the African American Union League organizer George Washington Cox of Tuscaloosa, Alabama, who spoke of the hopes and demands of freedpeople during Reconstruction: "The fact is, the colored people are very anxious to get land of their own to live upon independently; and they want money to buy stock to make crops. And we are aware . . . that the only way to get these necessaries is to give our votes to the party that are making every effort possible to bring these blessings about by Reconstructing the State."[44] In that year, Eric Foner maintains, "politics emerged as the principal focus of black aspirations.

In that *annus mirabilis*, the impending demise of the structure of civil authority opened the door for political mobilization to sweep across the black belt." Foner captures the exhilaration that the prospect of one man, one vote generated within the black community in 1867, a spirit, which, after the disenfranchisement of black voters that would accelerate at century's end, would not be rekindled in intensity until the voting registration drives led by the Student Nonviolent Coordinating Committee (SNCC) and other civil rights groups in the 1960s, culminating in the passage of the Voting Rights Act in 1965.

This belief among the freedpeople in the power of the suffrage, this realization that black power would manifest itself first and foremost through the power to vote, was noted widely at the time. One Northerner covering an early 1868 election in Alabama wrote that African Americans, "in defiance of fatigue, hardship, hunger, and threats of employers," with tattered clothes and without shoes, stood in line to vote, motivated by "the hunger to have the same chances as the white men."[45]

Frederick Douglass, among other abolitionists such as Senator Charles Sumner of Massachusetts, clearly understood the relation between freedom and the right to vote. Douglass first advocated for black suffrage as early as 1847.[46] In 1865, upon the end of the Civil War, he maintained that African Americans could not enjoy full freedom until they could vote. When William Lloyd Garrison, at the May 1865 meeting of the American Anti-Slavery Society, declared, "My vocation, as an Abolitionist, thank God, is ended," Douglass famously responded, "Slavery is not abolished until the black man has the ballot. While the Legislatures of the South retain the right to pass laws making any discrimination between black and white, slavery still lives there." Following the meeting, when Wendell Phillips replaced Garrison as president, the organization's publication added this motto to its masthead: "No Reconstruction Without Negro Suffrage."[47] As Douglass put it in his speech at the convention, "What the Black Man Wants":

> By depriving us of suffrage, you affirm our incapacity to form an intelligent judgment respecting public men and public measures; you declare before the world that we are unfit to exercise the elective

franchise, and by this means lead us to undervalue ourselves, to put a low estimate upon ourselves, and to feel that we have no possibilities like other men. Again, I want the elective franchise, for one, as a colored man, because ours is a peculiar government, based upon a peculiar idea, and that idea is universal suffrage.... [H]ere, where universal suffrage is the rule, where that is the fundamental idea of the Government, to rule us out is to make us an exception, to brand us with the stigma of inferiority, and to invite to our heads the missiles of those about us; therefore, I want the franchise for the black man.[48]

The only real way to guarantee the gains of Reconstruction, Douglass knew, would be through the ballot box.

"In what skin will the old snake come forth?" Douglass had asked rhetorically in his remarkable speech at the 1865 Anti-Slavery Society convention. The answer would surface soon enough, as part of a larger white supremacist discourse that unfolded in the form of the most disgusting claims about, and denunciations of, "the nature" of black people made in a wide variety of forms, including political speeches demanding the rollback of black voting rights, in bizarre treatises on the "science" of "race"—as part of the never-ending search for a scientific basis for American antiblack racism—in the depiction of deracinated or malicious black characters in short stories and novels, and, of course, in the omnipresent visual representations of black people as Sambos in popular art.

Nevertheless, as late as April 1870, Douglass could still express untrammeled optimism about the Negro's prospects for the future. Indeed, on April 20, 1870, he delivered a speech in Albany, New York, celebrating the significance of the ratification of the Fifteenth Amendment in ensuring the Negro citizen's future, despite the ups and downs that had characterized Reconstruction thus far. Given how brief the period of the Negro's possibilities of securing the rights and privileges of citizenship after 1870 would be, the title of Douglass's speech, "At Last, at Last, the Black Man Has a Future," makes its fetchingly upbeat tone all the more distressing:

> Our eyes behold it; our ears hear it, our hearts feel it, and there is no doubt or illusion about it. The black man is free, the black man is

a citizen, the black man is enfranchised, and this by the organic law of the land. . . .

At last, at last, the black man has a future. Heretofore all was dark, mysterious, chaotic. We were chained to all the unutterable horrors of never ending fixedness. Others might improve and make progress, but for us there was nothing but the unending monotony of stagnation, of moral, mental and social death. The curtain is now lifted. The dismal death-cloud of slavery has passed away. Today we are free American citizens. We have ourselves, we have a country, and we have a future in common with other men.[49]

OPPOSITION

Within three years, however, the signs would be unmistakable that support for Reconstruction was severely challenged. The depth of the reaction against demands that the Negro have the right to vote, and the sheer range of racist vehemence and terrorism that arose to neutralize that right once it had been enshrined in the Fifteenth Amendment, is stunning to contemplate. As David Blight reports, "At least ten percent of the black members of constitutional conventions in the South in 1867–68 became victims [of Klan violence], including seven who were murdered." White vigilantes lynched an estimated four hundred black people across the South between 1868 and 1871. In rural central Kentucky alone, white mobs lynched as many as two dozen African Americans each year between 1867 and 1871. Thirty-eight black people were lynched in South Carolina between the elections of 1870 and the spring of 1871. About thirty African Americans were killed in a single day in Meridian, Mississippi.[50] A key motivation for these lynchings was the attempt to intimidate black men from voting.

President Johnson, predictably, voiced his opposition to black access to the franchise early on. Johnson—who said of Abraham Lincoln's friend Frederick Douglass, after a meeting at the White House on February 7, 1866, that "he's just like any nigger, & he would sooner cut a white man's throat than not"—declared that "[t]he Negroes have not asked for the privilege of voting; [and] the vast majority of them have no idea what it means." Putting aside for the moment what to his mind was the outrageous "policy or impolicy of Africanizing the southern part of our territory," Johnson continued, "To force the right of suffrage out of the hands of white people and into the hands of the Negroes is an arbitrary violation of [the principle of federal non-intervention in matters over which the state should, constitutionally, have jurisdiction]."[51]

States' rights was just an excuse for Johnson; his aversion to black suffrage was as deep as his aversion to the idea of the fundamental equality of black people with white people. As he put the matter in his third address to Congress, on December 3, 1867:

But if anything can be proved by known facts, if all reasoning upon evidence is not abandoned, it must be acknowledged that in the progress of nations Negroes have shown less capacity for government than any other race of people. No independent government of any form has ever been successful in their hands. On the contrary, wherever they have been left to their own devices they have shown a constant tendency to relapse into barbarism. In the Southern States, however, Congress has undertaken to confer upon them the privilege of the ballot. Just released from slavery, it may be doubted whether as a class they know more than their ancestors how to organize and regulate civil society. Indeed, it is admitted that the blacks of the South are not only regardless of the rights of property, but so utterly ignorant of public affairs that their voting can consist in nothing more than carrying a ballot to the place where they are directed to deposit it.[52]

Johnson had marshaled the central tenets of white supremacist beliefs in an all-out effort to prevent black men from voting; it was, to paraphrase Malcolm X, a war between the ballot and the bullet, with the bullet destined to win.[53] The power of the idea of universal suffrage to summon the forces of darkness buried deep in the white racist imaginary is a monstrous thing to behold from our vantage point today. In a masterful manifestation of both antiblack racism and antisuffrage sentiment, Colonel Pat Donan, the editor of a Lexington, Missouri, newspaper, declared, "No simian-souled, sooty skinned, kink-curled, blubber-lipped, prehensile-heeled, Ethiopian gorilla shall pollute the ballot box with his leprous vote."[54]

By 1890, after a fierce and brave struggle, the momentum had tipped considerably away from advocates of black equality to the white supremacists' advantage, as the newly elected senator Ben Tillman, a Democrat from South Carolina, happily declared, "Democracy has won a great victory unparalleled. The triumph of Democracy and white supremacy over mongrelism and anarchy is most complete."[55] James Kimble Vardaman, the notorious future governor and US senator from Mississippi, admitted nakedly, when commenting on the motivation for the 1890 Mississippi Constitutional Convention, "There is no use to equivocate or lie about the matter. Mississippi's constitutional convention was held for no other purpose than to eliminate the nigger from politics; not the ignorant—but the nigger."[56] The right to vote was of such importance to the potential transformation of the enslaved to citizens that its failure to be enforced by the courts spelled the failure of Reconstruction and the beginning of a sad new era characterized by the deprivation of black rights.

No one understood this better than Booker T. Washington. With a straight face, he tossed any fear that he would be continuing the work of his ostensible predecessor, Frederick Douglass, into the dustbin of Southern history by declaring, near the very beginning of his 1895 Atlanta Cotton States and International Exposition address, that his audience—which overnight would turn into the whole of the country—need not be concerned about that: "Ignorant and inexperienced, it is not strange that in the first years of our new life we began at the top instead of at the bottom; that a seat in Congress or the state legislature was more sought than real estate or industrial skill; that the political convention or stump speaking had more attractions than starting a dairy farm or truck garden."[57] Other than an embrace of the merits of slavery itself, nothing could have amounted to a greater betrayal of Frederick Douglass's most fundamental principles and beliefs about the rights of African Americans than this single sentence delivered just seven months after Douglass had died. The mantle had been passed; and this aspect of Douglass's legacy had been trampled.

HOW DID RECONSTRUCTION FAIL?

Given the enormity of the sacrifice of lives in the Civil War to abolish slavery, how was Reconstruction—the program of transitioning those four million slaves into citizenship—allowed to fail? The dismantling followed a few different tracks, principally in the court system and the state legislature. We can approach this question from three vantage points: the political, the economic, and the legal. Politically, a combination of violence, fraud, the aftershocks of the Panic of 1873, and dissipating will and a shift in priorities in the North allowed Democrats (then the "white man's party") to take back control of the various state governments in the South, really from 1869 on. South Carolina, for example, was nicknamed Negro Country during slavery and was the "blackest" of all the states in terms of the relative size of the black voting population. After the election of 1876, in which the "Redeemer" government was ushered in, the new slate of Democrats in the state legislature closed the state university, which had been integrated—in fact, Harvard's first African American graduate, Richard T. Greener, taught in its law school— and reopened it in 1880, for white students only. It remained that way until it was finally desegregated close to a century later, in 1963.

Economically, implementation of the redistribution of the land owned by the traitorous planter class would have effected the single most dramatic change conceivable within the Southern economic landscape. As early in the war as 1861, a writer in the *Weekly Anglo-African*, a leading African American outlet in New York, had this to say about the importance of the ownership of land:

What course could be clearer, what course more politic, what course will so immediately restore the equilibrium of commerce, what course will be so just, so humane, so thoroughly conducive to the public weal and the national advancement, as that the government should immediately bestow these lands upon those freed men who know best how to cultivate them, and will joyfully bring their brawny arms, their willing hearts, and their skilled hands to the glorious labor of cultivating as their OWN, the lands which they have bought and paid for by their sweat and blood?[58]

Just three years later, the National Convention of Colored Men in Syracuse, New York, urged the freedmen to pursue "the accumulation of property."[59] White people also knew the importance of land ownership to African Americans. As A. Warren Kelsey wrote to a group of Northern textile manufacturers who had hired him "to investigate prospects for the resumption of plantation agriculture": "The sole ambition of the freedman at the present time appears to be to become the owner of a little piece of land, there to erect a humble home, and to dwell in peace and security at his own free will and pleasure. . . . That is their idea, their desire and their hope."[60]

In early 1865, African Americans had reason to believe that the federal government would support their desires. On January 12, General William Tecumseh Sherman, Secretary of War Edwin Stanton, and twenty local church leaders met in Savannah, Georgia, to discuss what to do with the land the Union military had seized on the southern coast. Sherman's primary goal was to find somewhere to put the slaves who kept running to Union lines, but the Baptist minister Garrison Frazier explained what freedpeople wanted: "I would prefer to live by ourselves, for there is a prejudice against us in the South that will take years to get over."[61]

Two days after this meeting, Sherman issued Special Field Order No. 15, which proclaimed lands in coastal South Carolina and Georgia "reserved and set apart for the settlement of the negroes now made free by the acts of war and the proclamation of the President of the United States." It granted freedpeople "possession of which land military authorities will afford them protection until such time as they can protect themselves or until Congress shall regulate their title."[62] Forty thousand freedpeople settled on four hundred thousand acres of this land by June.

One of the ministers at the Savannah meeting, Ulysses Houston, established a community on Skidaway Island, Georgia. All told, the federal government held possession of about 850,000 acres of confiscated Southern land after the war.[63]

It is difficult to imagine any act more revolutionary than the redistribution of land from the planters to the slaves in the former Confederacy. By the fall of 1865, Andrew Johnson, keenly aware of the fundamental transformation this would cause in the structure of the economy in the South and in the relations between black and white, reversed any plans for land redistribution. Only former slaves who had paid for their land were allowed to remain on it. Rumors of "forty acres and a mule" for all freed slaves proved unfounded. Still, African Americans continued to make land ownership a priority. As the freedman Bayley Wyat (also spelled Wyatt) put it succinctly in his "Freedman's Speech," delivered in 1866: "We has a right to the land where we are located. For why? I tell you. Our wives, our children, our husbands, has been sold over and over again to purchase the lands we now locates upon; for that reason we have a divine right to the land."[64]

Judges and legislators, on the federal and state levels, dismantled black rights in a number of overlapping ways. The Supreme Court played a crucial role. In *United States v. Reese* (1876), the court struck down key sections of the Enforcement Act of May 1870, which had attempted to outlaw any interference with a citizen's voting rights. The court said the Fifteenth Amendment did not guarantee any citizen the right to vote; it only prevented setting racial limitations on the vote. Otherwise, the states had the power to establish qualifications for voting as they saw fit. In *United States v. Harris* (1883), the court struck down a key section of the Ku Klux Klan Act of 1871, ruling that the Thirteenth and Fourteenth Amendments did not allow Congress to punish acts of private persons, only the actions of states.

In the *Civil Rights Cases* (1883), the court applied similar reasoning to strike down the Civil Rights Act of 1875, which had banned racial discrimination in the access to all manner of services and public accommodations. On October 19, 1883, John Mercer Langston delivered a powerful address in Washington, DC, surrounded onstage by luminaries, all of whom were in opposition to the ruling, among them Frederick Douglass, Richard T. Greener, Mississippi's former US senator Blanche K. Bruce, and Jeremiah Eames Rankin, a white abolitionist and the minister of Washington's First Congregational Church who would soon be named the sixth president of Howard University. Langston noted the impossibility of getting protections from Democratic state governments:

> The Supreme Court would seem desirous of remanding us back to that old passed condition. It advises that we appeal to the legislatures of the States for protection and defense of our rights. But let us be patient. Wait a little while, some one counsels. My God! How long a time are we to wait! . . . We need and demand protection, and if States should not protect us against abuse, against insults, against violation of our rights, Congress should and must. Hence the Civil Rights bill. . . . How is it possible for the Supreme Court then, able as its members are, learned in the law, to have reached the conclusion that the Civil Rights Act, under the circumstances, is unconstitutional? This is incomprehensible.[65]

Three days later, Douglass spoke in the nation's capital as well, but in terms of grief much more visceral than Langston's:

> We have been, as a class, grievously wounded in the house of our friends, and this wound is too deep and too painful for ordinary measured speech. . . . [W]hen a deed is done from slavery, caste and oppression, and a blow is struck at human progress, the heart of humanity sickens in sorrow and writhes in pain. It makes us feel as if some one were stamping upon the graves of our mothers, or desecrating our sacred temples of worship. . . .
>
> The cause which has brought us here to-night is neither common nor trivial. Few events in our national history have surpassed it in magnitude, importance and significance. It has swept over the land like a moral cyclone, leaving moral devastation in its track. . . .

While slavery was the base line of American society, while it ruled the church and the state, while it was the interpreter of our law and the exponent of our religion, it admitted no quibbling, no narrow rules of legal or scriptural interpretations of Bible or Constitution. . . . But now slavery is abolished. Its reign was long, dark and bloody. Liberty *now*, is the base line of the Republic. Liberty has supplanted slavery, but I fear it has not supplanted the spirit or power of slavery. Where slavery was strong, liberty is now weak. . . .

It is said that this decision will make no difference in the treatment of colored people; that the Civil Rights Bill was a dead letter, and could not be enforced. There is some truth in all this, but it is not the whole truth. . . . [The Civil Rights Bill] was a banner on the outer wall of American liberty, a noble moral standard, uplifted for the education of the American people. There are tongues in trees, books, in the running brooks—sermons in stones. This law, though dead, did speak. It expressed the sentiment of justice and fair play, common to every honest heart. Its voice was against popular prejudice and meanness. It appealed to all the noble and patriotic instincts of the American people. It told the American people that they were all equal before the law; that they belonged to a common country and were equal citizens. The Supreme Court has hauled down this flag of liberty in open day. . . .

The whole essence of the thing is a studied purpose to degrade and stamp out the liberties of a race. It is the old spirit of slavery, and nothing else.[66]

Judges also narrowed the scope and meaning of laws and amendments, especially the Fourteenth Amendment, so that they offered fewer and fewer protections. Though the facts of the *Slaughterhouse Cases* (1873) do not take on Reconstruction policy explicitly, the court, split 5–4, narrowed the application of the Fourteenth Amendment, holding that it only protects the rights derived from national citizenship—not state citizenship—and defined those rights as so narrow as to be almost meaningless. In *United States v. Cruikshank* (1876), which flowed out of the Colfax Massacre in Louisiana three years earlier, the court ruled that the Due Process and

Equal Protection Clauses of the Fourteenth Amendment applied only to state civil rights violations, not civil rights violations by individuals.

The most notorious example of the Supreme Court restricting civil rights was, of course, *Plessy v. Ferguson* (1896). Homer Plessy, a mixed-race man, was removed from a whites-only train car after he told the conductor he was one-eighth black when asked for his ticket—and jailed as a result. Plessy sued. The Louisiana Railway Accommodations Act of 1890 stated that railroad companies must "provide equal but separate accommodations for the white and colored races." Plessy and his team argued that the law violated the Fourteenth Amendment and awarded railroad employees too much power in determining the race of an individual. In his brief in favor of Plessy, Albion Tourgée—the novelist, newspaper editor, civil rights activist, and attorney and courageous judge in Reconstruction North Carolina, who worked on the Plessy case for free—wrote, "Justice is pictured blind and her daughter the Law, ought at least to be color-blind."[67]

In his majority decision, however, Justice Henry Billings Brown wrote: "Laws permitting, and even requiring, [the races'] separation in places where they are liable to be brought into contact do not necessarily imply the inferiority of either race to the other, and have been generally, if not universally, recognized as within the competency of the state legislatures in the exercise of their police power. The most common instance of this is connected with the establishment of separate schools for white and colored children." In his remarkable dissent, Justice John Marshall Harlan, the son of Kentucky slaveholders and once an opponent of emancipation, warned: "But in view of the Constitution, in the eye of the law, there is in this country no superior, dominant, ruling class of citizens. There is no caste here. Our Constitution is color-blind, and neither knows nor tolerates classes among citizens. In respect of civil rights, all citizens are equal before the law. . . . In my opinion, the judgment this day rendered will, in time, prove to be quite as pernicious as the decision made by this tribunal in the Dred Scott Case." Harlan did make a distinction when it came to Chinese people, whom he called "a race so different from our own."[68]

As the federal government signaled it would not interfere in the affairs of Southern states, and the Supreme Court overturned or defanged Reconstruction civil rights legislation, Southern Democrat lawmakers took the next logical step. Spurred on by the blueprint set by Mississippi in 1890, redeemed state governments created new constitutions. Virtually all of the former Confederate states threw out their Reconstruction-era constitutions—those that black people helped draft and which they voted to ratify—and wrote new ones that included disenfranchisement provisions, antimiscegenation provisions, and separate-but-equal Jim Crow provisions. Though "race neutral" in language, these new constitutions solidified Southern states as governed by legal segregation and discrimination.

And yet, despite its relative brevity and the enormous power and vitriol of the forces mounted against it, Reconstruction achieved remarkable historical precedents. Before examining in the next two chapters how Reconstruction was attacked and ultimately dismantled, it is useful to compare summaries of the period's most important accomplishments by two historians, Allen Guelzo and Eric Foner, whose approaches are markedly different. Guelzo argues that birthright citizenship stands out as its great achievement, even more important than the Equal Protection Clause of the Fourteenth Amendment.

While the due process protections in the Fourteenth Amendment were tremendously important in the quest to ensure black rights, Guelzo says that Chief Justice Roger Taney had attempted to use the Due Process Clause in the Fifth Amendment (one of the tools for protecting slave owners' property) as the justification for the *Dred Scott* decision, so it was already present in the Constitution, as applied to the federal government, not the states; the Fourteenth Amendment did the latter. However, the clarification that citizenship in the United States is based on location of birth (jus soli), not heredity (jus sanguinis), was revolutionary. Guelzo explained to me that "Taney had tried to assert jus sanguinis in *Dred Scott*, too, because the Constitution simply didn't offer a working definition of citizenship, either at the state or federal level. This is what entitled black people to vote, since their citizenship could now be based on the inarguable fact that they were born on US soil."[69]

Guelzo contends that even Webster's definition of "citizenship" entailed the right to vote. Webster had written in 1828 that a US citizen was "a person, native or naturalized, who has the privilege of exercising the elective franchise, or the qualifications which enable him to vote for rulers, and to purchase and hold real estate."[70] This definition alone, in Guelzo's reading, "did substantially more than any emancipation anywhere else" in the Western Hemisphere in the nineteenth century.[71] (Citizenship, despite Webster's definition, did not automatically confer upon an individual the right to vote. For example, women were citizens but could not vote until the ratification of the Nineteenth Amendment in 1920.)[72]

Furthermore, states Guelzo, Reconstruction "restored the Union without destroying federalism, without triggering a second civil war or a genocidal race war, and without punitive waves of executions for treason. Instead, it is one of the monumental ironies of Reconstruction that the victors—freed slaves, Northern whites—were more often the *targets* of violence and murder than the vanquished." That was most certainly a dramatic departure in the history of civil conflicts.[73]

One could say that there was a "double consciousness" in Guelzo's conclusions about Reconstruction, to adapt a concept articulated by W. E. B. Du Bois. While Reconstruction laid the groundwork for the large-scale embrace of white supremacist ideology in this country, it also, according to Guelzo, laid the groundwork for continued black resistance to it.

Eric Foner's summary of the significance of Reconstruction stresses a related point:

> Reconstruction provided space for the creation of key institutions of Black America—the independent church, schools and colleges, and stable families, which became the springboards for future struggle. Its [state] laws and Constitutional amendments [the 13th, the 14th, and the 15th] remained on the books, insuring that the Jim Crow system that followed, at least as a matter of law, remained a regional, not a national, system. The amendments, while flagrantly violated, remained, to quote [Massachusetts Senator Charles] Sumner, "sleeping giants" that could be awakened by subsequent generations. That

blacks retained the right to vote in the North became crucial when the Great Migration took place. Reconstruction was followed by a dire retreat, but it forestalled even worse outcomes, such as the system close to slavery envisioned by the Black Codes. One should not minimize the setback that Redemption represented, but we should not simply declare Reconstruction a failure and leave it at that.[74]

Foner concluded in his 2015 essay "Why Reconstruction Matters": "Citizenship, rights, democracy—as long as these remain contested, so will the necessity of an accurate understanding of Reconstruction. More than most historical subjects, how we think about this era truly matters, for it forces us to think about what kind of society we wish America to be."[75]

To some, it may seem that black people somehow went underground in 1877 and didn't appear again until 1954, the year that the US Supreme Court ended legalized segregation in public schools in *Brown v. Board of Education*. But Reconstruction initiatives continued to assert themselves even past *Plessy v. Ferguson*. There is a constant thread between the end of Reconstruction and the reemergence of the civil rights movement of the 1950s.[76]

The court cases and acts of legislation that enshrined Jim Crow as the law of the land did not unfold in a vacuum. The larger context for them was the ideology of white supremacy, the set of beliefs and attitudes about the nature of black people that arose to justify their unprecedented economic exploitation in the transatlantic slave trade. Following the Civil War, this ideology evolved in order to maintain the country's racial hierarchy in the face of emancipation and black citizenship. Anything but unmoored or isolated, white power was reinforced in this new era by the nation's cultural, economic, educational, legal, and violently extra-legal systems, including lynching. Among its root and branches were the paired mythology of white women's rape and black men's brutality, the convict-lease system, disenfranchisement, and the choking off of access to capital and property ownership. In many ways, this ideology still roams freely in our country today. The next two chapters of this book seek to explain how this process unfolded between the end of Reconstruction and the release of *The Birth of a Nation* in 1915, as antiblack racism effectively deconstructed the image and status of the so-called Old Negro, while the fourth examines the form of black agency inherent in successive attempts to define a New Negro in the face of the rise of the New South, a Negro perhaps better armed to do battle with the hideous forces inscribed in our nation's cultural psyche, forces poised to erupt spontaneously as they would do on so many occasions in American history since Reconstruction, as they did so gruesomely on June 17, 2015, within the sacred confines of Charleston, South Carolina's Mother Emanuel African Methodist Episcopal Church.

BACKLASH:
THE WHITE RESISTANCE
TO BLACK
RECONSTRUCTION

"Have you any <u>flesh</u> coloured silk stockings, young man?" From the popular series *Life in Philadelphia* by Edward Williams Clay, hand-colored etching with aquatint, 1829.

"Grand Celebration ob de Bobalition ob African Slabery," *Life in Philadelphia*, hand-colored etching, drawn and engraved by I. Harris, reissued in London from the original American print by Edward Williams Clay, ca. 1833–1834.

Jim Crow, etching, ca. 1835–1845. This image of the lively old black dancer enjoyed immense popularity as portrayed by the white comedian Thomas Dartmouth "Daddy" Rice.

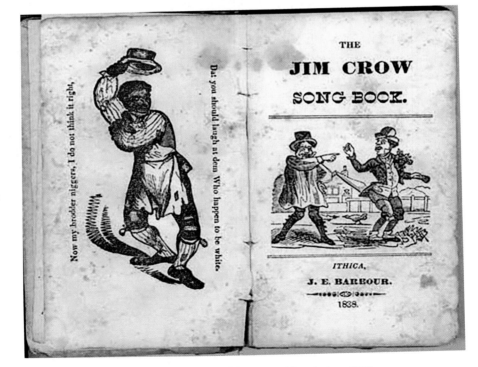

The Jim Crow Song Book, title page and frontispiece, 1838.

THE DIS-UNITED STATES—A BLACK BUSINESS

"The Dis-United States—A Black Business," political cartoon, *Punch*, 1856.

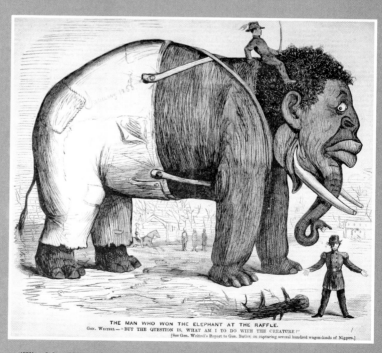

THE MAN WHO WON THE ELEPHANT AT THE RAFFLE.

GEN. WEITZEL.— "BUT THE QUESTION IS, WHAT AM I TO DO WITH THE CREATURE?"

[See Gen. Weitzel's Report to Gen. Butler, on capturing several hundred wagon-loads of Niggers.]

"The Man Who Won the Elephant at the Raffle," political cartoon, ca. 1862.

"Young Eph's Lament," song-sheet cover, 1863.

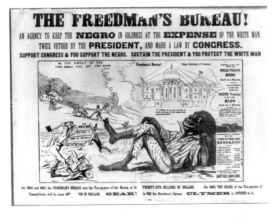

Anti-Freedman's Bureau political broadside, 1866.

"Holy Horror of Mrs. McCaffraty in a Washington City Street Passenger Car," political cartoon, *Harper's Weekly*, February 24, 1866.

"This Is a White Man's Government," Thomas Nast, *Harper's Weekly*, September 5, 1866.

"Reconstruction and How It Works," Thomas Nast, *Harper's Weekly*, October 1, 1866.

"The Two Platforms," Hiester Clymer campaign poster,
Pennsylvania gubernatorial race, 1866.

"We Accept the Situation," political cartoon, *Harper's Weekly*, April 13, 1867.

"Would you marry your daughter to a nigger?," political cartoon,
Thomas Nast, *Harper's Weekly*, July 11, 1868.

"One Vote Less," Thomas Nast, *Richmond Whig*,
published during campaigns of 1868 and 1872.

"Too Thin, Massa Grant," political cartoon, *Frank Leslie's Illustrated Newspaper*, September 14, 1872.

"The Union as It Was," Thomas Nast, *Harper's Weekly*, October 24, 1874.

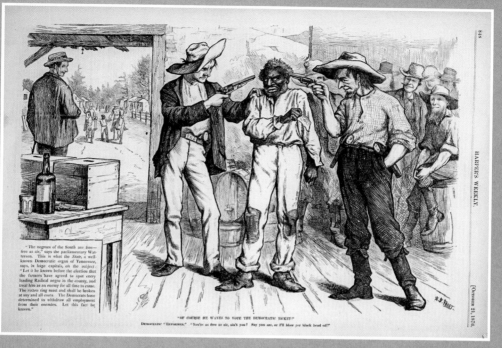

"Of Course He Wants to Vote the Democratic Ticket," Arthur Burdett Frost,
Harper's Weekly, October 21, 1876.

"In Self-Defense," Arthur Burdett Frost,
Harper's Weekly, October 28, 1876.

"The Ignorant Vote—Honors Are Easy," Thomas
Nast, *Harper's Weekly*, December 9, 1876.

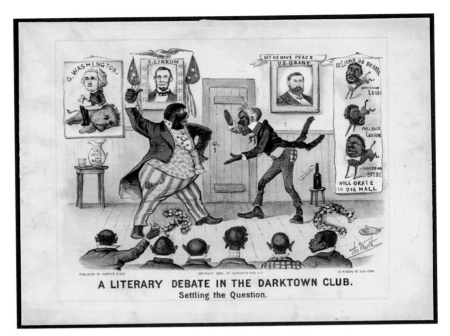

Darktown Comics, "A Literary Debate in the Darktown Club:
Settling the Question," Currier & Ives, 1885.

Darktown Comics, "A Literary Debate in the Darktown Club:
The Question Settled," Currier & Ives, 1885.

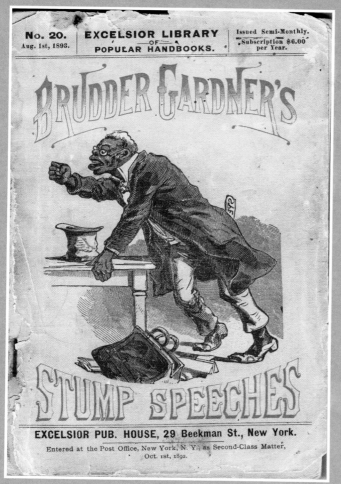

"Brudder Gardner's Stump Speeches," handbook with collection of minstrel speeches to be performed by white actors in blackface, August 1, 1893.

"A Warning," Norman Jennett, political cartoon, *Raleigh News & Observer*, August 30, 1898.

"Heroes of the Colored Race," chromolithograph, J. Hoover, Philadelphia, 1881. In center: Senator Blanche Kelso Bruce, Frederick Douglass, and Senator Hiram Rhodes Revels.

"Colored Chieftains," poster, George M. Rewell & Co., Cleveland, 1885.

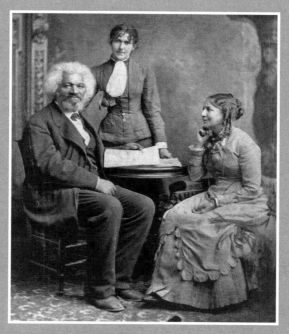

Frederick Douglass, his second wife, Helen Pitts,
and her sister Eva (standing), photograph, 1884.

Sulphur Bitters, the Great Blood Purifier, trading card featuring Douglass and Pitts,
chromolithograph by Mayer Markel & Ottman, New York, ca.1885.

Two

THE OLD NEGRO

Race, Science, Literature, and the Birth of Jim Crow

▼

When men oppress their fellow-men, the oppressor ever finds, in the character of the oppressed, a full justification for his oppression.

—FREDERICK DOUGLASS, "The Claims of the Negro, Ethnologically Considered," Western Reserve College Commencement, July 12, 1854

Between me and the other world there is ever an unasked question: unasked by some through feelings of delicacy; by others through the difficulty of rightly framing it. All, nevertheless, flutter around it. . . . To the real question, How does it feel to be a problem? I answer seldom a word.

And yet, being a problem is a strange experience,—peculiar even for one who has never been anything else, save perhaps in babyhood and in Europe. It is in the early days of rollicking boyhood that the revelation first bursts upon one, all in a day, as it were. I remember well when the shadow swept across me. . . .

—W. E. B. DU BOIS, "Of Our Spiritual Strivings," *The Souls of Black Folk*, 1903

The postwar American South fashioned a political and economic system in which freedpeople were, if no longer slaves, then not fully free either, suspended in a liminal state somewhere between enslavement and quasi-citizenship, as close as a person can be to being a slave without being legally defined as such. But how? If white supremacy, as I am arguing, was—to riff on a formulation of Stuart Hall's—the "free-floating signifier" in the post–Civil War discourse on race, in what forms did it express itself, and how did this perverse fiction that an entire group of human beings was inherently inferior, even subhuman, achieve sufficient popularity and authority to justify that group's disenfranchisement and that oxymoron "second-class citizenship"?[1]

The work of symbolically denigrating freedmen and freedwomen—who would come to be identified by the end of the century as the Old Negro—was a multipronged attack, fought on several fronts simultaneously, and deploying myriad odious images supported by numerous ideologically tainted discourses. Even, perhaps most shockingly, racial science—the use of ostensibly objective "measurements" of difference to define "race" and "race characteristics"—was called upon to "prove" fundamental, "natural," biologically based essential differences between black people and white people. And these "differences" in turn became evidence in the argument for de jure (legal) segregation. In this chapter I want to examine how the ideology of white supremacy took shape in four discourses: racial science, journalism, political rhetoric, and finally fiction and folklore.[2]

RACIAL SCIENCE AND SCIENTIFIC RACISM

Nineteenth–century racial science, often cited as justification for racial slavery, developed largely along two lines in response to a longstanding debate in Europe and the United States that had preoccupied scientists in the eighteenth century as well: What was the cause of the blackness of Africans? The Academy of Bordeaux had challenged respondents to address this conundrum in 1741. Furthermore, did white and black people, and the other "races of man," share a common point of origin (monogenesis), despite differences in skin color, hair texture, and facial features, or had there been distinct "races" from the very beginning of the creation of human beings (polygenesis)?

Religious proponents of monogenesis looked to the authority of the Bible as the basis for their belief in a hierarchical Great Chain of Being: although all people descended from a single Adam and Eve, the original people were white and therefore superior to black people and members of other races, who had "degenerated" from an original white archetype. There were different explanations for how and why this process of degeneration had occurred, and two of the biblically based theories involved a curse. One was that God had created a new, inferior race as a punishment, turning Cain black—branding him with the "mark of Cain" for killing his brother Abel.[3]

Paul Finkelman and Matthew Wilhelm Kapell point to a more popular explanation of the cause of blackness embraced by monogenists, one that was commonly discussed by black people as part of my own Christian upbringing:

> According to the story in the book of Genesis, Noah celebrated the end of his voyage in the ark by getting drunk. While Noah was in that state, his youngest son, Ham, "saw his father's nakedness," while his two brothers, Shem and Japheth, covered their father. When he awoke, Noah cursed not Ham but Ham's son Canaan, declaring "Cursed be Canaan; the lowest of slaves shall he be to his brothers." He went on to declare, "Blessed be the Lord, the God of Shem; let Canaan be a slave to them. May God enlarge Japheth, and let him dwell in the tents of Shem; and let Canaan be a slave to them." Nineteenth-century Southern theologians asserted that this curse rendered Canaan and his children black. They used this text not only to explain racial differences but also to endorse slavery.[4]

Monogenesis sputtered on into the mid-nineteenth century. In early 1850, for example, John Bachman, a professor of natural history at the

College of Charleston in South Carolina, published *The Doctrine of the Unity of the Human Race* and an accompanying article in the *Charleston Medical Journal*. The Lutheran Bachman repeated the idea that Shem was the "parent of the Caucasian race—the progenitor of . . . our Savior," while Ham was the parent of African-descended races.[5] Nevertheless, as Ibram X. Kendi explains, by the time Bachman's works saw the light of day, "northern and southern minds were made up for polygenesis."[6]

While monogenesis found its basis in religion, adherents of polygenesis turned to science to uncover the roots of different races. (That said, they conveniently ignored the evolutionary theories of Charles Darwin, which gained traction in the 1860s.)[7] In this sense, polygenesis grew in popularity during this period because it matched the broader ideological needs of both scientists and nonscientists alike, who sought justification for their racial beliefs and the larger social order. As Nancy Stepan puts it, "By the middle of the nineteenth century, a very complex edifice of thought about human races had been developed in science that was sometimes explicitly, but more often implicitly, racist. Race science, in brief, had a history and coherence of its own to its practitioners . . . an internal logic."[8] While Stepan's research focuses on the scientific scene in Britain, we can see that the ideas she encountered also circulated on this side of the Atlantic. Unpacking what she calls the "scientific discourse on race" is both fascinating as an intellectual exercise and key to understanding the particular forms that white supremacy assumed over the nineteenth century, for the science of race and antiblack racism were inextricably intertwined.

A key proponent of polygenesis was Louis Agassiz, a Swiss-born paleontologist and naturalist hired by Harvard in 1846 as a professor of natural history.[9] Harvard would have a long (and long-ignored) relationship with race-based science for the next several decades. Agassiz argued that all races were created at the same time but came from different "creation centers," which each had their own Adam (European Adam, African Adam, etc.). Even though the different races appeared simultaneously, Agassiz wrote in 1850, it would be wrong "to assume that races have the same abilities, enjoy the same powers, and show the same natural dispositions, and that in consequence of this equality they are entitled to the same position in human society."[10] Agassiz and many advocates of poly-genesis argued that people of different races were actually of different species.

Agassiz used a number of methods in his attempt to demonstrate racial differences. In March 1850 he traveled to Columbia, South Carolina, and commissioned a photographer to make daguerreotypes of a group of slaves. In comparing the likenesses of a nearly naked enslaved man named Renty with those of Agassiz himself, dressed in a dignified suit that signified his "social and professional status as a respected scientist," the writer Molly Rogers notes, "those of Renty were intended to deline-ate all that the naturalist is not—African, slave, subjected body. . . . In Columbia Agassiz sought evidence that would fit humans securely into God's plan like a jigsaw puzzle piece. . . . The daguerreotypes of slaves did not prove the theory of polygenesis. . . . Rather, they proved science itself by conforming to—and therefore appearing to confirm—Agassiz's ideas."[11]

Agassiz had begun as a proponent of monogenesis, but as the cultural anthropologist Lee D. Baker describes, two events "led him to believe Negroes were a separate species altogether."[12] The first was Agassiz's ini-tial encounter with black people, in a hotel in Philadelphia, where "all the domestics . . . were men of color. . . . [T]he feeling that they inspired in me," Agassiz wrote in a letter to his mother the year he arrived at Har-vard, "is contrary to all our ideas about the confraternity of the human type (genre) and the unique origin of our species." Despite "experienc[ing] pity at the sight of this degraded and degenerate race"—so much pity, in fact, that "their lot inspired compassion in me in thinking that they were really men"—"it is impossible for me to repress the feeling that they are not of the same blood as us." He detailed "their black faces with their thick lips and grimacing teeth, the wool on their head, their bent knees, their elongated hands"[13]—all visuals that would become hallmarks of the bestial (and beastly) imagery that flooded the press and publications of the Jim Crow era.

Agassiz's meeting with Samuel George Morton, a Philadelphia-based doctor and phrenologist, also inspired his transition from monogenist to polygenist. The science (today pseudoscience) of phrenology was founded by a German physiologist named Franz Joseph Gall in the early 1800s. (Gall preferred the term "craniology," but it's the term "phrenology" that has stuck.) Even before then, European scientists including Petrus Camper, Johann Kaspar Lavater, and Georges Cuvier had argued for a connection between various physical traits and mental capacity (and, it follows, diminished mental capacity). As David Bindman puts it, "The basis of scientific racism is that Africans have different shaped skulls which relates to the brain inside, which in turn defines their brain power and the power of moral decision." This late-eighteenth-century concept— measuring skulls to measure mental capacity and even moral character— caught fire in the United States during the middle part of the nineteenth century.[14]

Morton owned perhaps the world's largest collection of human skulls. His 1839 book, *Crania Americana; or, A Comparative View of the Skulls of Various Aboriginal Nations of North and South America*, ranked the different races from light to dark, ostensibly based on the shapes and sizes of their skulls. His schema included the Caucasian race at the top ("distinguished for the facility with which it attains the highest intellectual achievements"); Mongolians of East Asia; Malay people of South Asia and the Pacific Islands; Americans, or Native Americans, in the middle; and Ethiopians, or black people, at the bottom ("In disposition the negro is joyous, flexible, and indolent; while the many nations which compose this race present a singular diversity of intellectual character, of which the far extreme is the lowest grade of humanity").[15] In his 1981 book *The Mismeasure of Man*, Stephen Jay Gould destroyed Morton's argument by showing his errors in methodology and his tendency to prioritize whatever findings supported the idea that the white race was superior. But in his time, Morton was profoundly influential.[16] The general public bought what he was selling, and what he was selling was ideal for justifying the enslavement of black people.

In 1851, Samuel Cartwright, a New Orleans doctor and follower of Morton and Agassiz, published "Diseases and Peculiarities of the Negro Race" in *De Bow's Review*, a magazine concerned primarily with agriculture and industry in the South that had a decidedly proslavery bent. The diseases in his report afflicted only black people. One such ailment was "Drapetomania, or the disease causing negroes to run away," as he called it. "If the white man attempts to oppose the Deity's will, by trying to make the negro anything else than 'the submissive knee-bender,' (which the Almighty declared he should be,) by trying to raise him to a level with himself, or by putting himself on an equality with the negro, . . . the negro will run away; but if he keeps him in the position that we learn from the Scriptures he was intended to occupy, . . . the negro is spell-bound, and cannot run away."[17] Infantilization was the preventive medicine for drapetomania. "If treated kindly," Cartwright wrote, ". . . they are very easily governed—more so than any other people in the world. . . . They have only to be kept in that state and treated like children, with care, kindness, attention and humanity, to prevent and cure them from running away."[18]

The second disease Cartwright claimed to identify was "Dysaethesia Aethiopica, or hebetude of mind and obtuse sensibility of body . . . called by overseers, 'Rascality.'" Although the disease purportedly afflicted "free negroes" and all those living on "every spot of earth they have ever had uncontrolled possession over for any length of time," Cartwright's sole concern was to "describe its symptoms among slaves," whose aptitude "to do much mischief, which appears as if intentional, . . . is mostly owing to the stupidity of mind and insensibility of the nerves induced by the disease." Cartwright enumerated its supposed symptoms and chastised Northerners who found fault with slavery instead of with the descendants of slaves themselves:

Thus, they break, waste and destroy everything they handle,—abuse horses and cattle,—tear, burn or rend their own clothing, and, paying no attention to the rights of property, steal others, to replace what they have destroyed. They wander about at night, and keep in a half nodding sleep during the day. They slight their work,—cut up corn, cane, cotton or tobacco when hoeing it, as if for pure mischief. They raise disturbances with their overseers and fellow-servants without cause or motive, and seem to be insensible to pain when subjected to punishment. . . . The northern physicians and people have noticed the symptoms, but not the disease from which they spring. They ignorantly attribute the symptoms to the debasing influence of slavery on the mind without considering that those who have never been in slavery, or their fathers before them, are the most afflicted, and the latest from the slave-holding South the least.[19]

"The disease," Cartwright concluded, "is the natural offspring of negro liberty."[20]

Another important student of Morton was Josiah C. Nott, a proslavery doctor from Alabama. In 1854, Nott and the British ethnologist George Gliddon published *Types of Mankind: or, Ethnological Researches, Based upon the Ancient Monuments, Paintings, Sculptures, and Crania of Races*, a work of polygenesis that, according to Lee D. Baker, provided the "'quantitative' data" slavery supporters needed to bolster their arguments and beliefs.[21]

As Morton had done, Nott and Gliddon explained their view of polygenesis by dividing all of humanity into groups. They defined the term "group" as including "all those proximate races, or species, which resemble each other most closely in type, and whose geographical distribution belongs to certain zoological provinces; for example, the aboriginal *American*, the *Mongol*, the *Malay*, the *Negro*, the *Polynesian* groups, and so forth." Of polygenesis Nott and Gliddon were certain. "The horse, the ass, the zebra, and the quagga, are distinct species and distinct types: and so with the Jew, the Teuton, the Sclavonian, the Mongol, the Australian, the coast Negro, the Hottentot, &c. . . . [A]ll idea of common origin for any two is excluded."[22] Ibram X. Kendi further describes the book's contents: "For visual learners, they inserted an illustration of two columns of faces adjoining skulls: the 'Greek' at the top, the 'ape' at the bottom, the 'Negro' in the middle. The debate over 'the primitive origin of the races' was the 'last grand battle between science and dogmatism.' Who would win? 'Science must again, and finally, triumph!'"[23]

In 1854, in the same year that the debate over slavery raged in the

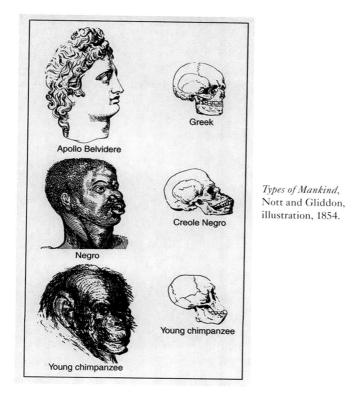

Types of Mankind,
Nott and Gliddon,
illustration, 1854.

expanding United States, stoked further by passage of the Kansas-Nebraska Act, which allowed settlers to choose to permit slavery in the Western territories by vote, and in the same year that America's leading white abolitionist William Lloyd Garrison, in Massachusetts on Independence Day, famously burned a copy of the US Constitution (and, perhaps less famously, a copy of the Fugitive Slave Law),[24] Nott and Gliddon's book, with its affirmation of polygenesis, its insistence that black people were a separate (and inferior) race from whites, was a runaway success.

Also in that year, on July 12, America's leading black abolitionist, Frederick Douglass, offered a critique of this group of race theorists in his commencement address at Western Reserve College, titled "The Claims of the Negro, Ethnologically Considered." Taking on "the Notts, the Gliddens [*sic*], the Agassiz, the Mortons," Douglass argued for the fundamental humanity of African American people: "When men oppress their fellow-men, the oppressor ever finds, in the character of the oppressed, a full justification for his oppression."[25]

These eminent scholars on the receiving end of Douglass's ire were not alone. Douglass used the occasion to skewer an editorial published by the editor John M. Daniel in the *Richmond Examiner*, a reliable and passionate defender of the merits of human slavery and white supremacy. (Edward Pollard, who literally wrote the book on the Lost Cause and who often found himself at odds with Douglass, would serve as the wartime editor of the *Examiner*, from 1861 to 1867.) Daniel's editorial, written seven years before the Civil War began, in a milieu in which works of scientific racism were gaining ever more ground, argued in bruising language that the so-called nature of black people justified their enslavement:

> The true defence of negro slavery is to be sought in the sciences of ethnology and natural history. The last defines the negro to be the connecting link between the human and brute creation. . . . From the most powerful family of the white race, we proceed by regular steps to the lowest type of the dark race, which is the negro; and close to him we find the chimpanzee of his native country, the first step in what we call brute creation. The difference between the last of the one series and the first of the other, is not greater—hardly so great— as between the last and the first of the human family itself.

And what are the implications of this "difference" between "man" and "brute" and their place on the Great Chain of Being; what is the relation, then, between "race" and rights? To Daniel the answer was obvious:

> To place the two on an equality; to treat two creatures so utterly different as the white man and negro man on the same system; to claim for them the same sphere of action; to call on them to exercise the same powers and do the same actions, is an effort to violate elementary laws, and to alter the course of Nature. . . .
>
> All arguments drawn from principles invented and intended for the white man, like aphorisms of our Declaration of Independence,

are, when applied to the negro, illogical. They involve the assumption that the negro is the white man, only a little different in external appearance and education. But this assumption cannot be supported. Ethnology and anatomy, history and daily observation, all contradict the idea in a way about which there can be no mistake. It is an assumption founded on an utter ignorance of the animal in whose supposed behalf it is made. Again and again we repeat it, the negro is not the white man. Not with more safety do we assert that a hog is not a horse. Hay is good for horses, but not for hogs. Liberty is good for white men, but not for negroes.[26]

That Africans and those of African descent were either not human or fully human was a cardinal tenet of proslavery thought and reveals the depths of depravity at the heart of white supremacist ideology. In his commencement address, Douglass quoted from Daniel's speech at length, and he railed against it unremittingly. "We bind him by law to the condition of the laboring peasant for ever, without his consent and we bind his posterity after him. Now, the true question is, have we a right to do this? . . . If the negro has the same right to his liberty and the pursuit of his own happiness that the White man has, then we commit the greatest wrong and robbery to hold him a slave—an act at which the sentiment of justice must revolt in every heart—and negro slavery is an institution which that sentiment must sooner or later blot from the face of the earth." Now, for a moment, Douglass addressed the audience directly: "After stating the question thus, the 'Examiner boldly asserts that the negro has no such right—BECAUSE HE IS NOT A MAN!'"

Before the war, Northern abolitionists, along with Douglass, repudiated the rejection of the African's common humanity with the European, of the Negro's with the white man's. Even Abraham Lincoln in his debates with Stephen Douglas took his opponent to task for assuming blacks were not human, while Lincoln insisted they were, and that they were entitled to the natural rights listed in the Declaration of Independence. Moreover, abolitionists, as foils to proslavery Southerners, used a range of images to promote recognition of African American humanity, starting with the ubiquitous icon "Am I Not a Man and a Brother?"

"Am I Not a Man and a Brother?," wood engraving,
late eighteenth century.

It's worth noting that black military service in the Civil War compelled many Northern white people to acknowledge the humanity of black people. But for those who wanted to defend slavery and do their best to restore it after its abolition, as closely as they could, the heroism of black soldiers was a threat rather than an inspiration.

Daniel's argument was the (barely) repressed element at the heart of antiblack racism that would surface with disturbing regularity throughout the remainder of the century, long after Reconstruction had been dismantled. After all, when the smoke cleared after Lee's surrender at Appomattox, cotton still had to be picked, and the Negro's labor had to be exploited as ruthlessly and as effectively as possible. Any expectation of "equal rights" or "equal protection of the law" had to be obliterated, and the massive potential of the black male vote in key Southern states thwarted, if the old order of a slave-based Confederate society was to be reestablished as seamlessly as possible.

POST-CIVIL WAR SCIENTIFIC RACISM

Just as scholars and writers in the first half of the nineteenth century appealed to science to justify slavery, postwar writers used science to oppose Reconstruction and equal rights for African Americans.

The political climate invited this. While elected and appointed officials weren't necessarily citing these scientists outright, in these postwar years, the so-called scientific findings that had been perpetuated for decades were given a voice in the popular press and in the chambers of government. On October 1, 1866, Benjamin Franklin Perry, the provisional governor of South Carolina, wrote about freedpeople in the *Charleston Daily Courier:* "The African, has been in all ages, a savage or a slave. God created him inferior to the white man in form, color, and intellect, and no legislation or culture can make him his equal. You might as well expect to make the fox the equal of the lion in courage and strength, or the ass the equal of the horse in symmetry and fleetness. His color is black; his head covered with wool instead of hair, his form and features will not compete with the Caucasian race, and it is in vain to think of elevating him to the dignity of the white man. God created differences between the two races, and nothing can make him equal."[27] Less than a year later, on June 3, 1867, in the *Columbia Phoenix,* Perry's fear was focused on the voting booth. "[I]t will be impossible to maintain a just, wise and permanent republican form of government where a majority of the voters are ignorant, stupid, demi-savage paupers. They ought to see, too, that the peace and quiet of the State cannot be preserved where there are two antagonistic races clothed with equal political powers, and the inferior race superior to it in numbers."[28]

Also in 1867, the writer and nominal political figure Hinton Helper, who had been appointed consul to Buenos Aires by Lincoln in 1861[29] and whose prewar pamphlet *The Impending Crisis* had argued that slavery was a disaster for poorer whites and the white South more broadly, painted an exceptionally ugly portrait of blacks. His language as well as his descriptions of the disease-riddled condition of the "sable individual before us" recalled that of the polygenists and phrenologists who flourished in the antebellum years. "The night-born ogre stands before us: we observe his low, receding forehead; his broad, depressed nose; his stammering, stuttering speech; and his general actions, evidencing monkey-like littleness and imbecility of mind. . . . Aye, in almost every possible respect, he is a person of ill proportion, blemish and disfigurement; and no truer is it that the Turk (in Europe) is the sick man of the East, than that the negro (in America) is the sick man of the West."[30]

Science—and racism—marched on. The lawyer-turned-anthropologist Lewis Henry Morgan, the founder of a secret society called the Grand Order of the Iroquois in upstate New York in the 1840s, first earned a reputation as an authority on race in the 1850s thanks to his research on Iroquois Native Americans. He would find his greatest acclaim in 1877, the year Reconstruction ended, with the publication of his most (in)famous book, *Ancient Society, or Researches in the Lines of Human Progress from Savagery through Barbarism to Civilization.* In *Ancient Society,* Morgan, then a professor at Yale, connected racial evolution with materialism, arguing that mankind passed in a linear fashion through three stages: savagery, barbarism, and civilization. Different races, Morgan argued, were at different points in this process, and their status was not fixed. As "with the production of inventions and discoveries, and with the growth of institutions, the human mind necessarily grew and expanded," he wrote; "and we are led to recognize a gradual enlargement of the brain itself," which signaled development.[31] Predictably, the white race—"the Aryan family"—received Morgan's highest praise, "represent[ing] the central stream of human progress, because it produced the highest type of mankind, and because it has proved its intrinsic superiority by gradually assuming control of the earth."[32]

The Gilded Age in the last quarter of the nineteenth century saw scientists such as Herbert Spencer and William Graham Sumner, a colleague of Morgan's at Yale, attempt to apply Charles Darwin's theory of evolution to biology. "Social Darwinism" was based on the idea of survival of the fittest—that the wealthy and powerful were thus because they were biologically and therefore culturally superior. Although Spencer and Sumner were concerned more with economics and the poor than with race, to the late-nineteenth-century racial theorists who followed them, it stood to reason that people of color were at the bottom of the social order because of their biology, and that race was a product of evolution, an immutable trait that could not be changed.[33] Randall Fuller explains that abolitionists had embraced Darwin's work as proof that slaves were human, but postwar white racial theorists interpreted the message differently: "[M]any people translated Darwin's theory to social issues, some arguing that privileged classes had no obligation to help those who had failed to adapt to an increasingly industrialized modern world. Such arguments not only justified the business interests of the Gilded Age, they exercised especially pernicious effects on race relations during the Reconstruction period and beyond."[34]

Frederick Hoffman, a German-born statistician and life insurance agent for Prudential in Newark, New Jersey, interpreted race difference statistically. Hoffman came to fame in 1896 (the year the US Supreme Court's decision in *Plessy v. Ferguson* read its "separate but equal" doctrine into the Constitution) with the publication of his heralded *Race Traits and Tendencies of the American Negro*. Citing data such as chest measurements, inferior vision, and susceptibility to respiratory diseases, Hoffman wrote of inherent "traits" among African Americans. Pounding the drumbeat of "facts," he then used that data to demonstrate black inferiority. He argued that the black population, now unshackled from what he considered the many benefits afforded by enslavement, stood in its own way of success, as well as that of the white population. He blamed "modern educational and philanthropic efforts [for] making it even more dependent on the white race at the present time than it was previous to emancipation":

All the facts prove that the colored population is gradually parting with the virtues and the moderate degree of economic efficiency developed under the regime of slavery. All the facts prove that a low standard of sexual morality is the main and underlying cause of the low and anti-social condition of the race at the present time. All the facts prove that education, philanthropy and religion have failed to develop a higher appreciation of the stern and uncompromising virtues of the Aryan race. The conclusion is warranted that it is merely a question of time when the actual downward course, that is, a decrease in the population, will take place. In the meantime, however, the presence of the colored population is a serious hindrance to the economic progress of the white race.[35]

Black scholars struck back. The following year, 1897, the Howard University professor of mathematics and sociology Kelly Miller, in a review for the American Negro Academy, argued: "The author's conclusion will not stand the philosophical tests of a sound theory. . . . The author fails to consider that the discouraging facts of observation may be due to the violent upheaval of emancipation and reconstruction, and are, therefore, only temporary in their duration."[36]

Working at the time on what would become his landmark sociological study, *The Philadelphia Negro* (1899), W. E. B. Du Bois, having secured a temporary appointment at the University of Pennsylvania two years after becoming the first African American to receive a PhD from Harvard, also reviewed the book, concluding: "To sum up briefly, the value of Mr. Hoffman's work lies in the collection and emphasis of a number of interesting and valuable data in regard to the American Negro. Most of the conclusions drawn from these facts are, however, of doubtful value, on account of the character of the material, the extent of the field, and the unscientific use of the scientific method." (Du Bois also managed to get in a dig at Hoffman's style: "As a piece of book-making this work invites criticism for its absence of page headings or rubrics, and its unnecessary use of italics. Moreover, Mr. Hoffman has committed the unpardonable sin of publishing a book of 329 pages without an index.")[37]

While in Philadelphia, Du Bois also authored "The Conservation of Races," an examination of past, present, and future conceptions of race and racial differences. Du Bois related why this topic was of such great importance: "The American Negro has always felt an intense personal interest in discussions as to the origins and destinies of races: primarily because back of most discussions of race with which he is familiar, have lurked certain assumptions as to his natural abilities, as to his political, intellectual and moral status, which he felt were wrong."[38] Du Bois exposed the inconsistency in the "scientific" justifications for racial difference:

> When we thus come to inquire into the essential difference of races we find it hard to come at once to any definite conclusion. Many criteria of race differences have in the past been proposed, as color, hair, cranial measurements and language. And manifestly, in each of these respects, human beings differ widely. . . . Unfortunately for scientists, however, these criteria of race are most exasperatingly intermingled. . . . The final word of science, so far, is that we have at least two, perhaps three, great families of human beings—the whites and Negroes, possibly the yellow race. . . . This broad division of the world's races . . . is nothing more than an acknowledgment that, so far as purely physical characteristics are concerned, the differences between men do not explain all the differences of their history. It declares, as Darwin himself said, that great as is the physical unlikeness of the various races of men their likenesses are greater, and upon this rests the whole scientific doctrine of Human Brotherhood.[39]

Written in a similar "fact-based" vein as Hoffman's *Race Traits and Tendencies of the American Negro* and in the same year was *The Surgical Peculiarities of the American Negro* (1896) by Rudolph Matas, a professor of surgery at Tulane University. Drawing on the work of the proslavery physician and polygenist Josiah Nott, Matas put forward the view that "[a]part from the inherent social weakness which must result from centuries of servitude and bondage, apart from the inferior intellectual, moral, and economic qualities, and only considering the phase of the race problem from a numerical point of view, the negro of the present day and for a long time to come is destined to furnish a large contingent of the indigent, dependent, and defective classes in the Southern States, and, with this prospect before us, his physiological, pathological, as well as sociological peculiarities are at present, even more than in the past, of deep interest to the thinking men, and especially to the medical men of the nation."[40]

Matas reached a number of conclusions—eleven, to be precise, printed in a list spanning the final two pages of his book—that illuminated key assumptions behind scientific racism, among them: "The North American negro, as he is known at present in the United States, is anthropologically, physiologically, and pathologically different from his original African ancestors and from his uncivilized brothers in the West Coast of Africa of the present generation." These differences were brought about by "A residence of nearly three hundred years on the Southern States of North America in contact with the white man and under the influence of civilization" and "acclimatization and adaptation to surroundings other than those of climate, and especially to miscegenation with the white race." (Matas's argument about the sui generis nature of the American Negro would be echoed, ironically, by the anthropologist Melville Herskovits in an essay he published in Alain Locke's *The New Negro* in 1925, and also by the sociologist E. Franklin Frazier, in a later debate with Herskovits, who would famously change his mind and become perhaps the leading proponent of his generation about cultural continuity between Africans and African Americans.)[41]

Matas continued, "[T]he general morbidity and mortality of the colored race was less than that of the white population" under slavery and through emancipation, but "since the colored race has been thrown upon its own resources . . . its morbidity and mortality have enormously increased." And although Matas found, "When viewed from the purely surgical operative standpoint, the white and the negro are practically alike," we must recall the professor's conclusion that "the degenerative tendencies of the colored race revealed by statistics, are due, essentially, to the influence of unfavorable hygienic surroundings; to unfavorable social (including moral) environment; to all the causes which lead to a bad heredity, vice, dependency, and degradation, and which are acting simultaneously upon an ethnologically inferior and passive race which is struggling for existence with a superior, aggressive, and dominant population."[42] In other words, environmental factors only compound fundamental "ethnological" differences, differences inscribed by nature.

If physical distinctions proved insufficient, historians of the era also used scientific ideas of "characteristics" to justify black inferiority, societal decline, and the collapse of Reconstruction. In the case of William Dunning and his students and colleagues at Columbia University, who collectively became known as the Dunning School, it was the innate differences of black people that had ensured Reconstruction's failure. Dunning wrote in the *Atlantic* in 1901: "The ultimate root of the trouble in the South had been, not the institution of slavery, but the coexistence in one society of two races so distinct in characteristics as to render coalescence impossible; that slavery had been a modus vivendi through which social life was possible; and that, after its disappearance, its place must be taken by some set of conditions which, if more humane and beneficent in accidents, must in essence express the same fact of racial inequality. The progress in the acceptance of this idea in the North has measured the progress in the South of the undoing of reconstruction."[43]

Dunning acknowledged two "distinct" races. Charles Carroll, a polygenist minister from Missouri, subscribed to no such belief. During the post-Reconstruction era in which these men were working, the religious basis that informed the monogenist and polygenist arguments of the middle part of the century had taken a back seat to the authority of science and the seeming objectivity of statistics. But with the publication of Carroll's *The Negro, a Beast; or, "In the Image of God"* (1900), a screed against miscegenation disguised as science, religion came racing back to the forefront. Carroll touted his work for its use of "Biblical and Scientific Facts Demonstrating that the Negro is not an Offspring of the Adamic Family."[44] On the title page, he stated his "findings" outright: "The Negro, a beast, but created with articulate speech and hands, that he may be of service to his owner—the White man."[45] Carroll equated evolution with atheism; whites and blacks were not people of different races descended from the same source but beings, one human and one otherwise, descended from different creatures altogether. Carroll declared:

All scientific investigation of the subject [of black-white relations] proves the Negro to be an ape; and that he simply stands at the head of the ape family, as the lion stands at the head of the cat family. When God's plan of creation, and the drift of Bible history are properly understood, it will be found that the teachings of scripture upon this, as upon every other subject, harmonize with those of science. This being true, it follows that the Negro is the only anthropoid, or man-like ape; and that the gibbon, ourang, chimpanzee and gorilla are merely negro-like apes. Hence, to recognize the Negro as a "man and a brother," they were compelled to declare man an ape. Thus the modern Christian, like the atheist, takes man, whom God created "in his own image," and takes the Negro, whom God made "after his kind"—the ape kind—and places them in the same family, as different "races" of one "species" of animal.[46]

Carroll refuted the idea that blacks descended from Ham; this would mean the Negro was a man, but nothing, in the minister's view, could be further from the truth. Yes, blacks had a place in the story of Noah, but not in that regard:

The Negro, being an ape, entered the ark with the rest of the animals; and as the descendants of Noah spread out over the earth they carried with them their negroes and other domestic animals, domestic plants, metallic implements, etc., and developed those superb civilizations the remains of which are found on every continent of the earth. . . . The extent and grandeur of these old civilizations indicate that for a long period after the Deluge these people respected the design of God in creating man, lived in obedience to his law and maintained the relation of master and servant between themselves and the Negro, and were happy and prosperous. . . . But in the course of ages they forgot God, descended to amalgamation, and this, in turn, gave birth to idolatry.[47]

This, in turn, gave birth to the unspeakable: race mixing. Amalgamation, as Carroll called it, was nothing short of a crime against God. "The offspring of Man and the Negro is not upon the earth in deference to Divine will, but in violation of Divine law. . . . Inasmuch as the immediate offspring of Man and the Negro is corrupted flesh, it follows that its ultimate offspring could never become pure. If mated continuously with pure whites for millions of generations, you could never breed the ape out, nor breed the spiritual creation in, the offspring of Man and the Negro."[48]

This corruption of God's plan put not only society at risk, but humanity itself. No good could come of race mixing, a "fact" borne out by Carroll's observations. "They prove that the Negro belongs to the flesh of beasts, from the fact that his offspring by a man, though mated continuously with negroes will not revert to the Negro, but approximates a lower grade of animal."[49] Miscegenation was an abomination, and as such, the offspring of such a union would not be entitled to the rights with which free people were imbued. "[T]he immediate offspring of man and the Negro—the mulatto—was doomed by Divine edict to instant death in the very moment of conception. Hence, neither the mulatto nor his ultimate offspring can acquire the right to live. This being true, it follows that these monstrosities have no rights social, financial, political or religious that man need respect; they have no rights that man dare respect—not even the right to live."[50]

EUGENICS AND PROGRESSIVISM

The most devastating form of scientific racism was yet to come in the twentieth century, advanced by the eugenics movement, which unfolded as the New Negro movement did. The British biologist Francis Galton coined the term "eugenics" in 1883 from the Greek "well born." Daniel J. Kevles writes of Galton: "All around him the technology of the industrial revolution confirmed man's mastery over inanimate nature."[51] Eugenics therefore reflected, ironically, impulses of progressivism—that man could shape and control nature through the application of science and technology. Galton was a supporter of "positive eugenics," or the use of selective breeding to create a genetically superior race and to eliminate "inferior" people. According to Galton, a half-cousin of Charles Darwin, "What

Nature does blindly, slowly, and ruthlessly, man may do providently, quickly, and kindly."[52] In 1904, he argued that eugenics must be "introduced into the national consciousness, like a new religion."[53] The poet and physician Oliver Wendell Holmes, Sr., a supporter of Galton's, wrote in 1875, years before the "science" was given a name, about the flip side of Galton's statement: "If genius and talent are inherited, as Mr. Galton has so conclusively shown, why should not deep-rooted moral defects . . . show themselves . . . in the descendants of moral monsters?"[54]

Where else could speculation like this lead but to negative eugenics, the overtly sinister cousin of positive eugenics? Supporters of negative eugenics called for outlawing interracial marriage, severely restricting immigration, and mandating sterilization.[55] In 1907 Indiana became the first state to pass a eugenics law in an effort "to prevent procreation of confirmed criminals, idiots, imbeciles, and rapists."[56] Four years later, in 1911, Harvard's president emeritus Charles Eliot wrote that Indiana "blazed the trail which all free states must follow, if they would protect themselves from moral degeneracy."[57] (Sterilization laws were new, but antimiscegenation laws weren't. In 1909 William H. Milton, a Democratic senator from Florida, introduced a resolution to ban interracial marriages. What was novel about the resolution was its basis on multiple "scientific" findings—including "Average weight of brain . . . gorilla 20 ounces, negro 35 ounces, European 45 ounces"—that established black people as a "distinct species.")[58]

Harvard emerged as a center of eugenics thought in the United States. As Adam S. Cohen writes: "Harvard administrators, faculty members, and alumni were at the forefront of American eugenics—founding eugenics organizations, writing academic and popular eugenics articles, and lobbying government to enact eugenics laws. And for many years, scarcely any significant Harvard voices, if any at all, were raised against it."[59] Support for eugenics found a home elsewhere in academe, at Stanford, Yale, and the University of Virginia, but according to Cohen, "Harvard was more central to American eugenics than any other university. Harvard has, with some justification, been called the 'brain trust' of twentieth-century eugenics, but the role it played is little remembered or remarked upon today."[60] It's understandable that this august university, my home for the last twenty-seven years, would find little to boast about in this part of its history.

A central figure in the American eugenics movement was Charles Davenport, the son of an abolitionist, who earned a PhD from Harvard in zoology and taught at the school. Davenport, like other burgeoning eugenicists, took the hereditary theories of Gregor Mendel, which were based on studies of plants and mice, and applied them to humans. In other words, Davenport theorized that traits such as skin color and mental capacity could be manipulated through reproduction. He thus supported sterilization and dedicated his work to cataloging the reasons why poor people, minorities, and criminals were unfit to reproduce.[61] He argued that "the most progressive revolution in history" could occur if "human matings could be placed on the same high plane as that of horse breeding."[62] In 1910, he opened the Eugenics Records Office in Cold Spring Harbor, New York, which became an intellectual hub for eugenics researchers. A year later his book *Heredity in Relation to Eugenics* became, in Siddhartha Mukherjee's words, "the movement's bible" and a classroom staple, widely read in the eugenics courses that were gaining popularity on college campuses and even at high schools.[63] In it Davenport wrote, "The eugenical standpoint is that of the agriculturalist who, while recognizing the value of culture, believes that permanent advance is to be made only by securing the best 'blood.'"[64] Ibram X. Kendi writes of the popularity of eugenics: "The eugenics movement created believers, not evidence. Americans wanted to believe that the racial, ethnic, class, and gender hierarchies in the United States were natural and normal."[65]

WORLD WAR I

United States involvement in World War I gave the nation's eugenicist scientists a vast new playing field on which to test their theories, theories whose veracity they never seemed to question. The US Army used an intelligence test designed by the Harvard psychology professor Robert

Yerkes, the results of which Stephen Jay Gould summarizes in *The Mismeasure of Man*. According to Gould, the finding that "[t]he average mental age of white American adults stood just above the edge of moronity at a shocking and meager thirteen . . . became a rallying point for eugenicists who predicted doom and lamented our declining intelligence, caused by the unconstrained breeding of the poor and feebleminded, the spread of Negro blood through miscegenation, and the swamping of an intelligent native stock by the immigrating dregs of southern and eastern Europe." Furthermore, "European immigrants [could] be graded by their country of origin," with fair Nordic populations planted firmly at the top of the scale and darker-complexioned Italians near the bottom. Not surprisingly, based on the available "science," "the Negro lies at the bottom of the scale," and in one experiment, "blacks were divided into three groups based upon intensity of color; the lighter groups scored higher."[66]

World War I led eugenicists to question the very future of the "white race." In 1916, Madison Grant published *The Passing of the Great Race; or, The Racial Bias of European History*. Grant, who would serve as the vice president of the Immigration Restriction League and would work in support of the National Origins Act of 1924,[67] wrote: "The great lesson of the science of race is the immutability of somatological or bodily characters, with which is closely associated the immutability of psychical predispositions and impulses. . . . Furthermore, race lies at the base of all the manifestation of modern society, just as it has done throughout the unrecorded eons of the past and the laws of nature operate with the same relentless and unchanging force in human affairs as in the phenomena of inanimate nature."[68]

Henry Fairfield Osborn, a eugenicist and the president of the American Museum of Natural History in New York City, wrote the preface to Grant's book. In it Osborn offered a summary of eugenicist thought: "Race has played a far larger role than either language or nationality in moulding the destinies of men; race implies heredity and heredity implies all the moral, social, and intellectual characteristics and traits which are the springs of politics and government. . . . The moral tendency of the hereditary interpretation of history is for our day and generation and is in strong accord with the true spirit of the modern eugenics movement in relation to patriotism, namely the conservation and multiplication for our country of the best spiritual, moral, intellectual and physical forces of heredity; thus only will the integrity of our institutions be maintained in the future."[69]

In 1920, a student of Grant's and yet another Harvard PhD, Lothrop Stoddard, published *The Rising Tide of Color against White World-Supremacy* (with an introduction from Grant). The book had a tremendous impact, with fourteen printings in its first three years, and it was praised by President Warren G. Harding.[70] It also made its way into fiction, enthusiastically endorsed by the character Tom Buchanan in F. Scott Fitzgerald's novel *The Great Gatsby* (1925), as "*The Rise of the Colored Empires* by this man Goddard." In Stoddard's volume (not the fictional Goddard's), the author warned that World War I had weakened white power by initiating the migrations of people of color into white lands: "To me, the Great War was the first White Civil War. . . . The subjugation of white lands by colored armies may, of course, occur, especially if the white world continues to rend itself with internecine wars. However, such colored triumphs of arms are less to be dreaded than more enduring conquests like migrations which would swamp whole populations and turn countries now white into colored man's land irretrievably lost to the white world. . . . Two things are necessary for the continued existence of a race: it must remain itself, and it must breed its best."[71]

Just as the white supremacist ideology seemingly infiltrated every corner of late-nineteenth-century life, eugenicist thought was by no means the philosophy of a fringe element. The movement in the United States won a significant legal victory in 1927, when the Supreme Court (in an 8–1 decision) upheld Virginia's sterilization law in *Buck v. Bell*. In his majority decision for the court, Oliver Wendell Holmes, Jr., wrote: "It is better for all the world if, instead of waiting to execute degenerate offspring for crime or to let them starve for their imbecility, society can prevent those who are manifestly unfit from continuing their kind. . . . Three generations of imbeciles are enough."[72]

DEFINING THE "NEGRO PROBLEM"

It was out of this fraught environment, in which science was being used to bolster racial stereotypes instead of to break them down, that Jim Crow was born. Novelists and scholars of the era would breathe life into the concept of the degraded, degenerate "Old Negro" in their works. And myriad writers—especially white American men—would attempt to define the "Negro Problem" and propose solutions to it, largely at the expense of the Negro's rights. Through this intertwining and overlapping of themes over decades, across genres and disciplines, we can begin to see how the patchwork of white supremacy was knitted into the suffocating blanket of Jim Crow, unfolding after decades of bad racial science and political debates about causes of—and solutions to—the so-called Negro Problem.

In the years that witnessed the demise of Reconstruction, the challenge to the quest for equal rights before the law, and the institutionalization of Jim Crow segregation, academics, politicians, and other political figures, most of them apologists for segregation, argued that black Americans indeed faced challenges, but black leadership or black self-determination would not be up to meeting those challenges. Instead, white Americans were morally obligated, in the most paternalistic way, to step in and solve the so-called Negro Problem *for* the Negro, not *with* him. Their motivation often flowed from a perverted sense of noblesse oblige. Consistently, these writers reiterated that racial discrimination was not the source of the Negro Problem. Moreover, their obligation to solve it arose not from a desire to right past wrongs, but from a belief that African Americans were unequipped to be the masters of their own destiny, a fact they believed to be rendered patently apparent during Reconstruction.

In fact, this position had been argued from the earliest days of Reconstruction. For example, in 1865, Christopher Memminger, the former secretary of the treasury for the Confederacy, said to President Andrew Johnson: "The African is virtually in the condition of the youth. . . . He is subjected to the guidance and control of one better informed. He is bound as an apprentice to be trained and directed; and is under restraint until he is capable of discharging the duties of manhood."[73] The rabidly proslavery writer George Fitzhugh went so far as to call the Freedmen's Bureau "merely a negro nursery. . . . The Negro Nursery is an admirable idea of the Federals, which, however, they stole from us. For we always told them the darkeys were but grown-up children that needed guardians, like all other children."[74]

Founded in Boston in 1857 by James Russell Lowell (who would serve as its first editor), Ralph Waldo Emerson, and Henry Wadsworth Longfellow, among others with impeccable abolitionist credentials,[75] the *Atlantic Monthly*, by the post-Reconstruction years, often provided a forum for white scholars working toward conceptualizing the so-called Negro Problem. The thinking presented in the *Atlantic* evolved—to use that word in a most ironic way—in the span of just a few years. Perhaps it is more correct to say that the emphasis shifted from the promotion of the Negro-as-separate-species theory to a less vitriolic, albeit dreadfully paternalistic, one. In February 1882, the magazine ran an article called "Negro Types," published anonymously but written by Jonathan Baxter Harrison in his *Studies in the South* series,[76] which unapologetically promoted the former: "the uncouth, strangely shaped animal-looking Negro or mulatto, who seems mentally, even more than by his physical characteristics, to belong to a race entirely distinct from that of the white race around them. He is not so much hostile or antagonistic as alien, unimpressible, inaccessible. He cannot be influenced or guided to any extent. He must have his way. He will only do so much work, and will labor only under conditions natural and desirable to him."[77] In July 1884, the magazine presented a special forum on "The Future of the Negro." And in November of that year, the Harvard paleontologist Nathaniel S. Shaler published his essay "The Negro Problem." In it Shaler proposed theories based on the inherited characteristics of racial difference, starting from a point of African American incapability:

First, I hold it to be clear that the inherited qualities of the negroes to a great degree unfit them to carry the burden of our own civilization; that their present Americanized shape is due in large part to the strong control to which they have been subjected since the enslavement of their blood; that there will naturally be a strong tendency, for many generations to come, for them to revert to their ancestral conditions. If their present comparative elevation had been due to self-culture in a state of freedom, we might confide in it; but as it is the result of an external compulsion issuing from the will of a dominant race, we cannot trust it. Next, I hold it to be almost equally clear that they cannot as a race, for many generations, be brought to the level of our own people. There will always be a danger that by falling to the bottom of society they will form a proletariat class, separated by blood as well as by estate from the superior classes; thus bringing about a measure of the evils of the slavery system—evils that would curse both the races that were brought together in a relation so unfit for modern society.[78]

Shaler, who had been trained by Louis Agassiz, believed that "American slavery, though it had the faults inherent in any system of subjugation and mastery among men, was infinitely the mildest and most decent system of slavery that ever existed. When the bonds of the slave were broken, master and servant stayed beside each other, without much sign of fear or any very wide sundering of the old relations of service and support."[79] Shaler cited black people's helplessness as a reason for white intervention: "The insensate greed of our ancestors took this simple folk from their dark land and placed them in our fields and by our firesides. Here they have multiplied to millions, and have been forced without training into the duties of a citizenship that often puzzles the brains of those who were trained by their ancestry to a sense of its obligations. Our race has placed these burdens upon them, and we, as its representatives, owe a duty to these black-skinned folk a thousand times heavier than that which binds us to the voluntary immigrants to our land."[80]

Shaler concluded by again minimizing the role that black people themselves could play in their own advancement. African Americans must open themselves up to white solutions. "If the negro is thoughtfully cared for," he wrote, "if his training in civilization, begun in slavery, is continued in his state of freedom, we may hope to find abundant room for him in our society. He has a strong spring of life within him, though his life flows in channels foreign to our own. Once fix in him the motives that are necessary for citizenship in a republic, and we may gain rather than lose from his presence on our soil. The proper beginning is to give him a chance to receive the benefits of the education that comes from varied and skillful industry."[81]

In response to a comment by General Samuel Chapman Armstrong, the founder of Hampton Institute and the mentor of Booker T. Washington, about the necessity of giving black people access to education, Shaler the educator balked at "the value to the negro of a high purely literary education. The time may come when such a training will bear the same relation to their inheritances that it does to those of the literate class of our own race, but as a rule the little colored girl was right: 'You can't get clean corners and algebra into the same nigger.' That combination is with difficulty effected in our own blood. The world demands the *clean corners*; it is not so particular about the *algebra*."[82]

The idea that (academic) education was lost on black people was certainly nothing new, as South Carolina's senator John C. Calhoun made clear when he declared that until he encountered a black man who had mastered Greek and Latin, he would not be convinced of the inherent equality of white and black people. According to his own testimony, Alexander Crummell, W. E. B. Du Bois's hero, took this as a personal challenge and matriculated at the University of Cambridge in part to prove Calhoun wrong.[83] At the turn of the century, Booker T. Washington practically built an empire, we might charitably say, by turning this idea on its head. But earlier, at the end of the Civil War, the Freedmen's Bureau teacher Elizabeth Hyde Botume recounted a comment leveled at her about the pointlessness of her work, an idea that recalls one of the tenets of scientific racism and demonstrates how widely and perniciously it had penetrated public opinion: "'I do assure you,' once said a Southern woman to me, 'you might as well try to teach your horse or mule to read, as to teach these niggers. They can't learn. . . . [T]he country niggers are like monkeys. You can't *learn* them to come in when it rains.'"[84]

Joel Williamson, a scholar of Southern culture, credits Shaler with conferring intellectual legitimacy on the idea that, post-slavery, African

Americans were "retrogressing" to what Shaler called "their ancestral conditions." Shaler, Williamson writes, was "[p]robably the first significant person to promote the theory of retrogression in a scientific way." At the same time, ironically, Shaler was one of W. E. B. Du Bois's "favorite professors" at Harvard. Apparently, Shaler expelled from his class a student "who objected to sitting next to Du Bois because of his color."[85]

THE NEGRO: A PROBLEM OF WHOSE MAKING?

The Negro Problem preoccupied Southerners who viewed Reconstruction as a terrible mistake, a period when white people were stripped of their dignity as (and because) black people were imbued with the inalienable rights of American citizens that should have remained alien to them. The diabolically clever Henry Grady, the editor of the *Atlanta Constitution*, considered the issue in his famous "New South" speech of December 22, 1886, which was an ingenious rebranding of the Old South in the guise of the New. Speaking before a crowd of Northerners in New York City, Grady envisioned a New South that looked more like the North—centered on an industrialized economy, trade, and education. He claimed that African Americans would have important roles in the New South, but his rosy, paternalistic description of how the South had allegedly solved the Negro Problem blatantly ignored the dangerous reality that black people faced: "He shares our school fund, has the fullest protection of our laws and the friendship of our people. Self-interest, as well as honor, demand that he should have this. Our future, our very existence depend upon our working out this problem in full and exact justice."[86]

Mistreatment of Southern black people, according to Grady, was not systemic but rather the result of a few bad actors. "The relations of the Southern people with the Negro are close and cordial," he said. "We remember with what fidelity for four years he guarded our defenceless women and children, whose husbands and fathers were fighting against his freedom. . . . Ruffians have maltreated him, rascals have misled him, philanthropists established a bank for him, but the South, with the

North, protects against injustice to this simple and sincere people." But there were limits to this seeming magnanimity. "To liberty and enfranchisement is as far as law can carry the Negro," Grady declared. "The rest must be left to conscience and common sense."[87]

One year later, however, on October 26, 1887, Grady defined these limits of conscience and common sense. At the Dallas, Texas, State Fair, in a speech called "The South and Her Problems," Grady romanticized slavery in exceptionally personal terms:[88]

I want no better friend than the black boy who was raised by my side, and who is now trudging patiently with downcast eyes and shambling figure through his lowly way in life. I want no sweeter music than the crooning of my old 'mammy,' now dead and gone to rest, as I heard it when she held me in her loving arms, and bending her old black face above me stole the cares from my brain, and led me smiling into sleep. I want no truer soul than that which moved the trusty slave, who for four years, while my father fought with the armies that barred his freedom, slept every night at my mother's chamber door, holding her and her children as safe as if her husband stood guard, and ready to lay down his humble life on her threshold. History has no parallel to the faith kept by the negro in the South during the war.[89]

For Grady, this beautiful relationship—the stuff of romance, so lovingly misrepresented, so frighteningly one-sided—was in jeopardy, threatened by the perils of black citizenship and black suffrage. "In less than twelve months from the day he walked down the furrow a slave," Grady said, "a negro dictated in legislative halls, from which Davis and Calhoun had gone forth, the policy of twelve commonwealths. . . . From the proven incapacity of that day has he far advanced? Simple, credulous, impulsive, easily led and too often easily bought, is he a safer, more intelligent citizen now than then?"[90] Grady answered his own question with a resounding "no," his proposed solution rooted in explicit white supremacy:

The clear and unmistakable domination of the white race, domi-
nating not through violence, not through party alliance, but through
the integrity of its own vote and the largeness of its sympathy and
justice through which it shall compel the support of the better classes
of the colored race—that is the hope and assurance of the South. . . .
Standing in the presence of this multitude, sobered with the responsibility of the message I deliver to the young men of the South, I declare that the truth above all others to be worn unsullied and sacred
in your hearts, to be surrendered to no force, sold for no price, com-
promised in no necessity, but cherished and defended as the covenant
of your prosperity, and the pledge of peace to your children, is that
the white race must dominate forever in the South, because it is the
white race, and superior to that race by which its supremacy is threatened. It is a race issue.[91]

It is not surprising that Grady staunchly opposed Republican Massachusetts Representative Henry Cabot Lodge's 1889–1890 bill to autho-
rize the return of federal officials to the South to ensure that African
Americans could vote freely. Boldly he made his case in Lodge's Boston.
As Harold E. Davis writes: "The Republican party after March 1889 controlled both the White House and Congress and was committed to Negro suffrage upon the practical proposition that blacks would likely vote
Republican. Grady and his partners at the newspaper saw in that prospect
a diminution of their influence. Thus, when he was invited to speak to the
Boston Merchants' Association, figuratively in Representative Lodge's
backyard, he had the opportunity to say to an important Northern audience that the South could manage its racial affairs without help."[92]

Grady died very young, at age thirty-nine, after delivering that final
speech in Boston. Six months after Grady's death, in June 1890, Representative Lodge fought back, arguing that the only way to solve the
Negro Problem was through the legislation he had introduced to *protect* black voting rights under the Fifteenth Amendment, which along
with the Fourteenth Amendment, was under siege. It was a last-ditch
effort to stem the tide of Jim Crow: "The first step . . . toward the

settlement of the negro problem and toward the elevation and protection of the race is to take it out of national party politics. This can be done in but one way. The United States must extend to every citizen equal rights."[93]

The world was watching, and the English historian James Bryce was quick to disagree with Lodge. In his December 1891 article "Thoughts on the Negro Problem," published in the *North American Review*, Bryce—claiming that as a non-American, he could see the problem "free from sectional feeling or political prepossession"—sided with Shaler, Grady, and countless others who confined African Americans to a state of arrested development and incompatibility with the responsibilities and privileges that were part and parcel of the white world, and of a free nation. "When it is remembered that the grandparents or great-grandparents of many of them were African savages," he wrote ". . . we must not be surprised that large masses, especially in Louisiana and Mississippi, remain at a low level of intelligence and morality, with rudimentary notions of comfort and still dominated by gross superstition."[94] Furthermore, any steps African Americans had taken themselves, in organizing schools and charitable societies, for instance, had "not brought the colored people any nearer to the whites."[95] Bryce conceded that black people had not received the rights granted them by the law, but he believed that Lodge's bill, which advocated for black suffrage, was misguided, "an attempt to overcome nature by law."[96] Rather than active enforcement of black rights, he wrote, "it will be better to let nature take its course." (Bryce's repudiation of Reconstruction would be quoted as far afield as Australia, New Zealand, and South Africa around the turn of the century as these far reaches of the British Empire instituted their own white supremacist policies.)

The following year, 1892, Thomas Nelson Page, whose fiction we will examine later in this chapter, published an essay called "The Negro Question." In it he covered similar territory to that of Shaler and Grady, putting forth the idea that black people were incapable of helping themselves. The capable "Negro" was the exception to the rule of low achievement and underdeveloped thought. "It is not argued that because a negro is a negro he is incapable of any intellectual development," Page wrote. "On the contrary, my observation has led me to think that under certain conditions of intellectual environment, of careful training, and of sympathetic encouragement from the stronger races he may individually attain a fair, and in uncommon instances a considerable degree, of mental development. . . . But the incontestable proof is that such cases of intellectual development are exceptional instances. . . . Where the negro has thriven it has invariably been under the influence and by the assistance of the stronger race."[97]

African Americans naturally contested the idea of the Negro as a problem, few more boldly than George Washington Williams. On April 16, 1884, the pioneering African American historian, minister, and Civil War veteran delivered an emancipation day address at the Asbury Church in Washington, DC, on the topic "The Negro as a Political Problem." He would take his facts from history, not from the "science" on which his white counterparts relied.

Williams began with an assessment of black people's brutal past and why he believed it was essential to dwell more on the future:

> Few, indeed, and odorless and colorless, are the flowers of memory that we as a race care to turn back and pluck. Passion flowers innumerable we might find. But were we to turn and touch them, every stamen and petal would instantly become vocal with a thousand tongues. They would tell the story of tribes cheated, villages burned, and murder perpetrated by the remorseless hand of gain. They would relate the story of the middle passage, of young men and innocent maidens, of old men and helpless women, forced into the horrible middle passage; how that the ocean became a voracious sepulchre for hundreds of thousands of the hapless victims of the slave-trade, and will forever chant a ceaseless requiem over their watery grave; they would voice the deep plaint of innocent womanhood led into captivity, of broken hearts and sundered families; they would tell the long and mournful story of a race's wrongs and sufferings,—of hope and piety, love and fear. . . . We must turn only to those facts

of history that may act as a tonic and inspiration for the discharge of duties present and future.[98]

Williams made the argument that whatever economic progress the country had made was an indirect result of the so-called Negro Problem and that white hypocrisy shaped the (im)moral course of the nation. Without the accumulated value made possible by centuries of slave labor, there would be no American power. "The Negro problem," he said, "was the other side of American materialism. . . . The greatness of the foremost Americans of the nineteenth century was distilled through the tears and bloody sweat of the Negro slave; and every ray of lasting glory that rests upon the brow of the Republic was born in the deepest vale of the slave's degradation. The republic of letters owes the Negro a debt of gratitude."[99]

What of the future? Williams called for new forms of black leadership, which would become a steady theme in debates over the Negro Problem and, later, over the New Negro:

> New leaders for the Negro race are needed. Not the time-serving lickspittle, not the self-seeking parasite, not the obsequious, cringing go-between, not swaggering insolence or skulking cowardice in leadership, nor any man who is either ashamed of being, or mean enough to deny that he is, a Negro. We want, we demand leaders, first of all, who are not ashamed of the race; who are possessed of brains, character, courage, zeal, and tact. We want leaders who know the history of the race's trials, struggles, and achievements; and who can, from that history, draw inspiration for the great work to be accomplished.[100]

Williams understood the Negro Problem for what it was: the product of centuries of white exploitation. Frederick Douglass, too, attacked the Negro Problem formula in one of his greatest speeches, "Lessons of the Hour," delivered on January 9, 1894, at the Metropolitan AME Church in Washington, DC. As only Douglass could, he eviscerated the premises of the argument and exposed the motivations of those who propagated it.

It is a formula of Southern origin, and has a strong bias against the negro. It handicaps his cause with all the prejudice known to exist against him. It has been accepted by the good people of the North, as I think, without investigation. It is a crafty invention and is in every way, worthy of its inventors. . . .

The device is not new. It is an old trick. It has been oft repeated, and with similar purpose and effect. For truth, it gives us falsehood. For innocence, it gives us guilt. It removes the burden of proof from the old master class, and imposes it upon the negro. It puts upon a race a work which belongs to the nation. It belongs to the craftiness often displayed by disputants, who aim to make the worse appear the better reason. It gives bad names to good things, and good names to bad things. . . .

I repeat, and my contention is, that this negro problem formula lays the fault at the door of the negro, and removes it from the door of the white man, shields the guilty, and blames the innocent. Makes the negro responsible and not the nation.[101]

Richard T. Greener, the first black faculty member, as of 1873, at the University of South Carolina (before its resegregation), agreed. In May of 1894, Greener inverted the language in a widely reprinted essay he called "The White Problem" and defined the problem as such: "A phase of the white problem is seen in the determination not only to treat the Negro as a member of a child-like race, but the grim determination to keep him a child or a ward. In every advance since emancipation, it has, with true Caucasian gall, been assumed that everything must be done for him." Greener was adamant that the opposite was true. Black people themselves, he said, created their own opportunities and ensured their own salvation. There existed "nothing which tended to unshackle the slave or remove the clogs from the free colored man, in which he was not the foremost, active, intelligent participant, never a mere recipient."[102]

Writing almost twenty years after Greener, the anthropologist Franz Boas, in *The Mind of Primitive Man* (1911), also expressed faith in the self-reliance of people of color—with a few caveats: "In short, there is every reason to believe that the negro when given facility and opportunity, will be perfectly able to fulfill the duties of citizenship as well as his white neighbor. It may be that he will not produce as many great men as the white race, and that his average achievement will not quite reach the level of the average achievement of the white race; but there will be endless numbers who will be able to outrun their white competitors, and who will do better than the defectives whom we permit to drag down and retard the healthy children of our public schools."[103] It was a backhanded compliment that seemed almost generous in the context of its times.[104]

PLANTATION LITERATURE

Visions of the New South, articulated by scientists, journalists, politicians, and academics of the post-Reconstruction era, portraying black people in a chronic state of childlike dependence, hinged on the continued vitality of the myths of the Old Negro whose devotion, labor, and loyalty propped up the Old South. In response to that demand, the era saw the flourishing of the genre of plantation literature, a kindred discourse to racial science, to musings about the so-called Negro Problem, and to the grotesque images circulating in American popular culture. In their fiction, the authors who traded in this mode of representation depicted black people in much the same way that those trafficking in pseudoscience (and later "Sambo art") did—infantile, easily led, insensate, yet dangerously brutal—the difference being that these writers "allowed" former slaves to speak ostensibly in their "own voices," or, more accurately, in the white author's ventriloquist mimicry of their black voices, employing dialect to illustrate low intellect coupled with high devotion. These writers argued that they were conveying to their readers what "real" black people—the Old Negro, the plantation Negro—really thought, and not what carpetbaggers and black agitators *wanted* black people to think.

The era's most celebrated popularizer of plantation folklore, Joel Chandler Harris, worked at Henry Grady's *Atlanta Constitution* from 1876 until 1900 before transitioning into fiction writing.[105] Paul M.

Gaston argues that Harris's depiction of one of the most famous black characters in American literature, Uncle Remus, the Redemption archetype of the contented black man—nearly identical to Grady's "shambling figure [trudging] through his lowly way in life"—allowed the New South and Old South myths to coexist. Jeremy Wells agrees that Harris used Uncle Remus both to bolster the myth of the Old South and to mark continuity with the New: "Having returned to the plantation on which he had once labored as a slave to work for his deceased master's sister and her family, Uncle Remus embodies the popular postbellum idea that plantation life and work were more preferable for black southerners than the alternatives, namely city life in an industrializing 'New South' or emigration to an industrialized North. He thus serves as a symbol of continuity and seems to prove, by virtue of his having stayed put, that slave life had never really been all that bad, even in Georgia. He suggests furthermore that Reconstruction had achieved very little and that efforts to advance black southerners' civil rights and material well-being had only interfered with a social system whose adherents knew best how to accommodate each other."[106] Recall Shaler's "old relations of service and support," and we can readily see the shape of the well-worn pattern.

Wells points out that many black people were drawn to Uncle Remus, reminding us that this benevolent, avuncular icon of slavery and Reconstruction, clearly meant to echo Harriet Beecher Stowe's Uncle Tom but from within a Lost Cause ideological frame, "was ranked 'one of the best characters in American literature' by no less a judge than the African American poet and critic Sterling A. Brown in 1937. Forty years earlier, Uncle Remus was called 'one of the very few creations of American writers worthy of a place in the gallery of the immortals' by William Malone Baskervill, an early historian of southern literature."[107] Harris's creation would have staying power through the first half of the twentieth century, and would have seemed to be the ideal center of an animated Technicolor film. And sure enough, in 1946, Disney adapted *Uncle Remus: His Songs and Sayings* for the big screen. The live-action/animated *Song of the South*, with its Christlike central character, played by James Baskett, sporting a white beard and a broad, accommodating grin, singing the Oscar-

winning "Zip-a-Dee-Doo-Dah" amid a menagerie of animated creatures, featuring Br'er Rabbit, Br'er Fox, and Br'er Bear (voiced in a thick,
often parodic black vernacular English by the well-known black actors
Johnny Lee, Baskett himself, and Nick Stewart, respectively), was a huge
hit—until it wasn't. Dogged by charges of racism, the film would be re-
luctantly shelved by Disney, which never released it on home video in
the United States, and apparently has no plans for a reboot. The ac-
tress Whoopi Goldberg, for one, believes that *Song of the South* should
be rereleased; that to keep it archived in a warehouse somewhere is to
hide our country's history.[108] This is precisely the same reason I believe
so strongly that racist representations of black people in the Jim Crow
era, which I shall investigate in more depth in the next chapter, *must*
be collected and studied, archived and critiqued, since they played such
a key role in the history of the emergence of white supremacy in the
war over the interpretations of Reconstruction. Sadly, these images remain with us today, as potent now as they were then, and they fall into
categories or types. Sterling A. Brown was one of the first scholars to
realize this.

In 1933, Brown published an article called "Negro Character as Seen
by White Authors." In it he pointed out that the white novelist and short
story writer Roark Bradford neatly and confidently divided his black
characters into three types: "the nigger, the 'colored person,' and the
Negro—uppercase N." Those were Bradford's words, and he considered
himself qualified to assign such categories because, as he said, "I was
born on a plantation that was worked by them; I was nursed by one as an
infant and I played with one when I was growing up." Brown knew that
Bradford was far from being an objective observer, and Bradford's representations of black characters were not, as he thought, anthropological
revelations of the social structure of enslaved people on the plantation.
Instead, Brown noted, they were demonstrations of the ways in which
antiblack racism and the ideology of Jim Crow manifested themselves in
literature. The black characters in white American literature, in other
words, were really reflections of contemporary white attitudes about
black people and not some sort of privileged, anthropologically exact

rendering of the realities of the black experience on the plantation based on close observation and, therefore, historical accuracy, as Southern writers such as Bradford proudly proclaimed. Quite perceptively, Brown pointed out that "his generalizations about *the* Negro remain a far better analysis of a white man than of *the* Negro."[109]

Brown used his critique of Bradford's work to publish his analysis of the constellation of stereotypes employed by "the majority of books about Negroes," stereotypes laid on thick to characters whose foibles and capacities, by and large, served as justifications for Jim Crow segregation. As Brown concluded, "Those considered important enough for separate classification, although overlappings *do* occur, are seven in number: (1) The Contented Slave, (2) The Wretched Freeman, (3) The Comic Negro, (4) The Brute Negro, (5) The Tragic Mulatto, (6) The Local Color Negro, and (7) The Exotic Primitive." "The Negro," he noted, "has met with as great injustice in American literature as he has in American life."[110]

Brown's typology, unfortunately, has just as much relevance today as it did in 1933 when he published it, demonstrating not merely the nagging staying power and inertia of racist stereotypes, but the sad fact that these characterizations continue to "do work" within our psychological and cultural subterranean racial landscape. Public expressions of hate speech in the wake of Barack Obama's presidency and Donald Trump's election often tap into this wellspring of stereotypes, many of them born in Reconstruction and reaching a warped form of maturity during Redemption. Depictions of black men and women as monkeys, for instance, have continued to percolate within the white racist id, finding expression in simian images of the first black president of the United States (as well as of his wife, First Lady Michelle Obama, famously referred to as an "ape in heels" by a West Virginia nonprofit official).[111]

Plantation literature ran wild with these stereotypes. Brown explains why these images of black people were, first and last, political, and the sinister role they played in the fall of Reconstruction. In *The Negro in American Fiction* (1937), the same book in which he rated Uncle Remus so highly, Brown describes "the plantation tradition [as] a signal victory in the Reconstruction. Although no longer needed to defend a tottering institution [slavery], it was now needed to prove that Negroes were happy as slaves and hopelessly unequipped for freedom, so that slavery could be resurrected in practice though not in name."[112] Accordingly, the plantation tradition was a powerful weapon in Lost Cause ideology, because as Brown explains, the old stereotypes embodied the selfsame "traits" that men of science had presented as "facts," measurements, and data to support—sometimes explicitly and sometimes implicitly—the idea that blacks were biologically inferior at best, a separate species at worst. As long as their "nature" could be controlled within the confines of slavery, the worst aspects of their natural characteristics could be contained. However, with premature emancipation and the manipulations of unscrupulous politicians, "The Negro was established as contented slave, entertaining child and docile ward, until misled by 'radical' agitators, when he became a dangerous beast."[113] Additionally, Brown continued, "the happy slaves are forever singing in the beautiful fields of white cotton, and forever black mammies fondle their little marses and missies and exude love for all the rich folks in Dixie, and body servants rescue the perishing, care for the dying, serve their beloved masters until death let them depart in peace, to serve in heaven, forever and ever."[114]

We can readily understand how useful these fictional depictions of the slave community were to claims about the dangers, excesses, and weaknesses of Reconstruction, as well as the perils of black voting rights, unfolding at the same time as did explicitly racist apologies for slavery. For example, in 1881, just a year after the Uncle Remus stories first appeared in book form, no less an authority on slavery than the former president of the Confederacy himself, Jefferson Davis, wrote of the descendants of Africans "fortunate" enough to be brought to the American South: "Never was there a happier dependence of labor and capital on each other." This happy dependence, Davis argued, needn't end just because slavery did, a common component of Lost Cause mythology. Indeed, fiction and folklore—because they were so popular and so easily and widely consumed—played a role as key to the rise and implementation of Jim Crow ideology as racial science and journalism did, if not more so, at least subconsciously. These interlocking narratives whose effect—if not intent—was to denigrate the status of the African American community, especially the freedpeople (90 percent of whom would still be living in the South as late as 1910), together formed the warp and weft of the fabric of white supremacy. Even the extraordinarily popular Uncle Remus was called upon to play his role.

Sterling Brown, an accomplished poet who turned to the black vernacular for its formal linguistic power, understood that the Uncle Remus tales were a repository of black vernacular storytelling, much of which had been viewed with some unease and ambivalence by some members of the black elite, as antiblack racism grew in vehemence during Reconstruction and Redemption, including the mocking of black intellect by rendering black speech in a racist vernacular dialect. What disturbed Brown was that Joel Chandler Harris, while valorizing the impressive mythmaking propensity of the slaves, was unable to resist employing Remus as a defender of Lost Cause ideology. At the same time that he was a vehicle for the transmission of black folklore, Brown writes, "Uncle Remus [was] the mouthpiece for defending orthodox Southern attitudes. . . . He defends the glory of the Old South, he admires his white folks, and he satirizes education for Negroes," as he does in the following diatribe: "Hit's de ruinashun er dis country. . . . Put a spellin'-book in a nigger's han's, en right den en dar' you loozes a plow-hand. . . . What's a nigger gwineter larn outen books? I kin take a bar'l stave an' fling mo' sense inter a nigger in one minnit dan all de schoolhouses betwixt dis en de State er Midgigin. . . . Wid one bar'l stave I kin fa'rly lif de vail er ignunce."[115]

Uncle Remus's rejection of book learning, a tenet of Reconstruction governments intent on implementing a system of public schools for the first time in the South, was the symbolic extension of the rejection of a life in freedom. That, perhaps, was the ultimate insult in the vast array of aspersions cast on the freedmen and freedwomen: had they their druthers, they'd "druther" be slaves than free. When Harris's character Mom Bi is freed from slavery at the end of the war, she returns to the plantation, irresistibly drawn back to the prison house in which she was enslaved: "I done bin come back. I bin come back fer stay, but I

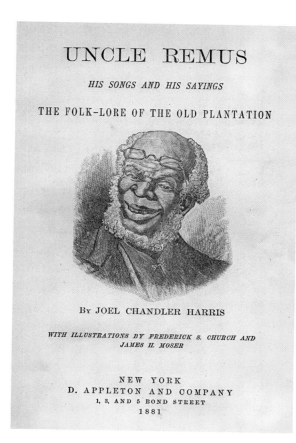

Uncle Remus: His Songs and His Sayings, Joel Chandler Harris, title page, illustrated by Frederick S. Church and James H. Moser, 1881.

free, dough!"[116] Free, but not free—by choice. Harris was by no means alone in his portrayal of the devoted former slave, who fondly recalls life on the plantation and who, if given the chance, would return to it in a heartbeat, a powerful theme within the genre of plantation literature, still another justification for the deprivation of black rights through Jim Crow.

The Negro's supposed nostalgia for her or his own enslavement found its way as a central theme into three salient examples, precisely in the very decade in which de jure segregation became the law of the land.[117] In 1891, the Baltimore native F. Hopkinson Smith published his first novel, *Colonel Carter of Cartersville*, which epitomized this theme of plantation literature.[118] Before becoming a writer, Smith, also an accomplished painter, had made his name as an engineer. After moving to

New York, he engineered a seawall around Governors Island and built the foundation of Bedloe's Island—Liberty Island, home of the Statue of Liberty. There is delicious irony in the idea that the man who literally built the foundation for the most iconic symbol of American freedom—and, perhaps more significantly, the symbol of the *promise* of freedom offered on these shores—romanticized and celebrated freedom's exact opposite in the printed word. In Smith's novel, the former slave Chad describes, in racist dialect, his affection for his master and his yearning for the time before emancipation. "Marsa John's" mercurial temperament in no way detracts from Chad's fondness for him. "Dem was high times," he muses. "We ain't neber seed no time like dat since de war."

> "My old marsa,"—and his eyes glistened,—"my old Marsa John was a gemman, sah, like dey don't see nowadays. Tall, sah, an' straight as a cornstalk; hair white an' silky as de tassel; an' a voice like de birds was singin', it was dat sweet.
>
> "'Chad,' he use' ter say,—you know I was young den, an' I was his body servant,—'Chad, come yer till I bre'k yo' head;' an' den when I come he'd laugh fit to kill hisself. Dat's when you do right. But when you was a low-down nigger an' got de debbil in yer, an' ole marsa hear it an' send de oberseer to de quarters for you to come to de little room in de big house whar de walls was all books an' whar his desk was, 't wa'n't no birds about his voice den,—mo' like de thunder."
>
> "Did he whip his negroes?"
>
> "No, sah; don't reckelmember a single lick laid on airy nigger dat de marsa knowed of; but when dey got so bad—an' some niggers is dat way—den dey was sold to de swamp lan's. He would n't hab 'em round 'ruptin' his niggers, he use 'ter say."[119]

In Grace King's 1893 short story "A Crippled Hope," published later as part of *Balcony Stories* (1914), a former slave is physically disabled by "lameness" and emotionally disabled, both by emancipation. King, whose writing focused primarily on her hometown of New Orleans, was a staunch advocate of the Lost Cause.[120] The character, who had "no other name than 'little Mammy,'" is positively mournful at the loss of her life in bondage:

> The negro-trader's trade was abolished, and he had vanished in the din and smoke of a war which he had not been entirely guiltless of producing, leaving little Mammy locked up behind him. . . .
>
> Free, she was free! But she had not hoped for freedom. The plantation, the household, the delicate ladies, the teeming children,—broomsticks they were in comparison to freedom, but,—that was what she had asked, what she had prayed for. God, she said, had let her drop, just as her mother had done. More than ever she grieved, as she crept down the street, that she had never mounted the auctioneer's block. An ownerless free negro! She knew no one whose duty it was to help her; no one knew her to help her. In the whole world (it was all she had asked) there was no white child to call her mammy, no white lady or gentleman (it was the extent of her dreams) beholden to her as to a nurse. And all her innumerable black beneficiaries! Even the janitor, whom she had tended as the others, had deserted her like his white prototype.[121]

At the turn of the twentieth century, three years after *Plessy v. Ferguson* wrote into law "separate but equal," when Jim Crow rule was well along at chipping away at every right black people had gained during Reconstruction, the native Kentuckian James Lane Allen published the novel *Two Gentlemen of Kentucky* (1899). The titular gentlemen are a white colonel and his loyal former slave, who views his master with "an expression of indescribable solicitude and love." The master, portrayed as kind and generous, comfortably casts himself in a God-like role, before which his worshipful slave willingly bows. Once again, we see the inability of the former slave, here named Peter Cotton, to see the antebellum years through anything but rose-colored glasses, or, in this case, an "ancient pair of silver-rimmed spectacles," prima facie evidence that

Jim Crow represented a quasi-return, a return to the natural order between the races:

> One after another the colonel's old servants, gathering their children about them, had left him, to begin their new life. He bade them all a kind good-by, and into the palm of each silently pressed some gift that he knew would soon be needed. But no inducement could make Peter or Phillis, his wife, budge from their cabin. "Go, Peter! Go, Phillis!" the colonel had said time and again. "No one is happier that you are free than I am; and you can call on me for what you need to set you up in business." But Peter and Phillis asked to stay with him. Then suddenly, several months before the time at which this sketch opens, Phillis had died, leaving the colonel and Peter as the only relics of that populous life which had once filled the house and the cabins. . . .
>
> In paying his servants the colonel would sometimes say, "Peter, I reckon I'd better begin to pay you a salary; that's the style now." But Peter would turn off, saying he didn't "have no use fur no salary." . . .
>
> "I've got to leave you, Peter. Don't you feel sorry for me?"
>
> "Oh, Marse Rom!" cried Peter, hiding his face, his whole form shaken by sobs.
>
> "Peter," added the colonel with ineffable gentleness, "if I had served my Master as faithfully as you have served yours, I should not feel ashamed to stand in his presence."
>
> "If my Marseter is ez mussiful to me ez you have been—"
>
> "I have fixed things so that you will be comfortable after I am gone. When your time comes, I should like you to be laid close to me. We can take the long sleep together. Are you willing?"
>
> "That's whar I want to be laid."[122]

These fictions, as pernicious as they were, turned out to be mere dress rehearsals for the power of literature not only to reinforce even the most reprehensible social attitudes, but to inspire the cruelest forms of white supremacist violence.

THE SPECTER OF RECONSTRUCTION

The author Thomas Nelson Page rose to fame for his novels that pine for the good ole days of the Old South, filling volume after volume with paeans to the Lost Cause. One of the central themes of Page's work is that black political participation would lay waste to the South in ways that even the "War of Northern Aggression" couldn't. As Mary Alice Kirkpatrick argues, "He idealizes a mythic world inhabited by chivalrous gentlemen and faultless southern belles, a system characterized by harmonious race relations and abiding loyalty between slaves and their masters. Page nostalgically hearkens back to the glory days of the antebellum South, hoping to reclaim the pastoral beauty of this untainted Eden."[123]

In one of his most famous works, the story "Marse Chan," Page uses the character of Sam, a former slave, to summarize his own view of plantation life and slavery: "Dem wuz good ole times, marster—de bes' Sam ever see! Dey wuz, in fac'! Niggers didn' hed nothin' 't all to do—jes' hed to 'ten' to de feedin' an' cleanin' de hosses, an' doin' what de marster tell 'em to do; an' when dey wuz sick, dey had things sont 'em out de house, an' de same doctor come to see 'em whar 'ten' to de white folks when dey wuz po'ly. Dyar warn' no trouble nor nothin'."[124] Sam embodies, quite unmistakably, one of Page's recurrent themes, a theme that echoed one of the tenets of anthropology and other branches of racial science, the theme that had so incensed Richard T. Greener: "the Negro as a member of a child-like race," shackled by the white person's "grim determination to keep him a child or a ward." Negroes were stuck—trapped in amber, as it were—in the childlike development of the human race, and, like children, they had to be led, nurtured, controlled. Children were not fit to rule themselves, not to mention ruling others, most certainly not their former masters. The depiction of the nature of the Negro under slavery, of course, was intended as a statement about their nature *after* slavery, especially the dire consequences of "Negro rule" in Reconstruction.

For both Page and Joel Chandler Harris, Reconstruction loomed large as the site of unprecedented evil, when the dormant beast asleep in the Negro had come unleashed. For them, the former slaves should be viewed with fear and suspicion and the Northern carpetbaggers who aided and abetted them with loathing. By the turn of the century, Reconstruction itself became a character in plantation fiction, and carpetbaggers became the agents of evil. For example, in Harris's book *Gabriel Tolliver: A Story of Reconstruction* (1902), the fictional Freedmen's Bureau agent, Gilbert Hotchkiss, earns special scorn for his diabolical role as catalyst in transforming the naturally docile slave into an angry and resentful ingrate, seeking vengeance for imagined injustices against the people who had loved them most, their benign masters: "Mr. Hotchkiss was absolutely sincere in believing that the generation of Southern whites who were his contemporaries were personally responsible for slavery in this country, and for all the wrongs that he supposed had been the result of that institution. He felt it in every fibre of his cultivated but narrow mind, and he went about elated at the idea that he was able to contribute his mite of information to the negroes, and breed in their minds hatred of the people among whom they were compelled to live."[125]

Obsessed with the evils of Reconstruction, moreover, Harris's narrator proclaims: "It is impossible, even at this late date, for any impartial person to read the debates in the Federal Congress during the years of 1867–68 without realizing the awful fact that the prime movers in the reconstruction scheme (if not the men who acted as their instruments and tools) were intent on stirring up a new revolution in the hope that the negroes might be prevailed upon to sack cities and towns, and destroy the white population."[126]

So-called Negro misrule had manifested itself in the Reconstruction constitutional conventions, at which the former Confederate states were forced to rewrite their constitutions to include suffrage for black men before they could be readmitted into the Union, which did so much to turn the world the planters had made upside down. Writing about the Georgia Constitutional Convention—"the mongrel convention," he calls it—Harris's narrator fumes:

> Beginning on the 20th, the election was to continue for three days, a provision that was intended to enable the negroes to vote at as many precincts as they could conveniently reach in eighty-three

hours. No safeguard whatever was thrown around the ballot-box, and it was the remembrance of this initial and overwhelming combination of fraud and corruption that induced the whites, at a later day, to stuff the ballot-boxes and suppress the votes of the ignorant. These things, with the hundreds of irritating incidents and episodes belonging to the unprecedented conditions, gradually worked up the feelings of the whites to a very high pitch of exasperation. The worst fears of the most timid bade fair to be realised, for the negroes, certain of their political supremacy, sure of the sympathy and support of Congress and the War Department, and filled with the conceit produced by the flattery and cajolery of the carpet-bag sycophants, were beginning to assume an attitude which would have been threatening and offensive if their skins had been white as snow.[127]

Page was similarly fearful of the black beast set free by Reconstruction and similarly outraged. In his novel *Red Rock: A Chronicle of Reconstruction* (1904), Page's character Reely Thurston expresses the author's own opinion of Reconstruction: "He had even ventured to express open skepticism as to the wisdom of the steps Mrs. Welch and her Aid Society had been taking in their philanthropic efforts on behalf of the freedmen; giving expression to the heretical doctrine that in the main the negroes had been humanely treated before the war, and that the question should be dealt with now from an economical rather than from a sentimental standpoint. He gave it as his opinion that the people down there knew more about the Negro, and the questions arising out of the new conditions, than those who were undertaking to settle those questions, from a distance, and that, if let alone, the questions would settle themselves."[128]

The function of these extremely popular views of plantation life and slavery was the projection of the antebellum past onto the Redemptionist present, the desire to achieve the myth of the eternal return. As Brook Thomas argues, "As much as he honors the 'Old South,' however, *Red Rock* is primarily concerned with the present and future order."[129] "Page," writes Matthew R. Martin, "manages a double vision that allows him to cheer for bigger cities while envisioning the return of a pastoral ideal, to mourn a way of life as lost forever yet see it as reborn."[130] Recall that Henry Grady, who Ethan J. Kytle and Blain Roberts rightly call "a tireless promoter of economic revitalization in the South and sectional reconciliation with the North," also traded in nostalgia, walking the line between the glorification of a righteous past and the exaltation of what he believed was the South's deservedly bright future.[131] This "double vision" was part of the key to Lost Cause ideology, and the restoration of the social roles and psychological demeanor of the Old Negro, too, was pivotal to that future, no matter what that process might cost.

BIRTH OF AN ICON

Perhaps no writer had a more lasting impact on the myth of the Old South and the dangers of free Negroes than Thomas Dixon, the most blatantly white supremacist of these authors. Dixon had worked as a lawyer, served in the North Carolina legislature, was a popular traveling minister, and, after leaving the ministry in 1895, became a full-time lecturer.[132] In 1902, he published the novel *The Leopard's Spots: A Romance of the White Man's Burden*, and three years later, he published his even more popular sequel, *The Clansman: An Historical Romance of the Ku Klux Klan*, which would become the basis for D. W. Griffith's landmark film a decade later, *The Birth of a Nation*.

Because of the extraordinary popularity of the novel and the ecstatic reception to Griffith's film, it can be argued that Dixon's interpretation of Reconstruction did more over the next several decades of the twentieth century to shape the country's understanding of that historical period, especially the supposedly noble origins of the Ku Klux Klan, than any other single factor. As David Blight writes, Dixon "provided the Klan and its violence with its most enduring romantic mythology. . . . Dixon's vicious version of the idea that blacks had caused the Civil War by their very presence, and that Northern radicalism during Reconstruction failed to understand that freedom had ushered blacks as a race into barbarism, neatly framed the story of the rise of heroic vigilantism in the South."[133] What *Uncle Tom's Cabin* had been to the abolition movement, *The Clansman* was to the Lost Cause and to Jim Crow white supremacist ideology.

Dixon was shameless in his defense of slavery and his admiration for the Klan. The Klan, he wrote, repeating the organization's own founding statement, was an "institution of Chivalry, Humanity, Mercy, and Patriotism." Its mission was "to aid and assist in the execution of the Constitution" and, rather like the Mafia's role in *The Godfather*, "to protect the weak, the innocent, and the defenseless from the indignities, wrongs and outrages of the lawless, the violent, and the brutal; to relieve the injured and the oppressed: to succor the suffering and unfortunate, and especially the widows and the orphans of Confederate Soldiers."

Dixon's novel characterized Reconstruction as an unmitigated disaster, the racial nightmare that white people were duty-bound to redeem: "The excitement which proceeded the first Reconstruction election in the South paralysed the industries of the country. When demagogues poured down from the North and began their raving before crowds of ignorant negroes, the plow stopped in the furrow, the hoe was dropped, and the millenium [*sic*] was at hand. Negro tenants, working under contracts issued by the Freedman's [*sic*] Bureau, stopped work, and rode their landlords' mules and horses around the county, following these orators."[134]

Dixon's novels afford an excellent opportunity to understand how thoroughly scientific racism and bad anthropology had penetrated popular forms of entertainment, especially novels, and thereby informed public opinion. For example, in *The Leopard's Spots*, Dixon sneers, "It seemed a joke sometimes as he thought of it, a huge, preposterous joke, this actual attempt to reverse the order of Nature, turn society upside down, and make a thick-lipped, flat-nosed negro, but yesterday taken from the jungle, the ruler of the proudest and strongest race of men evolved in two thousand years of history. Yet when he remembered the fierce passions in the hearts of the demagogues who were experimenting with this social dynamite it was a joke that took on a hellish, sinister meaning."[135] Dixon's novels were nakedly ideological; but for his readers, they were much more powerful and effective than the inaccessible works by revisionist historians, rich with page-turning storytelling that cloaked the fabrications of myth sanctioned by science in the guise of objective history. Even more, his novels were not only justifications for the history of white supremacy, but urgent calls to action *now*.

We might think of Dixon's novels as "how to" guides for white supremacists seeking to justify the logic of Jim Crow. Late in *The Leopard's Spots*, for example, a character states, in a diatribe reminiscent of Henry Grady's "New South" manifesto: "So long as the Negro is here with a ballot in his hands he is a menace to civilisation. The Republican party placed him here. The name Republican will stink in the South for a century, not because they beat us in war, but because two years after the war, in profound peace, they inaugurated a second war on the unarmed people of the South. . . . Their attempt to establish with the bayonet an African barbarism on the ruins of Southern society was a conspiracy against human progress. It was the blackest crime of the nineteenth century."[136] And that crime demanded, at all costs, to be revenged.

Racist words on the page were damaging, and damning, enough. As the popularity of novels such as those by Page and Dixon increased, technological advances made it possible to produce vivid visual imagery that could *literalize* the metaphorical imagery of novels and scientific tracts of black people as less than human, deforming representations captured through the lens of the black grotesque. A powerful visual rhetoric with a long history but newly empowered by chromolithography would arise as the century headed to a close, consisting of a startling range of images in a broad range of genres, with their own repeating forms and tropes, generated from within the haunted house of the subconscious American racist imagination. These visualizations of what plantation literature had defined as the "Old Negro" were perhaps the most powerful weapon in the arsenal of white supremacist ideology because of the subliminal power of endless repetition. And their collective impact—in advertisements, postcards, and trade cards, in blackface minstrelsy on the stage, and ultimately in stereotyped black characters in moving pictures—would play a pivotal role in persuading American society that black human beings were not only fundamentally different from white people, but irreversibly different *in kind*, and dangerously so, necessitating the erection of rigid boundaries and walls that demanded constant vigilance, with transgressions justifying the severest forms of vigilante punishment.

CHAINS OF BEING:
THE BLACK BODY
AND THE
WHITE MIND

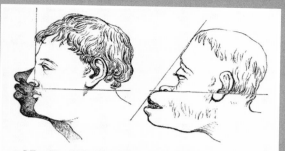

"Profile of Negro, European, and Oran Outan," illustration, *Crania Americana* by Samuel Morton, 1831.

[*Profile of Negro, European, and Oran Outan.*]

"Grades of Intelligence," *New Physiognomy* by Samuel Wells, 1871.

Fig. 142.—GRADES OF INTELLIGENCE.

FRANK LESLIE'S ILLUSTRATED NEWSPAPER.

OUR GODDESS OF LIBERTY.

WHAT IS SHE TO BE? TO WHAT COMPLEXION ARE WE TO COME AT LAST?

ALL WANTING FARMS,

9,000 acres good soil, mild climate, 34 miles south of Philadelphia. Price only $25 per acre. Also, improved farms. The place is growing more rapidly than most any other place in the United States. Thousands are settling. Address, C. K. LANDIS, Vineland, New Jersey.

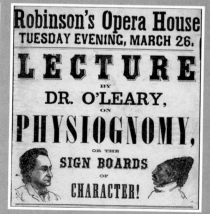

"Our Goddess of Liberty," political cartoon, *Frank Leslie's Illustrated Newspaper*, July 16, 1870.

"Lecture by Dr. O'Leary on Physiognomy, or the Sign Boards of Character!," an itinerant demonstration of scientific racism, broadside, ca. 1872.

HAECKEL'S EVOLUTION OF MAN.   PLATE XIV.

1. Chimpanzee

2. Gorilla.

3. Orang.   4. Negro.

"1. Chimpanzee. 2. Gorilla. 3. Orang. 4. Negro," Plate XIV, *The Evolution of Man* by Ernst Haeckel, 1879. Though a Darwinist, Haeckel, like Morton, claimed the parallel but independent evolution of different human species.

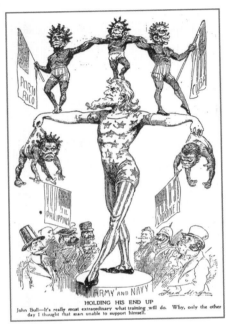

HOLDING HIS END UP
John Bull—It's really most extraordinary what training will do. Why, only the other day I thought that man unable to support himself.

"Holding His End Up," political cartoon, *Philadelphia Inquirer*, ca. 1899. An imperialist Uncle Sam holds up dark-skinned trophies of recently appropriated foreign lands: Puerto Rico, Hawaii, Cuba, the Philippines, and the Mariana Islands.

IRISH IBERIAN   ANGLO-TEUTONIC   NEGRO

Ireland from One or Two Neglected Points of View, illustration, H. Strickland Constable, 1888.

NEGROID SANE CRIMINALS
AND NEGROID CIVIL INSANE
MOSAIC OF METRIC DIFFERENCES

Criminal

Civil Insane

Criminal

Civil Insane

CRIMINALS
Shorter, broader, higher heads
Lighter skin color
More woolly, less frizzly hair
Higher, wider and more sloping foreheads
Thicker eyebrows
Longer, narrower faces and noses
Shorter ears
Less pronounced antihelices
Less rolled helices
Slightly lighter eyes
Less pigmented sclerae
More inner eyefolds
Higher eye-openings
Smaller brow ridges
Higher, narrower nasal roots, higher bridges
Thinner nasal tips
Thicker integumental and membranous lips
More pronounced lip seams
Broader jaws, less chin prominence
More pointed chins, more prominent malars and jaw angles
Fuller cheeks, more wrinkles
More prognathism

"Negroid Sane Criminals and Negroid Civil Insane," Francis Galton, ca. 1900.

"Mongrelization—End Of Civilization,"
postcard, 1968.

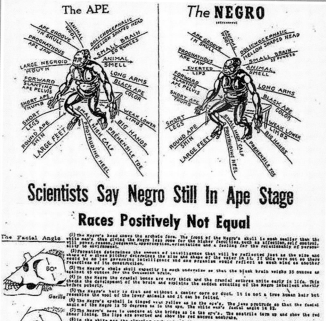

"Scientists Say Negro Still In Ape Stage," National Socialist White
Americans' Party flyer, handed out in Bellevue, Washington, 1995.

ILLUSTRATIONS FROM *THE NEGRO, A BEAST: OR, IN THE IMAGE OF GOD* BY CHARLES CARROLL, 1900. IN THIS VOLUME, CARROLL, A POLYGENIST MINISTER FROM MISSOURI, COUCHES HIS VICIOUSLY RACIST DOGMA OF ANTIMISCEGENATION IN BOTH RELIGIOUS TEACHINGS AND THE PSEUDOSCIENTIFIC "FACTS" THAT GAINED A WIDE AUDIENCE DURING THE SECOND HALF OF THE NINETEENTH CENTURY.

Book cover

"Adam and Eve in the Garden of Eden: Morning of the Creation of Man"

"Christ—The Son of God"

"Does Like Beget Like?"

"The Virgin Mary and the Child Christ"

"Adam and Eve in the Garden of Eden"

"The Beast and the Virgin"

DID NATURE BLUNDER?

Would you believe that the above negro was the daughter of pure whites? Never, though it was written in letters of fire upon the face of the heavens.

"Did Nature Blunder?"

WILL YOUR NEXT CHILD BE A NEGRO?

Your children are "bone of your bone" and "flesh of your flesh" then who can believe that the negro is an offspring of Adam and Eve, without fearing that their next child may be a negro.

"Will Your Next Child Be a Negro?"

THE EGG OF CREATION.

Were they both hatched from the same egg? If so, are they both in the image of their father? If they are both from the same egg, and both in the image of their father, then "like does not beget like", and it is possible for the Dove to produce an Ostrich.

"The Egg of Creation"

NATURAL RESULTS.

The screams of the ravished daughters of the "Sunny South" have placed the Negro in the lowest rank of the Beast Kingdom.

"Natural Results"

"Chorus—Sing, Darkeys, Sing," wood-engraved illustration, *Uncle Tom's Cabin Contrasted with Buckingham Hall*, Robert Criswell, 1852.

CHORUS—SING, DARKEYS, SING.

UNCLE TOM AT HOME.

" 'Aint she a peart young un?' said Tom, holding her from him to take a full-length view; then getting up, he set her on his broad shoulder, and began capering and dancing with her, while Mas'r George snapped at her with his pocket handkerchief, and Mose and Pete, now returned again, roared after her like bears, till Aunt Chloe declared that they fairly took 'er head off' with their noise."—Page 22.

"Uncle Tom at Home," wood-engraved illustration, George Cruikshank, for *Uncle Tom's Cabin*, John Cassell, London, 1852.

"Winter Holidays in the Southern States: Plantation Frolic on Christmas Eve," illustration, *Frank Leslie's Illustrated Newspaper*, December 26, 1857.

"I'se Gwine Back to Dixie," sheet music cover, C. A. White, lithograph, 1874.

"The Five Jolly Darkies Way down in Old Virginia/The Old Plantation," W. S. Reed Toy Co., Leominster, Massachusetts, lithographed paper on wood, ca. 1881–1896.

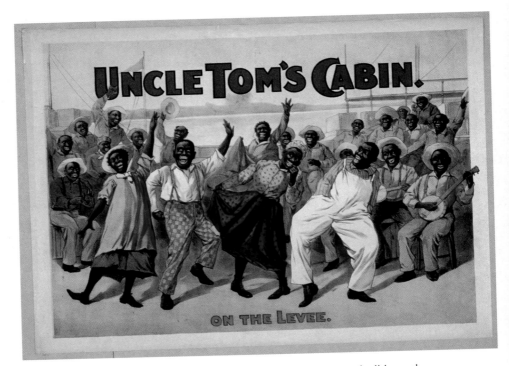

"Uncle Tom's Cabin. On the Levee," theatrical poster, color lithograph,
Currier Litho. Co., Buffalo, New York, ca. 1900.

TWO OF THE CENSORED ELEVEN *MERRIE MELODIES* AND *LOONEY* TOONS SHORTS,
A GROUP OF CARTOONS THAT WERE PULLED FROM DISTRIBUTION PRIOR TO 1948
BECAUSE OF THEIR BROAD STEREOTYPING OF BLACK PEOPLE.

"All This and Rabbit Stew" cartoon, starring Bugs Bunny, directed by Tex Avery, Warner Bros., 1941. The black hunter pictured here, in the role usually occupied by Elmer Fudd, is called Tex's Coon.

"Coal Black and de Sebben Dwarfs," film lobby card, directed by Robert Clampett, theatrical release by Warner Bros. and The Vitaphone Corporation on January 16, 1943. Here, Snow White and the Seven Dwarves are depicted derogatorily as darkies.

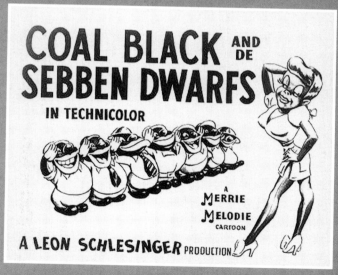

Jesse Washington after lynching, photograph, Fred Gildersleeve, published by the NAACP as "The Waco Horror," Waco, Texas, May 15, 1916.

The lynching of Isaac McGhie, Elmer Jackson, and Elias Clayton (on ground), photograph, Duluth, Minnesota, June 15, 1920.

The lynching of Thomas Shipp and Abram Smith, photograph, Marion, Indiana, 1930.

Three

FRAMING BLACKNESS

Sambo Art and the Visual Rhetoric
of White Supremacy

◡

I shall find it no hardship to say a good word for the portrait of Senator [Hiram] Revels. . . . We colored men so often see ourselves described and painted as monkeys, that we think it a great piece of good fortune to find an exception to this general rule. . . . This portrait, representing truly, as it does, the face and form of our first colored U. S. Senator is a historical picture. It marks, with almost startling emphasis, the point dividing our new form from our old condition. Every colored householder in the land should have one of these portraits in his parlor, and should explain it to his children, as the dividing line between the darkness and despair that overhung our past, and the light and hope that now beam upon our future as a people.

—FREDERICK DOUGLASS, Letter to Louis Prang, June 14, 1870

One cannot ignore the extraordinary fact that a world campaign beginning with the slave-trade and ending with the refusal to capitalize the word "Negro," leading through a passionate defense of slavery by attributing every bestiality to blacks and finally culminating in the evident modern profit which lies in degrading blacks—all this has unconsciously trained millions of honest, modern men into the belief that black folk are sub-human . . . a mass of despicable men, inhuman; at best, laughable; at worst, the meat of mobs and fury.

—W. E. B. DU BOIS, *Darkwater*, 1920

I am overdetermined from the outside. I am a slave not to the "idea" others have of me, but to my appearance. . . . I crawl along. The white gaze, the only valid one, is already dissecting me. I am *fixed*. Once their microtomes are sharpened, the Whites objectively cut sections of my reality. I have been betrayed. I sense, I see in this white gaze that it's the arrival not of a new man, but of a new type of man, a new species. A Negro, in fact!

The universal situation of the black man is ambiguous, but this is resolved in his physical existence. . . . [W]*herever he goes, a black man remains a black man.*

—FRANTZ FANON, *Black Skin, White Masks*, 1952

Frederick Douglass was among the first authors to notice that one is not born a slave; one is transformed into a slave. "You have seen how a man was made a slave," Douglass tells us at the structural center of his first slave narrative; "you shall see how a slave was made a man."[1] How, then, does a society attempt to transform a freedwoman or a freedman *back* into a slave? How can the speaking citizen-subject become transformed into the muzzled subcitizen object, in a state of nominal freedom, virtual neo-slavery, once again? Throughout American culture but especially in the South, with the onset of Reconstruction, white supremacists fabricated a racial melodrama that would be enacted within what the critical theorist Homi K. Bhabha describes as "a range of cultural, political, and historical discourses." These symbolic narratives of transgression unfolded in the American racial unconscious, in paired or binary constructs, fused, Janus-faced opposites: power and helplessness, fantasy and repugnance, desire and rejection, attraction and repulsion, seduction and violation, beauty and the bestial, the sublime and the grotesque, all within the larger, convoluted frame of the monstrous depravity and licentiousness of slavery.[2] The result was the genre of American popular culture sometimes called "Sambo art," representations of black women and black men as embodiments of all that was the reverse of Truth and Beauty, the Good and the Civilized.

White supremacist ideologues in the "redeemed" post-Reconstruction South fabricated a system of representation composed of a fixed set of signs and symbols, metaphors and metonyms, of which the racist types that Sterling Brown identified in plantation literature were just one subset in a much larger universe of genres, topoi, and tropes. The boundaries and borders of systems such as this, as Bhabha points out, were, ostensibly, fixed yet permeable, dependent for enforcement, paradoxically, upon the ease with which those boundaries and borders could be violated. And this paradox necessitated a range of mechanisms of control: obsessive, paranoiac vigilance; social, economic, and political domination; terrorist tactics ranging from actual acts of violence to—just as importantly—the cultivation of the *fear* of such violence; and the exaction of the most brutal forms of vigilante punishment for perceived violations. It was a system glued together by the unity of its inherent opposites.

Bhabha describes a similar system of contradictions that unfolded in societies dominated by European colonialism, in which "[t]he black is both savage (cannibal) and yet the most obedient and dignified of servants (the bearer of food); he is the embodiment of rampant sexuality and yet innocent as a child; he is mystical, primitive, simple-minded and yet the most worldly and accomplished liar, and manipulator of social forces." Opposition to arming black men and allowing them to serve as soldiers during the Civil War, to take one instance, often reflected these conflicting qualities: for some, black men were cowards who would run away at the first sight of a white soldier, while for others, black men were, at base, barely repressed savages who would, at the first opportunity, run amok and kill every white man in sight. Bhabha continues, "In each case what is being dramatized is a separation—*between* races, cultures, histories, *within* histories—a separation between *before* and *after* that repeats the mythical moment of disjunction." The "before" and the "after"—the event of disjunction—is that which marks the difference between the first and second American republics: the rise and fall of slavery and "the new birth of freedom," as Lincoln put it, as a result of the Civil War.

Bhabha argues that "the chain of stereotypical signification" in such a system "is curiously mixed and split, polymorphous and perverse, an articulation of multiple belief."[3] In the case of the black male and the black female, this split manifests itself most obviously through polar opposite fabrications of white and black sexuality: the beautiful and the beastly, the angelic and the diabolical, the pure and the licentious. The virginal sainted Mammy and the emasculated, neutered Uncle Tom, for example, stand against Gus the rapist from *The Birth of a Nation*, Frisco the gigolo, and Jezebel the whore. These archetypes of the "essences" of black character are perfect examples of "tropes of transgression," to borrow Kobena Mercer's phrase, embodying "the stereotype's twin poles of repugnance and fascination at the level of the collective unconscious."[4]

The extraordinary size and range of the archive of stereotypical images of African Americans that would be circulated through Reconstruction, Redemption, and the rise of Jim Crow emerged as everyday numbingly repeatable tropes of white supremacy that could be readily consumed and digested, processed and internalized, "within an apparatus of power," as Bhabha puts it. And the many latent, subliminal *and* conscious, cognizant manifestations of this apparatus were constructed from and reflections of a *totalizing rhetoric of terrorism*, expressed explicitly *and* implicitly, literally *and* figuratively, consciously *and* unconsciously. Fear and terror were the vehicle and tenor of Jim Crow's metaphors of white supremacy. Consider the common claim in Jim Crow America that "The Negro was a beast." Antiblack racists—through a veritable avalanche of imagery—produced an imaginary "Negro" through which to sublimate or divert a deep, almost primal sense of fear and terror, while simultaneously visiting real forms of terror and fear on actual human beings, the neighbors they sought to control, other human beings distanced through the designation of being "Negroes."[5]

In this chapter, I want to explore the range of representations of these stereotypes that came to be associated with the freedpeople of the South, the so-called Old Negro. It was to circumvent this circle of representational oppression that some African American intellectuals would feel the necessity, in the 1890s, during the decade in which segregation was made the law of the land in the US Supreme Court's decision on

Plessy v. Ferguson (1896), to recast themselves within the American racial melodrama as "New Negroes," as black people who were somehow sui generis, somehow de novo, a people within a people who were "new."

Sambo art has its basis in race rituals associated with slavery, initially in the form of caricature, as the symbolic accoutrement of justifications for eighteenth- and nineteenth-century slavery. Following the Civil War, it was summoned from its arsenal and used as full-force weaponry during the imposition of Jim Crow segregation. It is a commonplace that all art, to paraphrase the cultural critic Walter Benjamin, "always has its basis in ritual," but Sambo art is an example of one of this truism's most extreme, most debased forms: popular art in the service of racism, images called upon "for the purpose of establishing evidence," the evidence of the black person's absence of humanity.[6] The difference between the circulation of racist images of black people before and after the war, especially after Reconstruction, is the jaw-dropping extent of its sheer numbers, its remarkable *reproducibility*. Repetition of a range of offensive character types—ostensibly of "Negroes"—was an attempt to fabricate and stabilize a single black image, "the Negro," to reduce the complexity of actual black human beings and funnel it into fixed, unchangeable signifiers of blackness that even black people would see when they saw themselves reflected in America's social mirrors. The privileging of white culture and white people was directly tied to the denigration of black culture and black people in a mutually reinforcing relationship.[7]

What possible rationale demanded this many debased representations of the recently freed black people produced in the final third of the nineteenth century? How many ways can one call a woman or a man a "nigger" or a "coon"? How many watermelons does a person have to devour, how many chickens does an individual have to steal, to make the point that black people are manifestly, by nature, both gluttons and thieves? Why in the world was it necessary to produce tens of thousands, perhaps hundreds of thousands, of these separate and distinct racist images to demean the status of the newly freed slaves, in a set of fixed types or motifs, which reached their perverse apex with the characterizations of black people during Reconstruction in *The Birth of a Nation*, in the figures of deracinated black elected officials and, of course, the black male as rapist? The explanation comes in three words: justifying Jim Crow, or, in three different words, disenfranchising black voters.

The Reconstruction Amendments affirmed that African Americans were legally equal to white Americans (though women of neither race enjoyed all of the benefits promised by these amendments). Just as importantly, African Americans' behavior confirmed that they were capable of organizing for elections, cultivating land, forming stable social and cultural institutions, marrying, functioning as members of families, raising children, and suing in court to defend their rights—in short, the freedpeople exemplified all of the hallmarks of citizenship that defined an American. Despite centuries of enslavement and an equally long history of antiblack racist discourse, in twelve short years, the mass of the African American people (about 90 percent of whom were still in bondage in 1860, a year before the Civil War broke out) demonstrated that they were human beings just like everybody else. But all of that changed with Redemption. As W. E. B. Du Bois put it, "The slave went free; stood a brief moment in the sun; then moved back again toward slavery."[8] How was it that the emancipated were "moved back again toward slavery" after only a few years "in the sun"?

The assault was double-barreled: legally, as I outlined in chapter 1, through a series of court rulings and laws that narrowed the Reconstruction Amendments and neutralized the Civil Rights Act of 1875; and simultaneously, as explored in chapter 2, through multiple narrative forms of white supremacy, ranging from "scientific" conclusions about the nature of Negroes in the discourses of racial and social science, through depictions of black people in fiction and folklore, political rhetoric, and journalism. To these written forms of negative imagery, we cannot underestimate the enormous importance of this massive number of negative Sambo images, intended to naturalize the visual image of the black person as subhuman and thereby subliminally reinforce the perverted logic of the separate and unequal system of Jim Crow itself. Given the intensity and range of the assault, we should not be surprised at how effective it was. Images of real black people, as Frederick Douglass noted in his response to seeing the portrait of Senator Hiram Revels, were so vastly outnumbered that they didn't have a meaningful chance at countering the fabrications of racist imagery.

Stereotypes of black people within each of these discourses interpenetrated each other, as it were. Nineteenth-century racial science reflected characterizations of black people inherited from eighteenth-century natural philosophy, such as racist speculations by David Hume and Immanuel Kant and Thomas Jefferson. Social science reinforced observations about black people's habits and character from travel accounts and individuals' journals. Zoologists or natural historians such as Louis Agassiz used the emerging art of photography as visual proof of dubious theories of the evolution of human beings. Legal opinions grounded their reasoning in the irrefutability of what we now can see were the commonplaces of scientific racism. The Negro's image was trapped in a viciously claustrophobic circle, and so, therefore, were actual Negroes, the freedmen and freedwomen so recently liberated from inherited bondage.

For example, consider the naked racist underpinnings laid bare in these commonplaces about the nature of Negroes, which Justice Joseph McKenna quoted from the prior Mississippi Supreme Court opinion in his own majority opinion for the 1898 US Supreme Court in *Williams v. Mississippi* (ruling that discrimination must be found in the text of a state's laws, not just in their administration): "By reason of its previous condition of servitude and dependencies, this race has acquired or accentuated certain peculiarities of habit, of temperament, and of character, which clearly distinguished it as a race from the whites; a patient, docile people; but careless, landless, migratory within narrow limits, without forethought; and its criminal members given to furtive offences, rather than the robust crimes of whites."[9]

Embedded in this single quotation are assertions made about black people from—among many other sources—Hume (about a black person's "national character"—that black people have created "no arts, no sciences");[10] Kant and Jefferson (about a black person's inherent or biologically based lack of intelligence or forethought: "this fellow was quite black from head to foot," as Kant put it, "a clear proof that what he said was stupid")[11]; Samuel Cartwright (that black people, naturally, were "submissive knee-benders"); and Thomas Nelson Page (that black people were characterized by "their amiability and their docility"). In other words, this single quote could stand as a summary of some key, shared tenets of white supremacist beliefs at the turn of the century, accumulated through several disciplines and discourses over the previous century and a half. "The convention," McKenna's quotation of the earlier court's opinion continues, "discriminated against [the negro race's] characteristics and the offenses to which its weaker members are prone." The supposedly biological and behavioral characteristics of black people referred to by McKenna—incidentally not a Southerner himself, but a native of Philadelphia, Pennsylvania, the so-called Cradle of Liberty—in the *Williams v. Mississippi* decision were reflected and caricatured throughout the American consumer market in an astonishing array of imagery. Following the Civil War, because of the technological innovation of chromolithography, it became cheap to mass-produce multicolor advertisements. By the 1890s—precisely when Jim Crow was hardening—one of the most popular means of advertising products to American consumers was to juxtapose the product or its virtues with supremely demeaning images of African Americans. So popular were they with the public, so widespread was their utilization, in the South, the North, and beyond the nation's borders, that virtually anywhere a white person saw an image of an African American, she or he was encoded in one of these stereotypes as somehow laughably ignorant, subhuman, devoid of thought and reason, ruled by one's senses, as would be an animal.[12] The collective image of the black person in American popular culture functions like a visual mantra reinforcing the negativity of difference.

In other words, when a white person confronted an actual black human being, he or she was "an already read text," to use Barbara Johnson's insightful definition of a stereotype.[13] It didn't matter what the individual black man or woman said and did, how much education he or she had, or whether they were from the North or the South, because negative images of them in the popular imagination already existed, and were already *fixed*, imposed upon them like hoods or masks. This practice of xenophobic masking, as it were, still exists.

Take, for example, the experiences of the novelist Chimamanda Ngozi Adichie. Upon her arrival at an American college from her home-land of Nigeria, she recalls that her American roommate "felt sorry for me before she saw me. . . . My roommate had a single story of Africa, a single story of catastrophe. In this single story, there was no possibility of Africans being similar to her in any way, no possibility of a connection as human equals." Fed a steady diet of images of Africa as "a place of beautiful landscapes, beautiful animals, and incomprehensible people, fighting wars, dying of poverty and AIDS, unable to speak for them-selves, and waiting to be saved by a kind, white foreigner," Adichie's roommate had no choice, she is saying, but to view her as a stereotype. "That is the way to create a single story," Adichie explains, "show people as one thing, as only one thing, over and over again, and that is what they become."[14] As Homi K. Bhabha puts it, "[T]he stereotype . . . is a form of knowledge and identification that vacillates between what is always 'in place,' already known, and something that must be anxiously repeated . . . as if the essential duplicity of the Asiatic or the bestial sexual license of the African that needs no proof, can never really, in discourse, be proved." And it is precisely for this reason, Bhabha argues, that "the stereotype must always be in *excess* of what can be empirically proved or logically construed."[15] Hence the demand to repeat the circulation of these im-ages in a seemingly endless loop. In the long reactionary era after Recon-struction, these racist stereotypes were subconsciously foisted on the face of actual African Americans, imposing on them Jim Crow's "mask of blackness." And the supposed truth of these images, sanctified by racial science, was called upon to justify the rollback of the gains black people had made during Reconstruction.

The fears and anxieties of black people from within what we might think of as the postwar American collective unconscious were projected onto a host of everyday, ordinary consumer objects, including postcards and trading cards, teapots and tea cozies, children's banks and children's games, napkin holders and pot holders, clocks and ashtrays, sheet music and greeting cards, products such as Aunt Jemima pancake mix and Pears' Soap, "Pick the Pickaninny" songs, puzzles and dolls, Valentine's

Day cards (many featuring iterations of watermelon-devouring and chicken-stealing "coons")—a veritable deluge of Sambo imagery spilling forth into virtually every form of advertisement for the most unremarkable of items. One particularly outlandish variation on the theme even illustrates the history of evolution by showing the transmutation of a watermelon into a "coon."

The most horrifying subgenre of antiblack imagery—all too realistic—consisted of postcards of lynchings, which became ever more popular in the early years of the twentieth century. One example is "The Dogwood Tree," depicting five black bodies hanging from one tree in Sabine County, Texas, on June 22, 1908. (The caption printed on the card lists the wrong date.) Between 1889 and 1918, according to the NAACP's *Thirty Years of Lynching in the United States,* more than three thousand lynchings took place precisely as these racist images of black people increased in popularity. I'm not arguing a simple cause-and-effect relationship between images on postcards and lynching; but I am arguing that the collective, cumulative effect of these racist images, in addition to other powerful socioeconomic forces, emboldened otherwise law-abiding people to commit the most abominable crimes.

As Carter G. Woodson, the black Harvard-trained historian who inaugurated

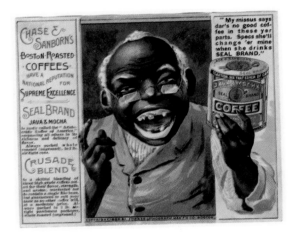

Chase & Sanborn's Boston Roasted Coffees, advertisement, lithograph, 1888.

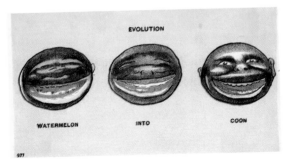

"Evolution—Watermelon into Coon," postcard, postmarked October 4, 1909.

Negro History Week in 1926 (the precursor to Black History Month), wrote in his classic text, *The Mis-Education of the Negro* (1933):

> To handicap a student by teaching him that his black face is a curse and that his struggle to change his condition is hopeless is the worst kind of lynching. It kills one's aspirations and dooms him to vagabondage and crime. It is strange, then, that the friends of truth and the promoters of freedom have not risen up against the present propaganda in the schools and crushed it. This crusade is much more important than the anti-lynching movement, because there would be no lynching if it did not start in the schoolroom. Why not exploit, enslave, or exterminate a class that everybody is taught to regard as inferior?[16]

SCENE IN SABINE COUNTY, TEXAS, JUNE 15, 1908.

The Dogwood Tree.
This is only the branch of the Dogwood tree;
An emblem of WHITE SUPREMACY.
A lesson once taught in the Pioneer's school,
That this is a land of WHITE MAN'S RULE.
The Red Man once in an early day,
Was told by the Whites to mend his way.
The negro, now, by eternal grace,
Must learn to stay in the negro's place.
In the Sunny South, the Land of the Free,
Let the WHITE SUPREME forever be.
Let this a warning to all negroes be,
Or they'll suffer the fate of the DOGWOOD TREE.
Copyrighted — *Pub. by Harkrider Drug Co., Center, Tex.*

Lynchings in Sabine County, Texas, photo postcard with "The Dogwood Tree" poem, 1908.

Antiblack racism found its daily, mundane existence through this imagery, drowning out the complex realities and achievements of actual black people. Chromolithography was deployed, with malice and brilliance, to sell commercial products through the lure of incongruously juxtaposed black caricatures, rendered in four-color imagery. The novelty swept the marketplace—and amplified antiblack racism. Subconsciously, consumption was inextricably intertwined with the legalization of racial segregation, the denigration of black people, and the stripping of black rights in Redemption constitutional conventions, whose dubious qualifications on voting, for instance, and segregated educational facilities, were upheld by the courts. As the historian

Thomas Holt concludes in an insightful analysis of the role of minstrelsy in naturalizing everyday antiblack racism, "it is precisely within the ordinary and everyday that racialization has been most effective, where it makes race [a process] that fixes the meaning of one's self before one even had had the opportunity to live and make a self . . . capable of communicating at a glance accumulated stores of racialized knowledge."[17]

MISCEGENATION

We can see how this symbolic system was put to work within a larger structure of oppression by considering the history of the image of the black male as sexual predator and rapist, which is an outgrowth of the irrational fears of miscegenation that emerged before the war and, as we might expect, dramatically expanded and morphed afterward. Caricatures of the dangers of interracial courting and seduction were common in antebellum America, and perhaps not surprisingly made several appearances as anti-Republican propaganda during Abraham Lincoln's 1864 presidential reelection campaign. One of the most popular

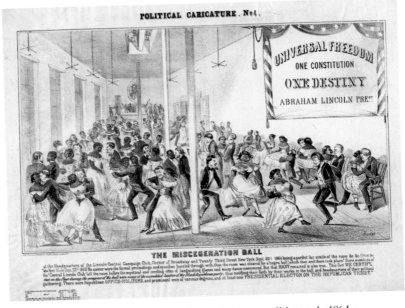

"The Miscegenation Ball," Kimmel & Forster, lithograph, 1864.

images was "The Miscegenation Ball," printed in 1864, along with "Practical Amalgamation," "The Fruits of Amalgamation," and "Miscegenation or the Millennium of Abolition," which echoed tropes from a three-part series called *Amalgamation Waltz*, drawn by Edward W. Clay in 1839.

At the beginning of Lincoln's second campaign, a scandalous hoax calling for forced race mixing was published, cooked up by two Democratic journalists. Titled *Miscegenation: The Theory of the Blending of the Races Applied to the White Man and the Negro*, it was roundly denounced, as was a widely circulated pamphlet *What Miscegenation Is! What We Are to Expect Now that Mr. Lincoln is Re-elected"* (1864), written by "L. Seaman," with this titillating cover image:

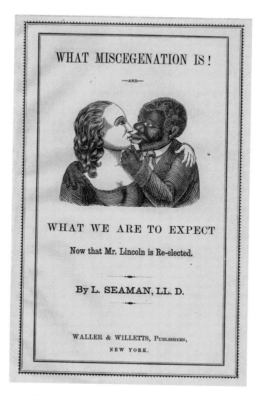

What Miscegenation Is! by L. Seaman, LL.D.,
book cover, ca 1864–1865.

Miscegenation, called "amalgamation" throughout much of the century, was the white supremacist's nightmare, because it constituted the violation of the supposedly immutable fixed boundaries between white and black, between the "human" and "subhuman." In December 1863, two journalists from the *New York World*, David Goodman Crosby and George Wakeman, published the seventy-two-page satiric pamphlet *Miscegenation* featuring an abolitionist narrator obsessed with the mixing of the races. Some, like the proslavery white supremacist writer and publisher John H. Van Evrie of New York, didn't recognize it as satire, taking the argument at face value and seeking to refute it. In 1864, he issued his response in the pamphlet *Subgenation: The Theory of the Normal Relation of the Races; An Answer to "Miscegenation"*:

> The elevation of humanity is to be reached by placing the races in their natural relation to each other—in a word, by subgenation.
>
> Do not be startled, reader; but every negro in the North ought at once to be placed in a position of subgenation—that is, enslaved, as it has been called in our ignorance of the laws of races. At present, the negroes of the North are non-producers. . . . According to the Census Reports, crimes among them are over six or eight times more frequent than among the white population. They are also rapidly perishing under the present policy, the births not being equal to the deaths. The truth is clear as noonday—God's eternal laws of subgenation are being outraged. No one has a right to try to make those equal whom God has made unequal. Never can we have a true democracy, never can humanity be elevated and ennobled, or freed from poverty and its attendant crimes, until the laws of God are respected and obeyed, and embodied in our legal and social system. The equality of all whom God has created equal (white men), and the inequality of those He has made unequal (negroes and other inferior races), is the corner-stone of American democracy, and the vital principle of American civilization and of human progress. . . .
>
> The very conception of love—upon which all lawful intercourse of the sexes is founded—is impossible, eternally impossible, between whites and blacks.[18]

In August of that year, S. S. Nicholas spoke at the Democratic National Convention and offered what the historian Forrest Wood calls "the benevolent racist position": "The scheme of miscegenation and amalgamation is one of equal folly. The law of nature against the propagation of hybrids vindicates its supremacy by a visible deterioration from both races, before reaching the octoroon, when propagation entirely ceases. Besides, the scheme is so disgustingly revolting to the strong natural instincts of our people, as to render its proposal a gross insult to the nation. If our abolition men and women will insist on having it tried with their personal aid, it is to be hoped that our country will not be disgraced by the experiment, but that it may be made in some foreign land. This natural revulsion is not to be conquered by its fierce denunciation in the halls of Congress as 'a base prejudice.'"[19]

Writing in response to a September 23, 1864, *New York World* report titled "Miscegenation in Earnest," Van Evrie, that proponent of "subgenation," criticized New York City's Central Lincoln Club as allegedly fostering miscegenation by allowing both whites and blacks to attend:

> Full a hundred and fifty of coal black wenches
> Tripped gracefully on the fantastic light toe;
> Some on the platform and more on the benches,
> Each damsel squeezed tightly her Republican beau.
> On the rostrum they sat, both ogling and teasing,
> And some waddled lazily around the hall;
> The smell was so strong that it set us a sneezing
> So we started away from the Miscegen Ball.[20]

On August 1, 1865, Francis Preston Blair, Sr., the journalist and long-time politician who cofounded the Republican Party but returned to the Democrats as a result of his disillusion with Reconstruction, shared his sense of alarm about the proverbial "mixing of the races" in a letter to President Andrew Johnson: "What can come of this adulteration of our Anglo-Saxon race and Anglo-Saxon Government by Africanization, but the degradation of the free spirit & lofty aspirations which our race inherited from their ancestry and brought to this continent; and turn that whole portion of it engaged as manual Operatives into that class of mongrels which cannot but spring from the unnatural blending of the blacks & whites in one common class of laborers and giving to both an assimilation through that color, which has unhappily marked servitude during all generations from the days of Ham."[21]

The threat of miscegenation was often linked to the threat of rape, pervading every corner of Southern life, and striking particular fear in the symbolic space of the voting booth. Several writers tied the right of black men to vote to the right to rape: As an editorial from the *New York World* published on November 14, 1867, put it: "The Republican Party carried through Congress the Reconstruction act which compels the Southern States to make all male negroes over twenty-one years of age voters. . . . It swept in its ample reach all the lazy, licentious, brutalized elements of the black population in the South. . . . [N]o sensible member of the Republican party, conspicuous for his intelligence and soundness of judgment on everyday affairs, would approve of this scheme of at once making voters out of uneducated, unreflecting, thriftless field-hands of the South."[22]

On March 28, 1868, an editorial in the *Bossier (LA) Banner* newspaper was even more explicit: "IF YOU DON'T want negro equality forced upon you, go to the polls and vote against the proposed Constitution, framed by the social banditi, domestic bastards, catamites, scalawags, slubberdegullions, cow thieves and jay-hawkers of Louisiana. . . . If you don't want your wives and daughters to be insulted by insolent and depraved negro vagabonds, go to the polls and vote against the new constitution. . . . If you are opposed to amalgamation and miscegenation, vote against the new constitution."[23]

Proximity between the races, especially on public transport, could only lead to disastrous results, since the libidos of black males, according to racist dogma, could not be restrained. On July 9, 1890, just one day before the Louisiana legislature passed the Separate Car Act, the state segregation law at issue in *Plessy v. Ferguson* (1896), the *New Orleans Times-Democrat* editorialized on the evil inherent in mixed train cars: "A man that would be horrified at the idea of his wife or daughter seated by the side of a burly negro in the parlor of a hotel or at a restaurant cannot see her occupying a crowded seat in a car next to a negro without the same feeling of disgust . . . who believes that the white race should be kept pure from African taint will vote against that commingling of the races inevitable in a 'mixed car' and which must have bad results."[24]

THE "NATURAL" PROPENSITY TO RAPE

Race mixing in public transportation, like the integration of black and white students in public schools, the argument went, only increased the opportunities for black males to rape white women, and therefore should be opposed, at all costs, since black men ostensibly could not control what was seen to be genetic or biological impulse. One of the fullest explanations of the need for lynchings as punishment and deterrent for rape was published in the *Memphis Daily Commercial*, on May 17, 1892. Titled "More Rapes, More Lynchings," the editorial bears reprinting because it encapsulates commonly held attitudes about the "natural" inclination of black men to rape white women: "The frequency of these lynchings calls attention to the frequency of the crimes which cause lynching. The 'Southern barbarism' which deserves the serious attention of all people North and South, is the barbarism which preys upon weak and defenseless women. Nothing but the most prompt, speedy and extreme punishment can hold in check the horrible and beastial [sic] propensities of the Negro race. There is a strange similarity about a number of cases of this character which have lately occurred."

These rapes form a pattern, the editorial continued:

In each case the crime was deliberately planned and perpetrated by several Negroes. They watched for an opportunity when the women were left without a protector. It was not a sudden yielding to a fit of passion, but the consummation of a devilish purpose which has been seeking and waiting for the opportunity. . . . No man can leave his family at night without the dread that some roving Negro ruffian is watching and waiting for this opportunity. The swift punishment which invariably follows these horrible crimes doubtless acts as a deterring effect upon the Negroes in that immediate neighborhood for a short time. But the lesson is not widely learned nor long remembered. . . . The facts of the crime appear to appeal more to the Negro's lustful imagination than the facts of the punishment do to his fears. He sets aside all fear of death in any form when opportunity is found for the gratification of his bestial desires.

Nor was this "propensity" to rape likely to change; the structures that had kept black men in check during slavery had been destroyed. "There is small reason to hope for any change for the better. The commission of this crime grows more frequent every year. The generation of Negroes which have grown up since the war have lost in large measure the traditional and wholesome awe of the white race which kept the Negroes in subjection, even when their masters were in the army, and their families left unprotected except by the slaves themselves. There is no longer a restraint upon the brute passion of the Negro."

There was only one alternative: "What is to be done? The crime of rape is always horrible, but [for] the Southern man there is nothing which so fills the soul with horror, loathing and fury as the outraging of a white woman by a Negro. It is the race question in the ugliest, vilest, most dangerous aspect. The Negro as a political factor can be controlled. But neither laws nor lynchings can subdue his lusts. Sooner or later it will force a crisis. We do not know in what form it will come."[25]

It seems there was no end to the torment inflicted upon white people by that question "What is to be done?" In 1909—as it happens, the year the NAACP was founded—the *Charlotte News* printed an article called "White Women in Danger," in response to what it felt to be the ultimate manifestation of the "Negro Problem": the insatiable, omnipresent black rapist. According to the paper, three times in two days, a "black brute" attempted to carry out his "fiendish designs" on four different "young ladies," each one spared only by her "remarkable presence of mind" and, in one case, her ability to wield a lamp as a weapon, "crashing it over the head of the midnight marauder." The crisis had been averted this time, the paper acknowledged, and therefore the "peace-loving people" of Charlotte could respond with restraint. But what about next time? Because surely there would be a next time. The editorial advocated for the enforcement of the city's "rigid law against vagrancy." Otherwise, there was no telling what might happen:

> What home is safe so long as shiftless negroes are allowed to make the city their rendezvous? What lady is safe on the streets after the twilight hour?
>
> Had the unspeakable crime been actually committed the city would have been thrown into a furor of excitement. Nor would men have been content with anything save the most thorough purging of the city of all classes of criminal vagrants. We should have turned heaven and earth to track down the culprit, and every step possible to be taken would have been made to free the city of would-be criminals and insure the future safety of our women. . . .
>
> Charlotte is populated with a peace-loving people. And yet, unless something is done to throttle this outcropping of criminality, we dare not contemplate eventualities, if once the citizenship becomes aroused over the commission of some heinous crime.[26]

It doesn't require much imagination to guess what those "eventualities" might be. By 1909, and for years before and after, they usually involved the murder of a black man.

The idea that white women could possibly desire black men was anathema to white supremacist ideologues, of course. In August 1898, the *Daily Record*, a black newspaper in Wilmington, North Carolina, published an editorial that would enrage white citizens to the point that they would attack the press and, in the process, trigger a riot and overthrow the local government. Alex Manly, the paper's publisher and editor, had been a vociferous advocate of black advancement and political power. In this editorial, he published a bold and courageous response to widespread claims by white supremacists that lynching and the threat of lynching were the only way to control the bestial sexual appetites of black men, and therefore protect the purity of white women. Specifically, the editorial in Manly's paper questioned the assumption that white women were unconditionally innocent. This was the offending line: "White women are not any more particular in the matter of clandestine meetings with colored men than are white men with colored women." Manly and the *Daily Record* voiced the startling and outrageous idea that sexual desire could be color-blind.

The opposition to Manly's editorial was led by the local white newspaper, the *Wilmington Messenger*. Yet only a decade earlier, the paper had offered support for the rights of the freedpeople and criticized white Southerners who promoted what it called "The Absurdity of Disfranchisement": "About the most absurd proposition that has occupied public attention lately, is the foolish suggestion of disfranchising the colored people of the South. . . . There is just as much sense in suggesting the restoration of the Southern Confederacy, or the re-enslavement of the negroes. Men who indulge in speculation on such problems as the re-enslavement or repression of races of men who have acquired freedom and the power of citizenship through intervention and influence of revolution, forget that revolutionary forces never recede. The world does not move backward. Issues of doubt to day become the settled facts of tomorrow. The hand of progress is never set back on the dial of time. Discussion of the re-enslavement of the black race in the United States is about twenty-four years behind time."[27]

By 1898, the *Messenger* had embraced militant white supremacy, and in its response to Manly, not a trace remained of the supportive sentiments published ten years prior. Adopting a hardline racist stance, the paper intoned: "If it does not make every decent man's blood boil, then the manhood is gone, and with it Anglo-Saxon loyalty to the pure and noble white women of our land. We hope the white men will read again and again that brutal attack . . . and swear upon the altar of their country to wipe out negro rule for all time in this noble old commonwealth."[28] The *Messenger* editorial would be blamed as the spark that ignited what became the Wilmington race riot of 1898, resulting in the death of as many as sixty black people (an official count escapes tally) and in Manly being run out of town. It also resulted in Democrats installing themselves in power by staging a coup against the local Fusionist government of Populists and Republicans, demonstrating that the threat of rape and the defense of white womanhood were used by white Democrats as a metaphor for deeper economic and political power relations, and as an excuse to reverse the gains in equal rights that black people had made under Reconstruction.

Rape caused lynching; black men raped. The twisted logic was as simple as that: lynchings would have to continue until the black beast was tamed and contained, which required racial segregation to be fully instituted and enforceable.

In the nineteenth century, before the end of the Civil War, the fear and guilt of the slave owner in the New World most frequently found its expression in the demonization of the revolution in Haiti and in the characterization of its brilliant military strategists, especially Toussaint Louverture and Jean-Jacques Dessalines, as cannibals and savages and, of course, rapists. Nat Turner and his companions were described in similarly derogatory ways after his bloody rebellion in 1831 in Southampton Country, Virginia, though curiously not as rapists.[29] But once the specter of black power manifested itself in the United States during Reconstruction as the irresistible power of the black ballot, the stereotype of the ruthless, homicidal black savage was bifurcated, transformed into a Janus-faced figure, polar opposites in resonance and signification.

Black people had long recognized the duality white racist mythology ascribed to them. As early as 1834, a group of black leaders addressed these contradictory representations of the essentialized "nature" of black people. At the Fourth Annual Convention for the Improvement of the Free People of Colour, held that year, the conference summary complained that "[the American Colonization Society] sometimes represents us as the most corrupt, vicious, and abandoned of any class of men in the community. Then again we are kind, meek, and gentle."[30] This latter stereotype, of course, of the comforting, deracinated, emasculated Sambo figure continued in circulation in American society, ranging in manifestation from Uncle Tom in *Uncle Tom's Cabin* and Uncle Remus in the Brer Rabbit stories to Uncle Ben on boxes of instant rice. At the other extreme stands the terrifying virility embodied in the Haitian revolutionaries and in American slave revolts such as those by Nat Turner, as well as Gabriel's in Richmond, Virginia, in 1800, and Denmark Vesey's in Charleston, South Carolina, in 1822, which struck fear in the hearts and minds of defenders of slavery. But the supplement or surplus to American anxieties about black virility—the psychological element that could not be neutered in harmless avuncular stereotypes such as Uncle Tom and Uncle Ben, or Hoke in *Driving Miss Daisy*, each one brilliantly parodied by Samuel L. Jackson's character, Stephen, in *Django Unchained* (just as Jamie Foxx's character, Django, parodies the vengeful-slave/Nat Turner stereotype)—was the creation of the white racist fiction of the unbridled, incorrigible, depraved heterosexuality of the black male, now refigured as the congenitally inveterate rapist, projected onto black male human beings, trapped by their "nature" in a permanent state of lust, poised to violate, unpredictably and spontaneously, the purity and sanctity of white virginal womanhood.

This stereotype of the omnipresent black rapist is a classic instance of repression and projection: the repression of the frequency of rape during slavery. Rape did commonly take place in the netherworld of the plantation, but not in the way that its occurrence would be projected during Redemption. We now know, thanks to developments in DNA analysis, that one in three African American males carries a Y-DNA signature inherited from a direct white male ancestor (say, a great-great-great-grandfather) and that the average African American autosomal admixture is about 25 percent European. These startling results could only reflect the frequency of the rape of black women by white men during slavery. The science is irrefutable and telling, and the creation of the stereotype of the black male as rapist can be seen as repression of the guilt and crime of rape, projected onto black males, in a most bizarre American manifestation of Freud's concept of the "return of the repressed." "What is forgotten [or denied] is not extinguished but only 'repressed,'" he wrote; "its memory-traces are present in all their freshness, but isolated by 'anticathexes' . . . they are unconscious—inaccessible to consciousness." Freud famously called these "derivatives of the unconscious," and they can manifest themselves in many familiar forms, including slips of the tongue but also fantasies. I argue, in other words, the stereotype of the black male as rapist, one of the common themes of Sambo art imagery, is an instance of this mechanism of repression, which

Freud calls "substitutive satisfaction . . . , the distinguishing characteristic [of which] . . . is the far-reaching distortion to which the returning material has been subjected as compared with the original."[31]

An editorial in the *Memphis Evening Scimitar* published on June 14, 1892, argued as if it were self-evident that "the violation of white women by Negroes . . . is the outcropping of a bestial perversion of instinct."[32] In other words, since black males are uncontrollable rapists, then it must be possible to lynch them at any time; to protect the sanctity of white society, white society must be ever vigilant. Frantz Fanon expands this notion of "lynching" from the literal to the figurative: "But the black man is attacked in his corporeality. It is his tangible personality that is lynched. It is his actual being that is dangerous." Fanon's observations here are helpful in understanding the creation of the stereotype of the black man as rapist, the excuse for a large proportion of lynchings in the American South following Reconstruction. As he puts it in the baldest terms, "Isn't lynching the black man a sexual revenge?"[33] Moreover, Fanon continues:

> The civilized white man retains an irrational nostalgia for the extraordinary times of sexual licentiousness, orgies, unpunished rapes, and unrepressed incest. In a sense, these fantasies correspond to Freud's life instinct. Projecting his desires onto the black man, the white man behaves as if the black man actually had them. . . . The black man is fixated at the genital level, or rather he has been fixated there. . . . To have a phobia about black men is to be afraid of the biological, for the black man is nothing but biological. Black men are animals. They live naked. And God only knows what else. Whoever says rape, says black man.[34]

Such a blistering insight could easily have been applied to Jim Crow America. It is no doubt true that, in the heinous history of rape, some black men were inexcusably guilty of raping some white women. But Jim Crow was never really concerned with evidence or proportionality, was it? During its rise, the myth of the omnipresent black rapist—spawned from the wildly exaggerated fears about the vulnerability of white women and the brutalities that could be visited upon them at any time by black men everywhere and anywhere—became part of the collective unconscious, to use Fanon's term, of the post-Reconstruction American South. Simply put, the thought that the ultimate fantasy of black males was to rape white women became an obsession—so, too, the desire to erase it through extralegal means.[35]

BLACKFACE

The historian Brian Roberts perceptively ties the growth of blackface performance to the use of rape as an excuse for lynching, especially after a decade of states' rights constitutional conventions and the imposition of Jim Crow laws: "By the turn of the century, blackface was everywhere in American culture, from stage to product packaging to the very term—'Jim Crow'—associated with the nation's system of racial hierarchy. By this time, blackface was well on its way to becoming America's gift to the world." Blackface, Roberts argues, with its depiction of "black characters as bodies without minds," allowed for an almost mystical displacement of desire from the white victimizer, as it were, onto the real victim, the black male: "In blackface performance," Roberts writes, "the black character became a vessel for a host of desires: for authentic masculinity, for sexual potency, for violent self-assertion, for liberation from culture itself. . . . What made blackface a part of the American racial state was the way it maintained hierarchies. . . . Some of the most beloved elements of blackface—the blackface character's physicality, his love of violence, his dangerous masculinity—would become rationales for many of America's worst crimes of racial oppression."[36]

An intriguing exception to the depiction of the black male as fearsome, salacious predator was a poster printed in Paris in 1905. The image can almost be read as a visual representation of Alex Manly's quote about the possibility for a reciprocity of desire between black men and white women. Designed by Louis Galice, *The Frisco* is one of the earliest instances of the phenomenon that Homi K. Bhabha calls "the return of the look." In the scenario, a lecherous but well-dressed black man, ostensibly a black American called Frisco, ogles in the most exaggerated manner a

The Frisco, theatrical poster by Louis Galice, 1905.

younger, elegantly dressed, refined white woman emerging from a "Conservatoire." She carries a black violin case. A quick glance at her face reveals her mutual fascination with the black man, engaging in an equally sexualized return of his gaze. To underscore the point, the poster features three outsize black phallic images: Frisco's top hat, his cane, and the woman's black violin case, all directing the gaze of the viewer to Frisco's groin, as it were.

The Frisco serves to deconstruct the black-male-as-lecher stereotype,

The New Smart Set, theatrical poster, 1906.
Advertisement for performance of *A Sure Winner* by
the vaudeville company The New Smart Set, led by
the African American impresario Sherman H. Dudley.

revealing, as Bhabha puts it, that "the stereotype is at once a substitute and a shadow," a substitute for white male rape in slavery as well as a shadow by which "the stereotyped Other reveals something of the 'fantasy' (as desire, defence) of that position of [white male] mastery."[37] It is not a surprise that this depiction of the doubling of the return of the gaze was created and circulated in France; little like it was in circulation in the United States at the height of Jim Crow. Something so daring would have been much more scandalous than Manly's editorial.

And yet, a year later, Cincinnati's US Lithograph Company produced *The New Smart Set* poster, which casts the black male and white female in roles similar to those depicted in *The Frisco*. Three black men, clownish despite their apparent wealth, leer at a white woman, who, instead of looking fearful, casts a sidelong glance at the men, her gaze particularly drawn to the leader of the pack, who sports a badge that says "Owner." In this illustration, the phallic black cane of *The Frisco* has been doubled: the aforementioned black male "Owner" and the white woman both sport dark brown walking sticks.

How many times had a white male slave owner eyed a black woman lasciviously? Both posters deconstruct the black male stereotypes that had been in wide circulation in the United States for at least the previous century. These are blackface performances with a marked difference: each one illustrates a stereotype of a black man and a white woman that at once reinforces but also calls into question the American stereotypes of black men's rape fantasies.

THE BIRTH OF A NATION

Soon, blackface performance at the turn of the century would find an outlet in the exciting, emerging new medium of moving pictures. The fantasy of black male–white female rape would continue to be drawn upon to titillate white Americans as the century progressed, becoming even more deeply inscribed in the American cultural imagination through D. W. Griffith's *The Birth of a Nation*. The film is one of the most blatantly racist motion pictures ever produced. Released in 1915, at the height of Jim Crow, it served as the perfect, dazzling cinematic representation of a bundle of Lost Cause myths, fabrications about the evils and excesses of Reconstruction, and denigrating stereotypes about black people (especially black men), all summoned to demonstrate on a big screen how the birth of the Ku Klux Klan and the deconstruction of Reconstruction saved White America.

As we saw in chapter 2, the pioneering Hollywood director D. W. Griffith obtained the film rights to Thomas Dixon's novel *The Clansman*. Griffith, who was sympathetic to Dixon's framing of history, married the author's incendiary themes to his own talent for spectacular, cutting-edge filmmaking.[38] The result was the blockbuster of the age, *The Birth of a Nation*, a title as famous as it is infamous.

The first part of *The Birth of a Nation* was not based on *The Clansman*. Instead, the film opens on a Civil War–era drama revolving around members of two different family clans, the Stonemans of Washington, DC, and the Camerons of fictitious Piedmont, South Carolina. The Camerons represent idealized visions of the Old South, while the Stonemans oppose slavery. It is the stuff of melodrama. Philip Stoneman falls in love with Margaret Cameron, while Ben Cameron becomes infatuated with Elsie Stoneman, whom he knows only through a photo. Though the two families maintain a close relationship, the Civil War divides them, like the Union itself. Tod Stoneman, fighting for the Union, and Duke Cameron, fighting for the Confederacy, die together in battle. The

Confederate Ben Cameron is injured but survives, and while in the hospital he finally meets Elsie Stoneman, who works there as a nurse. Elsie asks President Lincoln for Stoneman's pardon.

The political center of the film features Griffith's "take" on Reconstruction as a miserable failure. Specifically, he leveraged the character of Austin Stoneman, a Radical Republican leader of the House of Representatives (based on Thaddeus Stevens), to exemplify the era's corruption and racial horrors. Stoneman supports Silas Lynch, a mulatto carpetbagger who emerges as the film's archvillain. Lynch becomes the state's lieutenant governor at the same time that white South Carolinians are stripped of their right to vote and African Americans seize control of the government.

There are subtle nods to actual historical actors here, even if the interpretation was wrongheaded and racist. In Reconstruction-era Louisiana, Oscar J. Dunn had, in fact, become the first black lieutenant governor in 1868, and he was succeeded upon his death in 1871 by another African American, P. B. S. Pinchback. The name Lynch also calls to mind two of the real heroes of Reconstruction. James Lynch served as Mississippi's first black secretary of state, while John Roy Lynch of Natchez, Mississippi, served in Congress and wrote the seminal account of the period, *The Facts of Reconstruction* (1913), as an early corrective to the Lost Cause myth that Dixon and Griffith promoted. But in these early decades of film, the spectacle trumped the written record, even—or especially—one based on the firsthand experiences of a black officeholder.

The historian Leon F. Litwack describes D. W. Griffith's revision of Negro rule in *The Birth of a Nation* as follows: "Impudent, ungrateful, venal black men, their ambitions bloated by emancipation and civil rights, terrorize helpless whites, shoving them off the sidewalks, blocking their access to the ballot boxes, and leering at their women. Blacks brandish signs reading 'Equal Rights, Equal Politics, Equal Marriage.' They ridicule and chain their old masters. They abuse those 'faithful souls' (the Cameron servants) who still take pride in their white folks. They make a mockery of democratic government, sitting shoeless in legislative chambers, drinking whiskey from bottles, and eating chicken off the bone while enacting a statute legitimizing interracial marriage."[39]

These propagandistic tropes did not come out of nowhere; they had their roots in the Reconstruction period. Take, for instance, the work of two Northerners, James Shepherd Pike and Thomas Nast, whose weariness and skepticism toward Reconstruction grew obvious during the 1870s. In 1874, Pike, a former Radical Republican from Maine who had worked at the *New York Tribune*, published *The Prostrate State: South Carolina under Negro Government*, a vicious assault on Reconstruction and black-run government.[40] Pike put forth an argument that would become increasingly popular: Reconstruction has failed, and the failure should be attributed to African Americans. He described the government of South Carolina as "barbarism overwhelming civilization by sheer physical force. It is the slave rioting in the halls of his master, and putting that master under his feet. . . . At some of the desks sit colored men whose types it would be hard to find outside of Congo; whose costume, visages, attitudes, and expression only befit the forecastle of a buccaneer."[41]

Incredibly, Nast had come to national fame through his cartoons protesting slavery and discrimination. But, Eric Foner argues, "[c]hanges in graphic artist Thomas Nast's depiction of blacks mirrored the evolution of Republican sentiment in the North." His 1874 *Harper's Weekly* cartoon "Colored Rule in a Reconstructed (?) State" depicted black legislators in South Carolina as overweight, screaming caricatures, calling one another "thieves, liars, rascals, and cowards." A white man rests his head on his hand in resignation, while Columbia signals her disappointment: "You are aping the lowest Whites. If you disgrace your race in this way you had better take back seats."[42]

Although forty years lay between Nast's cartoon and Griffith's film, the scenes of the legislature on paper and on screen played on the same fears and stereotypes of the barbaric black man who had taken his unrightful place in the halls of power. As if this wasn't bad enough, Griffith also used his film's plot to illuminate and ignite white Southerners' most blood-boiling emotions about the threats to white womanhood. Recall the scene from *The Birth of a Nation* described above, in which the black legislators are "eating chicken off the bone while enacting a statute legitimizing interracial marriage." In that one scene, Griffith's film projected onto the screen the tandem fear of black political engagement and

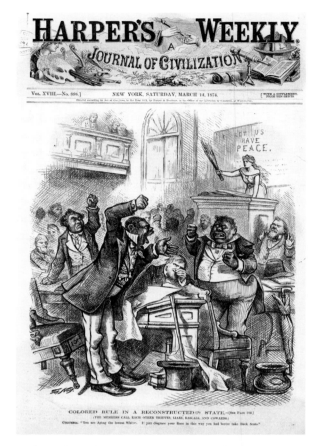

"Colored Rule in a Reconstructed (?) State," Thomas Nast,
Harper's Weekly, March 14, 1874.

miscegenation. Whether black men lusted after political power or white
women more remained an open, entangled question. In *Birth*'s most notorious (and perennially painful-to-watch) scene, one of the Cameron
family's former slaves, the character Gus, attempts to rape Flora Cameron. A lengthy chase scene ensues, and Flora opts to jump off a cliff
rather than succumb to Gus's lascivious assault. She dies in the arms of
her brother, Ben Cameron, who organizes the Ku Klux Klan to ride on
and lynch Gus. As the story unfolds, the black-run government in
South Carolina arrests Ben Cameron for his role in the Klan. Yet, in

a remarkable turn, his loyal black servants break him free before going into hiding together.

Flora is not the only white woman in danger. Alongside the Cameron saga, the villainous Silas Lynch sets his sights on Elsie Stoneman, whom he intends to force into marriage. "I will build a black empire," says Lynch, "and you as my queen shall rule by my side." A black militia then occupies Piedmont. All this is too much for Austin Stoneman, who, sickened by the prospect of a black man marrying his own daughter, turns his back on Reconstruction. At the climax of the film, the liberated Ben Cameron mobilizes the KKK to rescue Elsie from Lynch's clutches and to rescue the Camerons from political exile. In Griffith's world, this denouement was the definition of redemption and reconciliation between the Camerons and Stonemans, and thus between the Union and the former Confederacy. As a coda, white "Redeemers" close the door on Reconstruction, taking back power in Piedmont and disenfranchising their black population.

The Birth of a Nation was a sensation as soon as it premiered in Los Angeles, California, on February 8, 1915. President Woodrow Wilson famously viewed the film at a private White House screening. As it happened, Wilson was a friend of Thomas Dixon's. They had been classmates at Johns Hopkins. The first Southern-born president after the Civil War, Wilson had also written negatively about Reconstruction in his multivolume work, *A History of the American People* (1902), passages from which were excerpted on a trio of title cards that appeared in Griffith's silent film:

> Adventurers swarmed out of the North, as much the enemies of the one race as of the other, to cozen, beguile, and use the negroes. . . . In the villages the negroes were the office holders, men who knew none of the uses of authority, except its insolences. —Woodrow Wilson.

> The policy of the congressional leaders wrought . . . a veritable overthrow of civilization in the South . . . in their determination to "put the white South under the heel of the black South." —Woodrow Wilson.

> The white men were roused by a mere instinct of self-preservation . . . until at last there had sprung into existence a great Ku Klux Klan, a veritable empire of the South, to protect the Southern country. —Woodrow Wilson.

Although Wilson's much-discussed support of the film has been called into question—his endorsement of the film being "like history written with lightning" is likely apocryphal—there can be no doubt of the president's racism. Wilson allowed members of his administration to bring Jim Crow to various departments, including the Treasury and the Post Office Department, and black leaders like Du Bois turned on him for good reason after endorsing him in 1912. If any further evidence of his racism was needed, those were indeed Wilson's words used on the title cards in the Griffith film.[43]

The film spurred the NAACP to organize protests, including massive demonstrations in New York and Boston, and letter-writing campaigns to the National Board of Censorship of Motion Pictures. The spirited African American leader William Monroe Trotter, a Harvard graduate (he earned a bachelor's degree magna cum laude, was the first black person elected there to Phi Beta Kappa, and also earned a master's degree) who had helped launch the Niagara Movement with W. E. B. Du Bois and others in 1905, was the key to organizing the resistance to the film, thereby adding a new definition to the concept of the New Negro. In his native Boston, Trotter was punched by a plainclothes policeman and arrested attempting to buy a ticket at a segregated theater, and he organized a demonstration against the film in front of the Massachusetts State House, just above the memorial to Robert Gould Shaw and the 54th Regiment on Boston Common.[44]

David Blight explains the significance of *The Birth of a Nation* as such: "The lasting significance of this epic film is that by using powerful imagery, buttressed by enormous advertising and political endorsement, it etched a story of Reconstruction that has lasted long in America's historical consciousness. The war was noble on both sides, the film says, but

Reconstruction in the South was directed by deranged radicals and sex-crazed blacks, especially those mulattos given unwarranted political power. The very lifeblood of civilization, of familial survival, was at stake for the exploited South; hence, white Southern men had to take law and history into their own hands."[45]

Dick Lehr concludes that the protest against *The Birth of a Nation*, though ultimately unsuccessful in banning the film, was one of the most important factors in galvanizing black political protest against Jim Crow in the second decade of the century and served dramatically to increase the membership of the NAACP as it struggled to make headway as an effective force in the fight against segregation. As its membership shot up because of the protest against the film, I believe it helped the organization's leaders, especially Du Bois as editor of the *Crisis*, to see the enormous potential that the organization could have over the long run in fighting antiblack racism, to recognize the need for a systematic attack on de jure Jim Crow segregation through a blend of activism and the production of, as Du Bois would recall, culture and the arts. Furthermore, it focused attention on the shockingly damaging role that this new form of media—film—played in shaping public opinion about African Americans. *The Birth of a Nation* also helped inspire the rebirth of the Ku Klux Klan, which, as it mobilized and attracted new members in the 1920s, not only fed on antiblack racism but, increasingly, on rampant anti-Semitism and anti-immigrant sentiments in the country as well. It is no surprise, then, that a new New Negro movement would emerge just a few years later in the call for a "renaissance" that would identify the arts as the key to transforming the image of the race and, therefore, American race relations. In other words, the fight that Trotter and the NAACP embarked upon in 1915 to combat the pernicious influence of the emerging industry of film—unprecedented in its reach and its power to inflict harm by recasting the long history of negative images of the race in a potent new form—helped plant the seeds for the counterrevolution in image formation that lay at the heart of the New Negro Renaissance in the twenties. At least, that was the hope that shapers of the renaissance, especially its architect, Alain Locke, embraced.[46]

THE UNITED STATES
OF RACE:
MASS-PRODUCING
STEREOTYPES AND FEAR

Lautz Bro's & Co's Stearine Soap, advertisement, 1874.

"CREME"

Oat Meal Soap, is a pure and elegant article for the toilet.

The special merit of Oat Meal as a soap ingredient, is that it will cleanse, whiten, soften and smooth the skin, and prevents the hands from chapping. This soap is sold at the remarkably low price of ten (10) cents per box of three cakes.

THE PEOPLE'S MFG. CO.,

BUFFALO, N. Y.

TO CARD COLLECTORS.—There are six different designs in this set. We will mail the complete set to any address, on receipt of three cent stamp.

"Creme" Oat Meal Toilet Soap, advertisement, 1881.

Dingman's Electric Soap, advertisement, ca. 1880s.

Pears' Soap, advertisement, ca. 1884.

Chlorinol Bleaching Soda, advertisement,
R. Armstrong Ltd., Preston, Lancashire,
UK, 1908.

"No Dinner?," Rising Sun Stove Blacking,
advertisement, Morse Bros., Canton,
Massachusetts, 1870–1890.

"I Say Snow Flake, Dat Stove Was Blacked with Rising Sun
Did You Eber See De Like?," Rising Sun Stove Blacking,
advertisement, Morse Bros., Canton, Massachusetts, 1870–1890.

California Fig Bitters,
advertisement, 1900.

"The Little Nigs Are Nearly
Late for School," *The Little Nigs
of Tiny Town*, cartoon strip, 1907.

Cream of Wheat, advertisement featuring the black cook Rastus, illustration by Edward V. Brewer, 1921.

Aunt Jemima Pancake Flour, "All you need for perfect pancakes," print advertisement, *Saturday Evening Post*, May 10, 1919. This durable image of Aunt Jemima is based on a sketch of Nancy Green by A. B. Frost, 1893. Green, the original Aunt Jemima, was born into slavery in 1834.

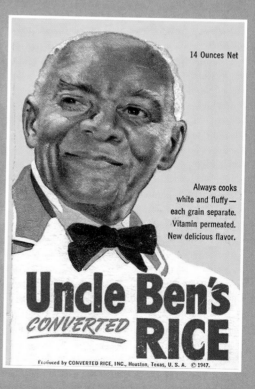

Uncle Ben's Converted Rice, package, early design, 1947.

"Alligator Bait," photolithograph, McCrary & Branson,
Knoxville, Tennessee, 1897 or 1900.

"Darky's Prayer, Florida," postcard,
early twentieth century.

"Free Lunch in the Jungle," postcard, 1907.

"Alligator Bait, on the Chagres River, Panama Canal," postcard,
I. L. Maduro, Jr., publisher, early 1940s.

"The Jolly Darkie Target Game," box cover, McLoughlin Bros.,
New York, ca. 1890–1915.

"Alabama Coon, A Jolly Game," target game, die-cut lithographed cardboard,
J. W. Spear & Sons, London/Bavaria, early 1900s.

African Dip game at the Panama Pacific International Exposition, 1915.

Playing cards from a pack of 72, 1930s.

"Hit the Nigger Baby," Camp Minikani, near Milwaukee, Wisconsin, YMCA brochure with "Special Events," 1942.

Special Events ... During every camp period there are one or more of the "special days" when the usual program of hikes, trips and sports is put aside for gala hours of "all out fun" packed with surprises and new treats.

The specialties of last summer, some traditional, some spontaneous, included: All Camp Carnival, Across the Lake Swim, Camper Rule Day, Parents' Campfire, Old Timers Day, Return of Chief Heinecker, and Closing Banquet each period.

"Be Mah Valentine—I'll be hanged if yo' is goin' to say NO!," greeting card, ca. 1920s.

"Jolly Nigger Bank," enameled cast iron, original design by Shepard Hardware Company, Buffalo, New York, 1880s.

"I Always Did Spise a Mule," mechanical bank, enameled cast iron, J & E Stevens Co., Cromwell, Connecticut, 1897.

"Smilin' Sam from Alabam, The Salted Peanut Man," mechanical vending machine, enameled cast iron, General Merchandise, Chicago, 1931.

FOR THE SUNNY SOUTH.
AN AIRSHIP WITH A "JIM CROW" TRAILER.

"For the Sunny South," illustration, *Puck*, February 26, 1913.

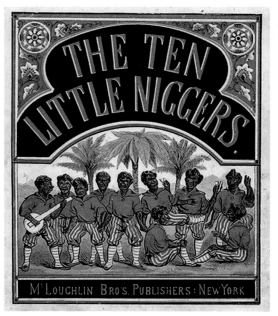

"The Ten Little Niggers," songbook cover, McLoughlin Brothers, New York, ca. 1870–1876.

Let's Hurry! or We'll Miss the Public Lynching!, parody book cover, *Bad Little Children's Books: KidLit Parodies* by illustrator Bob Staake, writing under the pseudonym Arthur C. Gackley, published by Abrams, 2016.

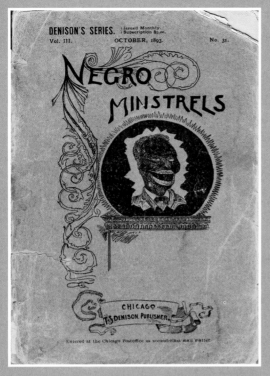

"Negro Minstrels," *Denison's* Series,
Vol. III, No. 31, T. S. Denison & Company,
Chicago, October 1893.

Hello! My Baby, theatrical poster for George
Thatcher's Greatest Minstrels, 1899.

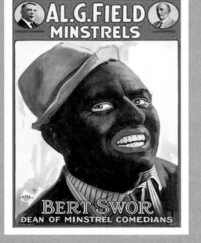

Bert Swor, Dean of Minstrel Comedians,
Al. G. Field Minstrels, theatrical poster,
early 1900s.

"Songs of the Sunny South," political cartoon, with
Booker T. Washington among those lynched, 1912.

"Hungry!: A Comedy a la Mode for Two Blackface Comedians," *Denison's Blackface Plays*, script books in two editions, T. S. Denison & Company, Chicago, 1917 (left), late nineteenth century (right).

"Two Coons in a Wreck," *Denison's Blackface Plays*, script book, T. S. Denison & Company, Chicago, 1920s.

Black man eating a watermelon, a dog pulling down his pants; written on back by sender: "This one takes the blue ribbon. Eh. Oscar," postcard, early twentieth century.

"No Race Suicide," postcard, Ullman Mfg. Co., New York, 1905. Message on back: "Hello—Well, how would you like to have the stork leave you such a nice present! 'All things come to those who wait,' Your Cousin Lola"

"A Dream of Paradise," postcard, H. Horina, J. I. Austen Co., Chicago, ca. 1907–1915.

"I am taking life easy in . . . ,"
continued in red ink by sender,
". . . the country," postcard,
postmarked October 8, 1906.

"I'se gwine back to Dixie!," embossed
postcard, published for European
distribution, Otto Schloss, Berlin,
printer and publisher, 1910.

"I'm afraid of the dark!," *Black Kids Comics*
series, postcard, Bamforth & Co., Peekskill,
New York, postmarked July 1937.

"A Trick in Hearts," postcard, postmarked September 11, 1912, Lake City, Minnesota. In background, images of a watermelon and the African American boxer Jack Johnson.

"I'm an American, same as you," postcard, Henry Heininger, 1917 or earlier.

"Sambo in a Watermelon Brings Greetings from Dixie Land," postcard, 1906. With handwritten sentiment from sender: "I think the nigger looks like you."

"Here's Some Assorted Chocolates," *Black Kids Comics* series, postcard, Bamforth & Co., printed in USA, postmarked Toronto, September 1923. Message on back: "Which one do you want and I'll send it down."

"A Team Fast on the Snow," hand-colored lithograph,
from the *Darktown Comics* series, Currier & Ives, 1883.

"A Team Fast to the Pole," hand-colored lithograph,
from the *Darktown Comics* series, Currier & Ives, 1883.

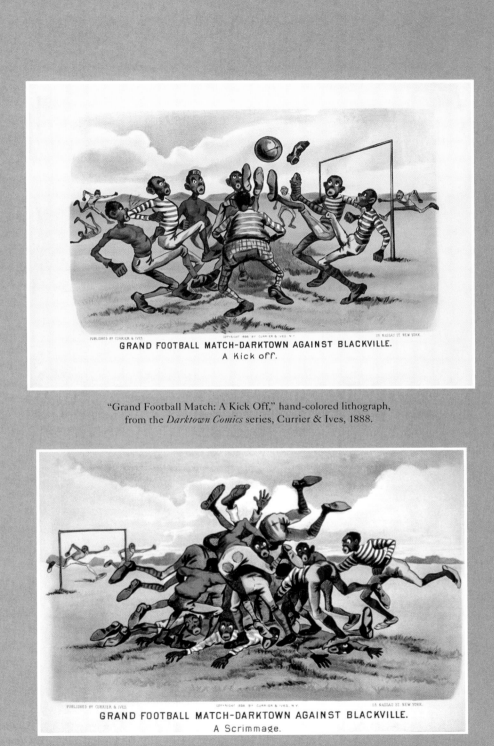

"Grand Football Match: A Kick Off," hand-colored lithograph, from the *Darktown Comics* series, Currier & Ives, 1888.

"Grand Football Match: A Scrimmage," hand-colored lithograph, from the *Darktown Comics* series, Currier & Ives, 1888.

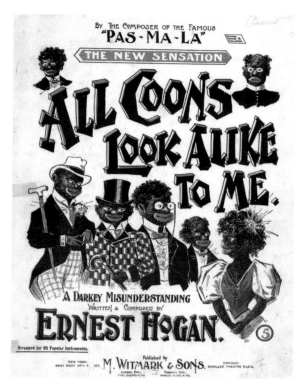

"All Coons Look Alike to Me,"
Ernest Hogan, lyrics and music,
song-sheet cover, M. Witmark &
Sons, New York, Chicago, 1896.

"The Mischievous Nigger: A Negro
Farce," by Charles White, *Amateur
Series*, T. S. Denison & Company,
Chicago, 1890s.

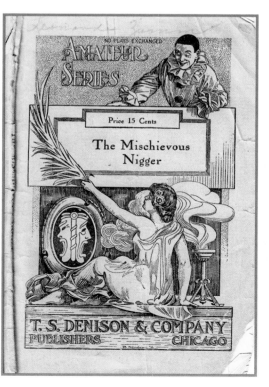

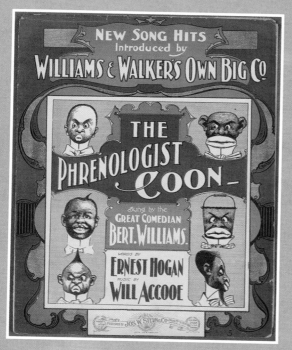

"The Phrenologist Coon—sung by the Great Comedian Bert Williams," Hogan and Accooe, song-sheet cover, Jos. W. Stern & Co., New York, 1901.

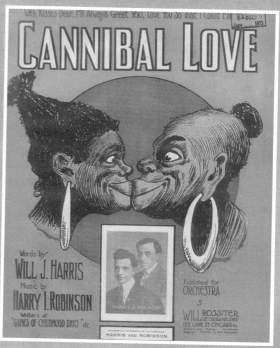

"Cannibal Love," song-sheet cover, Will Rossiter, Chicago, 1909.

"Human Confederate Flag," postcard, 1907. Schoolchildren form a living flag in front of a statue of Robert E. Lee, Richmond, Virginia.

Walter Long in blackface as the freedman and soldier Gus, confronting Flora Cameron in the woods, film still, 1915.

Gus captured by Klansmen and subsequently lynched, film still, 1915.

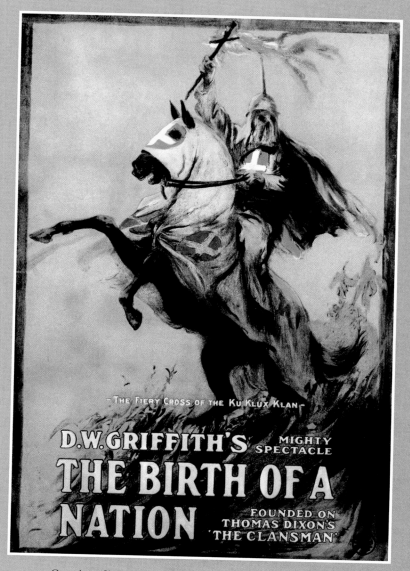

One-sheet film poster, distributed by the Epoch Film Co., 1915.

The Barbarian by Chas. R. Allen, illustrated by H. J. Ward, book cover, Spicy-Adventure Stories, 1934.

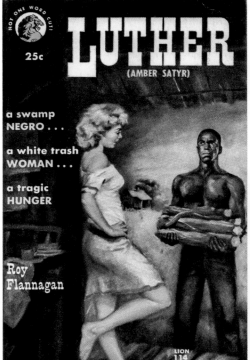

Luther (Amber Satyr) by Roy Flannagan, book cover, Lion Books, mid-twentieth century.

How Sleeps the Beast by Don Tracy, book cover, Lion Books, 1950.

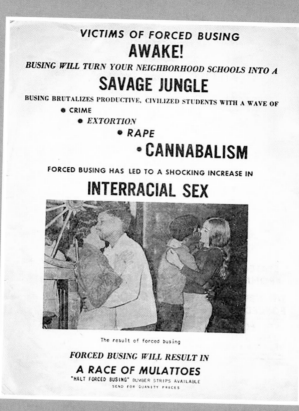

"Victims of forced busing AWAKE!," flyer,
published by Statecraft Enforcers, 1970s.

Four

THE NEW NEGRO

Redeeming the Race from the Redeemers

—

IS HE A NEW NEGRO?

Booker T. Washington at the Cotton States Exposition

Bishop Turner Says There Is No New Negro, but a New White Man.

—L. W. B, "Is He a New Negro?" (Chicago) *Inter Ocean*, October 2, 1895

Prof. B. T., or Bad Taste Wash had made a speech. . . . The white press style Prof. Bad Taste the new Negro, but if there is anything in him except the most servile type of the old Negro we fail to find it in any of his last acts. . . . So let the race labor and pray that no more new Negroes such as Prof. Bad Taste Washington will bob up.

—*CLEVELAND GAZETTE*, quoting *Atlanta Advocate*, November 2, 1895

With the Negro rapidly in process of class differentiation, if it was ever warrantable to regard and treat the Negro en masse, it is becoming with every day less possible, more unjust and more ridiculous.

—ALAIN LOCKE, "Enter the New Negro," 1925

THE BIRTH OF THE NEW NEGRO

One of the most fascinating responses to the collapse of Reconstruction and the institutionalization of Jim Crow segregation in the 1890s was the creation of a new leadership class within the race defined as individuals who fit the description of a "New Negro." These New Negroes—young, educated, post-slavery, modern, culturally sophisticated, and thoroughly middle class—would be more effectively equipped, the argument went, to combat the mounting injustices that the mass of black people were facing as racist Redemption policies became more deeply entrenched throughout the South than the so-called Old Negro possibly could have been. We can think of the concept of the New Negro as a metaphorical form of "reconstruction"—not an official government program or part of the historical period that we know as Reconstruction, which ended in 1877, but an attempt, almost two decades after the fact, to transform the image of the upper classes of race, the denigration of which played such a key role in justifying the subjection not only of the freedmen and freedwomen throughout the South but of black people in the North as well.

In the waning years of the nineteenth century, the rise of Jim Crow, premised on the long-held claim that all black people had been created (un)equal and reinforced by the several forms in which white supremacist ideology manifested itself, saw de jure (legal) segregation become the law of the land. Social customs, the law, and vigilante lawlessness marched arm in arm to instate severe restrictions on all aspects of Negro life throughout the redeemed South. By 1900, the Negro's gains under the Thirteenth, Fourteenth, and Fifteenth Amendments and various Reconstruction Acts had largely disappeared in the former Confederacy. Not only had the US Supreme Court in 1896 validated "separate but equal" in *Plessy v. Ferguson*, but the right to vote had become a distant memory for a huge percentage of Southern black people. Because black voters could have an enormous impact on election outcomes—some 90 percent of all African Americans lived in the South in 1900—just as they demonstrated during Reconstruction, it was of the utmost importance to rob them of the possibility of voting in Southern elections.[1] And robbed they were.

By the end of the decade, for instance, Louisiana had fewer than

6,000 registered black voters, down from a high of 130,000, and Alabama had 3,000, down from 181,000.[2] These figures are typical of those for other states in the former Confederacy, states in what was called the Black Belt. Hundreds of thousands of black men, most of them former slaves or their children, had been disenfranchised by the end of the decade. Of course, economic suppression, linked to the dismantling of voting rights, was also a key part of the establishment of Jim Crow, with the most vivid example seen in two forms of what has been called neo-slavery: sharecropping and convict leasing. Boundaries were policed legally and extralegally: the threat of terror was real and expressed itself in its most extreme form through lynchings, which were on the increase as part of a violent campaign to intimidate black men from trying to register to vote or assume a place in their societies as equal citizens.

In response to this onslaught, black men and women attempted to fight back in various ways, including nurturing their own segregated social and cultural institutions, especially churches, schools, colleges, self-help organizations, and fraternal organizations. And black intellectuals, creative artists, and political activists increasingly grappled in their responses to the so-called Negro Problem. White writers had given the "problem" plenty of thought, too, as we've seen, but their solutions—often condescending—invariably involved programs imposed by white people *onto* the black community. With Frederick Douglass's passing in February 1895, what kind of African American would stand up to the Negro Problem? What kind of African American would confront the broader issues of discrimination, inequality, and poverty throughout the Black Belt?

Even before the term was articulated for the first time, one set of answers to the Negro Problem coalesced around the necessity of a new kind of black person—a "New Negro"—to fight the Redemptionist attack facing the race. Whether intentionally or not, however, the construct of a New Negro implicitly acknowledged some of the stereotypes about the Old Negro—at one extreme, that fanciful creature of plantation literature and proslavery propaganda who thrived under slavery, and then, once slavery ended, pined for its return; and at the other extreme, the uneducated, landless former slaves who, through no fault of their own, had failed to thrive under freedom, had failed to "rise," as the black middle class would put it.

Divisions of class or caste within the black community had manifested themselves long before the Old Negro/New Negro divide was named, as we might expect, reaching back to slavery, with the proverbial distinctions within the slave community between house and field, between enslaved people by occupation, and between mixed-race descendants of white fathers (and, to a much lesser extent, white mothers) and those without white ancestry. As Henry Bibb, an escaped slave and noted abolitionist and newspaper publisher, freely admitted in 1849, "The distinction among slaves is as marked, as the classes of society are in any aristocratic community. Some refusing to associate with others whom they deem to be beneath them, in point of character, color, condition, or the superior importance of their respective masters."[3]

As the percentage of free Negroes increased—about 10 percent of the overall black population by 1860—distinctions between the enslaved and the free were also drawn by some free black people. Eric Foner cites an example where distinctions by caste and color merged in "the Charleston free elite [which] was no less conscious of the gap separating themselves not merely from the slaves, but from the city's poorer free blacks—a gap institutionalized in organizations like the Brown Fellowship Society, which excluded men with dark skins."[4] The "Minutes of the Fourth Annual Convention for the Improvement of the Free People of Colour," in 1834, openly admitted that "the present form of society divides the interest of the community into several parts. Of these, there is that of the white man, that of the slave, and that of the free colored man," before concluding "how very lamentable it is that there should be, anywhere on earth, a community of castes, with separate interests!"[5]

Many black leaders pushed back against this tendency, as did Henry Highland Garnet, a minister and abolitionist who had escaped from slavery as a child via the Underground Railroad. In his 1843 speech "An Address to the Slaves of the United States of America," he declared, "While you have been oppressed, we have also been partakers with you; nor can we be free while you are enslaved. We, therefore, write to you as being bound with you."[6] Moreover, "An Address to the Colored People of the United States," written by Frederick Douglass, Henry Bibb, W. L. Day, D. H. Jenkins, and A. H. Francis and published five years later, stated the relationship between enslaved and free people more bluntly: "In the Northern states, we are not slaves to individuals, not personal slaves, yet in many respects we are slaves of the community. . . . It is more than a figure of speech to say, that we are as a people chained together."[7] Black people, the argument went, were bound together by antiblack racism, whether in the South or in the North, whether enslaved or free. Nevertheless, distinctions were drawn; class mattered within the black community, and "class" could be defined, as Henry Bibb said, in a variety of ways, even on the plantation.

Frederick Douglass was an unabashed abolitionist, of course, and a champion of the slaves. But even his attitudes toward his enslaved sisters and brothers could be quite conflicted and complex, and these attitudes at times reflected both conscious and unconscious presuppositions about class and caste differences within the enslaved and free segments of the black community. In 1854, he underscored the pivotal role of the rise and progress of the free Negro community both in the larger estimation of the status of black people on the Great Chain of Being, but also within the abolition movement. "The true antidote . . . for black slaves," he maintained, "is an enlightened body of black freemen."[8]

A year later, in a major speech at Shiloh Presbyterian Church (chaired by his friend and fellow black abolitionist, the Glasgow University–educated medical doctor James McCune Smith), Douglass confessed his deep concern about "doubt among ourselves"[9]—a remarkably honest thing to admit out loud before an integrated audience, even today. Just a month before, Douglass had declared, in all capital letters, that "OUR ELEVATION AS A RACE IS ALMOST WHOLLY DEPENDENT UPON OUR OWN EXERTIONS. If we are ever elevated," he continued, "our elevation will be accomplished through our own instrumentality."[10] And he confessed, on several occasions, that it was the depth and degree of "our instrumentality" that quite concerned him, because generations of slavery had had its effects: "[O]ppression . . . deadens sensibility in its victims," he ruefully admitted in 1858. "I detest the slaveholders, and almost equally detest a contented slave. They are both enemies of freedom."[11]

For some free people of color, emancipation of their enslaved brothers and sisters could, surprisingly, be met with some trepidation, even if they welcomed unambiguously the collapse of slavery. "In cities like

New Orleans, Mobile, Savannah, and Charleston," Eric Foner writes, "affluent mulatto elites responded with deep ambivalence to the new situation created by emancipation. . . . Free blacks welcomed the end of slavery, but many resented the elimination of their unique status and feared being submerged in a sea of freedmen." Black, brown, and mulatto could constitute competing, even warring, caste categories, as the Reverend Henry McNeal Turner put it in 1866, even in his own church.[12]

These age-old class divisions within the black community assumed a dramatic, often disturbing new form following the end of Reconstruction, as the old Confederate elites and their descendants and defenders regained control of the economy and politics of their states at the expense of Negroes' rights and economic opportunities. For some African Americans, as matters became increasingly desperate, countering the worst aspects of white supremacism during Redemption meant drawing a sharp line between the Negro of slavery and the Negro of freedom, as well as between the classes that had arisen among their descendants since the Civil War. If the fiction of social custom and the law was now that all blacks were unequal, perhaps a case could be made that class mattered within the race, even more than race mattered to the class of white people. Perhaps, in other words, all black people weren't exactly alike, and therefore distinctions should be made between what effectively amounted to the Old Negro and the birth of a different kind of black person, a *New* Negro.

We can think of the metaphor of the New Negro, though coined at the height of Jim Crow, as the trope of black Reconstruction almost two decades after the Reconstruction era had ended, as Negroes fought to take back their image from the choking grasp of white supremacy in another kind of civil war, a war by other means; in this case, a war of representation, at times fought through culture and aesthetics. Despite the twists and turns in its several iterations between 1894 and 1925, we should never forget that the concept of the New Negro was employed by children of Reconstruction in the grip of Redemption.

Ironically, this movement of black self-(re)invention would be given its name by a white man. In 1894, in an essay called "The New Negro" printed in the journal *American Missionary*, the abolitionist Reverend W. E. C. Wright, a graduate of Oberlin College, a former professor at

Berea College, and a district secretary of the American Missionary Association, introduced the New Negro as the product of missionary education, his achievements measured by his acquisition of wealth: "It is the new Negro of the era of freedom, not the old Negro of a slave civilization, that is here and there emerging into a capitalist or a large planter, or a contractor, or a successful merchant, or a professional man."[13]

During the following year, after Wright coined the term "new Negro," on June 29, 1895, the black newspaper the *Richmond Planet*, headed by editor John Mitchell, Jr., offered a definition of the New Negro that exposed the fault line in the class structure of the black population. The *Planet* editorial suggested that black men of a certain social class (the New Negroes) might be more suited to equality in the eyes of the law than others (the Old Negroes). "The lowly and the illiterate do not specially desire to exercise the privileges, because they have neither money, the education nor the time to enjoy them, but there are others who do. We have a class of colored people, the 'New Negro,' who have arisen since the war, with education, refinement and money. They refuse to be kept in the relative condition once occupied by their ancestors, the slave of 250 years. The same delicate sensibilities that exist in the white man are present with them."[14]

This "class of colored people" would bear a strong resemblance to the elite group that Henry Lyman Morehouse would define, a year later in *The Independent* magazine, as "the talented tenth [man]"—"an uncrowned king in his sphere," as the historian Evelyn Brooks Higginbotham was the first to point out. Seven years later, W. E. B. Du Bois would popularize Morehouse's concept as "The Talented Tenth," the august "natural aristocrats" who Du Bois argued would, among other things, liberate the best parts of the race from the worst parts of the race.[15] As Du Bois put it, famously: "The Negro race, like all races, is going to be saved by its exceptional men. The problem of education, then, among Negroes must first of all deal with the Talented Tenth; it is the problem of developing the Best of this race that they may guide the Mass away from the contamination and death of the Worst, in their own and other races."[16] But this is getting a bit ahead of ourselves in the evolution of the concept of an elite within the race, its differentiation and its role and, possibly, its privileges. Du Bois would publish his riff on Morehouse's concept in

1903, in a book titled *The Negro Problem*, ironically edited by his nemesis, the celebrated, problematic Booker T. Washington. But Du Bois's concept is very much a part of, and a refinement of, a New Negro discourse that began almost a decade earlier.

Less than three months after the *Planet* editorial ran, on September 18, 1895, Booker T. Washington took the stage at the Cotton States and International Exposition in Atlanta and delivered his infamous "Atlanta Compromise" speech. The most frequently quoted line of that speech—"In all things that are purely social we can be as separate as the fingers, yet one as the hand in all things essential to mutual progress"—essentially accepted Jim Crow or de jure segregation in social and political matters, with the hope that this accommodation would appease the radical segregationists and enable the mass of black people in the South slowly but steadily to achieve economic progress through manual labor and the trades. Washington passionately advocated for a practical industrial education over the impractical liberal arts: "No race can prosper till it learns that there is as much dignity in tilling a field as in writing a poem," he said. "It is at the bottom of life we must begin, and not at the top."[17] With his "Atlanta Compromise" speech, Washington launched himself into the leadership position of the nation of Negroes left vacant by Frederick Douglass, who had died seven months earlier. The equation of "writing a poem" with the Negro's social mobility would pit Washington against the philosophy embodied by the Harvard-trained Du Bois and by Du Bois's role model, Alexander Crummell, a graduate of the University of Cambridge and the founder in 1897 of the American Negro Academy. Within weeks of his speech, Washington would be anointed in the white press as the manifestation, the embodiment, of the New Negro himself, a term he would employ in the title of a book he would soon publish.[18]

A month after Booker T. Washington's speech, Professor John Wesley Edward (J. W. E.) Bowen stood in the entrance of the Cotton States and International Exposition's Negro Building—a triumph of black workmanship—and delivered "An Appeal to the King," which concluded with a section called "The New Negro." Born enslaved in New Orleans in 1855, Bowen earned a bachelor of sacred theology degree in 1885 at

Boston University, where he would become the first African American to earn a PhD. After teaching at Baltimore's Morgan College and Washington, DC's Howard University, he became the first African American professor at Gammon Theological Seminary in 1893, which had been founded ten years earlier by the Methodist Episcopal Church to prepare black clergymen.[19] Bowen challenged Washington on the matter of education. All forms of education, he believed, not merely vocational, were critical to the future of the New Negro.

To Bowen, the extraordinary Negro Building where he stood, built by "a people just thirty years in freedom," was proof of African Americans' advancement and promise. Bowen said one need look no further than the statue positioned at the building's entrance, *A Negro with Chains Broken but Not Off*, to recognize that the New Negro was up to the task of proving his worth to whites. "This statue was born in the fruftful [*sic*] brain of a Negro, Mr. [W. C.] Hill of Washington. His frame is muscular and powerful; his eye is fixed upon his broken but hanging chain; his brow is knit in deep thought. This is the new Negro. What is he doing? He is thinking! And by the power of thought he will think off those chains and have both hands free to help you to build this country and make a grand destiny of himself. . . . This Negro, when educated in all of the disciplines of civilization and thoroughly trained in the arts of civil and moral life, cannot fail to be an invaluable help to our American life."[20] Bowen's "Appeal" would not fall on deaf ears; its logic would become embedded in a much larger movement hanging on the valorization of "respectability."

"THE POLITICS OF RESPECTABILITY"

Away from podiums and lecterns, middle-class black people in the North and in the South fought back symbolically against the rollback of the gains of Reconstruction in the decade in which de jure segregation was legalized, through a complex cultural discourse of their own design. It was a shared ideology expressing itself in a variety of ways, from the black women's club movement to sermons in churches to editorials in the black press. This was an interracial discourse in which a small group of educated black people—Du Bois's Talented Tenth—attempted to show their white class counterparts that they were "exceptions to the rule"; that they were superior to the mass of black people and equal to the best of white America; that they embodied the same middle-class social and moral Victorian values and aspirations that the white middle class did, and were therefore deserving of equal treatment in every way. They were, in other words, attempting to demonstrate what they were not. To describe this response, this movement, Evelyn Brooks Higginbotham coined the term "the politics of respectability."[21]

The politics of respectability stressed the embrace of white Victorian middle-class social and moral values, and it emphasized that black people should comport themselves in public as thoroughly middle class.[22] As we might expect, they dressed like middle-class white Americans, and they were careful to speak in standard English as opposed to black dialect. The public face and voice of black people were carefully crafted to refute the negative, racist stereotypes ubiquitously in circulation throughout American society. The key terms that peppered this discourse included "rising," "progress," and "elevation." The politics of respectability was quasi-religious, stressing conservative moral values and sexual restraint in an effort to counter the stereotypes of black people—men and women both—as genetically immoral, licentious, and degenerate. Much of it was aimed at what might be called the valorization of the mother—the restoration of the dignity of black women, who tended to be depicted in American popular culture either as mammies or as Jezebels. As Fannie Barrier Williams, the founder of the National League of Colored Women (the forerunner of the National Association of Colored Women) in 1894, wrote in praise of the strides black women had made in education and in church work, "It is sufficient for us to know that the daughters of women who thirty years ago were not allowed to be modest, not allowed to follow the instincts of moral rectitude, . . . have so elevated the moral tone of their social life that new and purer standards of personal worth have been created, and new ideals of womanhood, instinct with grace and delicacy, are everywhere recognized and emulated."[23] Williams was describing what John Henry Adams, Jr., would dub ten years later "the New Negro Woman."

The politics of respectability was essentially led by those who had benefited from the flip side of Washington's program of industrial education, the college-educated black upper class, whose collective cultural response to the vile caricatures of black people commonplace at the turn of the century was to demonstrate counterimages and thereby prove that these racist stereotypes were not true. As a result, one of the most important tasks that these New Negroes faced was battling these racist depictions of African Americans. "Sambo art" was designed to define the race, and it was a crucial component of the larger effort to erase Reconstruction and inaugurate a separate and decidedly unequal, legally bifurcated America, one face of it white, "civilized," and economically mobile, the other face of it black, primitivist, and permanently poor.

Black thinkers found themselves in a bind, determined to dispel the stereotypes that plagued African Americans but unable to turn a blind eye to some of the perceived failings they acknowledged to be true among their own. Bowen wrote ruefully, "Our notions of these [sacred family] relations, on the whole, are not what they should have been," but, he proudly noted, "the race is making a heroic effort to expel from its system all the virus of degrading sin and thus far we have made progress."[24] In his 1897 essay "The Conservation of Races," W. E. B. Du Bois himself confirmed race differences and repeated the alleged shortcomings of African Americans, stressing the potential of black people of the present and future to do better. "The first and greatest step toward the settlement of the present friction between the races lies in the correction of the immorality, crime, and laziness among the Negroes themselves, which still remains as a heritage of slavery."[25]

To counter these images—both those inflicted from without and perpetuated from within—adherence to the politics of respectability alone wasn't enough. Du Bois prescribed that black people had to fix themselves under the leadership of a black intelligentsia "united to stop the ravages of consumption among the Negro people, united to keep black boys from loafing, gambling and crime; united to guard the purity of black women and to reduce the vast army of black prostitutes that is to-day marching to hell; and united in serious organizations, to determine by careful conference and thoughtful interchange of opinion the broad lines of policy and action for the American Negro."[26]

Thus, the New Negro leader would be a black man or woman

embodying all the virtues of the race and none of the vices, a hero armed with a college degree and a three-piece suit or an elegant dress and hat. The New Negro phenomenon would last well into the 1920s. Although the New Negro adhered to a basic formula dictated by the politics of respectability, he and she would have many manifestations—many faces, literally—presented to the world visually, first through photography and later, at the height of the New Negro or Harlem Renaissance, through other forms of art and literature. At the turn of the century, in the same year in which Booker T. Washington was defining *A New Negro for a New Century*, Du Bois would appoint himself to convey to the larger white world—indeed, through an international platform—what the New Negro phenomenon looked like.

EVERY PICTURE TELLS A STORY: DU BOIS'S EXHIBIT OF AMERICAN NEGROES

Du Bois had long stood at the forefront of the counterattack against negative images of black people in writing; now he armed himself with carefully curated images designed to disarm a public that had grown used to encountering black stereotypes in every medium, at every turn. In April 1900, he presented the Exhibit of American Negroes (popularly referred to as the American Negro Exhibit) at the Paris Exposition in France.

The exhibit was a stunning collaboration among Du Bois, Thomas Junius Calloway, Daniel Alexander Payne Murray, and Andrew F. Hilyer. Calloway and Du Bois had been classmates at Fisk University in Nashville, Tennessee. When Calloway got the idea for this exhibit, he was the president of Mississippi's Alcorn Agricultural and Mechanical College, and Du Bois was a professor of sociology at the historically black Atlanta University. Murray was an assistant librarian at the Library of Congress, one of the first African Americans to work in a professional capacity at the institution. Hilyer was among the first black graduates of the University of Minnesota and a representative of the National Negro Business League. These men personified the New Negro in living color—educated, articulate, and successful.

When the United States announced its plan for its exhibits at the

Paris Exposition—financed with a $1.25 million allocation from Congress—the project included not a single contribution of the American Negro. Calloway, a lawyer and educator who had served as a state commissioner for the Atlanta exposition of 1895 where Booker T. Washington delivered his "Atlanta Compromise" speech, recognized the symbolic importance of black inclusion at the Paris Exposition. During the winter of 1899, he sent an urgent letter to "over one hundred representative Negroes in various sections of the United States," including Washington, saying that it was essential that the American Negro be present at the greatest world's fair in history because that, he stressed, "will attract attention . . . and do a great and lasting good in convincing thinking people of the possibilities of the Negro."[27] Calloway knew—and black leadership fully understood—that it "was strategically imperative that Negroes be seen as a proud, productive, and cultured race at Paris," as David Levering Lewis, Du Bois's biographer, puts it, rather than "as a mass of rapists," in Calloway's words.[28]

Calloway's strategy worked. Booker T. Washington intervened with President William McKinley, and George Henry White, a Republican from North Carolina and the last black representative in the US Congress in the Jim Crow era, championed the cause there, managing to secure an allocation of $15,000 ($10,000 less than he had asked for) to fund the exhibit. Named special commissioner, Calloway recruited Du Bois to design it. Du Bois would later say that it was "an honest, straightforward exhibit of a small nation of people, picturing their life and development without apology or gloss, and above all made by themselves."[29]

For the display, Du Bois and his collaborators selected 363 black-and-white photographs that represented black achievement since the yoke of slavery was lifted in 1865. Du Bois chose portraits of individuals to represent a variety of skin tones, hair textures, and facial structures (particularly aquiline noses, often shown in profile) to combat the stereotypical ideas being advanced in American popular culture (and in American science) of what black people looked like. "There are several volumes of photographs of typical Negro faces, which hardly square with conventional American ideas," wrote Du Bois, making a veiled reference to the many light-complexioned subjects of his exhibit.[30] The black men and women in these photographs—students, professionals—were almost exclusively photographed indoors, and when they were outdoors, they were dressed in fine clothes and posed on the steps of well-appointed buildings, not out in a field picking cotton or standing in weather-beaten attire outside a ramshackle cabin. Additionally, he created pie charts to illustrate the social and economic progress through occupations held by black people since emancipation; he also included photographs of the exteriors of churches and universities and the interiors of libraries and laboratories. Every image, every graph was included to prove the existence of the New Negro.

The organs of opinion in the black community celebrated Du Bois's achievement. *The Colored American* concluded, triumphantly, that through these images, "The people of other countries will know the Negro American better and think more of him hereafter than they have done before." Moreover, the editorial said, "Few things have been done for us in the last two decades that have counted so much for our dignity and capacity as the winning of so many prizes."[31] The exhibit was a triumph on a grand scale for Du Bois personally: the entire collection earned a Grand Prix, as well as a total of fifteen gold, silver, and bronze medals, and a gold medal for Du Bois himself.[32]

The art historian Deborah Willis says that with their "images of self-empowerment, self-determination, and self-recovery," these photographs themselves constitute a double *mythos*, which Du Bois would call a "double consciousness": "the one projected on the black community . . . by its own members" to counter the one projected on the black community "by the dominant culture."[33] As Du Bois wrote three years later in *The Souls of Black Folk* (1903): "This American world . . . yields [the Negro] no true self-consciousness, but only lets him see himself through the revelation of the other world. It is a peculiar sensation, this double-consciousness, this sense of always looking at one's self through the eyes of others, of measuring one's soul by the tape of a world that looks on in amused contempt and pity. One ever feels his two-ness,—an American, a Negro; two souls, two thoughts, two unreconciled strivings; two warring ideals in one dark body, whose dogged strength alone keeps it from being torn asunder."[34]

THE LOOK OF RESPECTABILITY

In 1903, as we have seen, Du Bois would unveil his concept of the Talented Tenth (the polar opposite of what he called the "submerged tenth" in *The Philadelphia Negro*),[35] referring to the best and brightest African Americans as the vanguard who would lead the progress of their race. From the beginning, he counted artists among this cohort. David Levering Lewis explains that earlier that year, in an article called "The Advance Guard of the Race," Du Bois "identified the poet Paul Laurence Dunbar, the novelist Charles Waddell Chesnutt, and the painter Henry Ossawa Tanner, among a small number of other well-educated professionals, as representatives of this class. The Talented Tenth formulated and propagated a new ideology of racial assertiveness that was to be embraced by the physicians, dentists, educators, preachers, businesspeople, lawyers, and morticians who comprised the bulk of the African American affluent and influential—some 10,000 men and women out of a total population in 1920 of more than 10,000,000."[36]

In the Paris exhibit, Du Bois had offered up images of black people cloaked in the politics of respectability. He was not the only black writer to do so. In 1904, the illustrator and art instructor John Henry Adams, Jr., would publish a pair of articles about the nature of New Negro women and men in the *Voice of the Negro* magazine accompanied by "rough sketches" that called to mind the portraits in Du Bois's exhibit. The first, "A Study of the Features of the New Negro Woman," appeared in the August 1904 issue.[37] He described this New Negro Woman "as a growing factor for good . . . and strong in every attribution of mind and soul."[38] In his companion October 1904 essay on "The New Negro Man," Adams lingered over his subject's countenance: "Here is the real new Negro man. Tall, erect, commanding, with a face as strong and expressive as Angelo's Moses and yet every whit as pleasing and handsome as Rubens's favorite model. There is that penetrative eye about which Charles Lamb wrote with such deep admiration, that broad forehead and firm chin."[39]

Adams's fixation on personal appearance reflected Du Bois's. Both used the physical characteristics of the individual to illuminate the larger character of the race. In a sense, Adams was beating white people at their own game. Black hair and black skin, black faces and black heads, had been lampooned mercilessly in Sambo art, ridiculed in racial science; now he lavished praise on them instead of derision and contempt.

Du Bois's Talented Tenth, his New Negroes, were fiercely engaged in a battle over interpretation, fighting back against the onslaught of popular images that rendered black human beings as things, as beasts. As he expressed it in 1960, looking back at this period in a reflection on his years at Harvard, he and his colleagues saw themselves as combatants in a culture war: "Eventually, in mass assault, led by culture, we Negroes were going to break down the boundaries of race; by at present we were banded together in a great crusade, and happily so."[40] In the short term at least, this wasn't a war they were winning: while they could occupy the summit of black achievement, prestige, and even wealth within the black community, they could not, at this nadir in American history, achieve meaningful upward social mobility within the larger American society.

To that end, unable to overcome the structures of oppression, black leaders embraced individual agency, will, and achievement as the most potent way to fight back against this tidal wave of antiblack racism. There was a sound and a look of respectability as requisite as its other components. Black dialect was scrubbed from the voices of black leaders, with no echo of the plantation remaining. Booker T. Washington and W. E. B. Du Bois sounded, for all intents and purposes, like Victorian white men. Madam C. J. Walker profited handsomely from this emphasis on personal hygiene and grooming, captured in Washington's "gospel of the toothbrush."[41] "Improved appearance responsible," one of her most well-recognized ads proclaimed, for the "Amazing Progress of Colored Race."[42]

"BRUTAL DRAWING OF THE COLOR LINE"

Establishment of class difference between themselves and lower-class African Americans was to some of the New Negroes (but not all, certainly) of central importance to their self-portrayal to the world outside. This group within the larger group initially believed that through their own achievements they could escape the clutches of laws and social practices that sought both to confine all black people under the same second-class citizen status and to define all black people, regardless of class or other kinds of differ-ence, as "Negro"—as the same. One of the most extreme examples of this New Negro resistance to the equation of class and race appeared in Charles W. Chesnutt's novel *The Marrow of Tradition* (1901), written five years after the legal implementation of "separate but equal" in *Plessy v. Ferguson*. In it Chesnutt—whom Du Bois had included among the very first exemplars of the Talented Tenth—narrates from the perspective of a black doctor sent to the "black car" after riding in the "white car" with a fellow white doctor:

> They were noisy, loquacious, happy, dirty, and malodorous. For a while Miller was amused and pleased. They were his people, and he felt a certain expansive warmth toward them in spite of their obvious shortcomings. By and by, however, the air grew too close, and he went out upon the platform. For the sake of the democratic ideal, which meant so much to his race, he might have endured the affliction.
>
> He could easily imagine that people of refinement, with power in their hands, might be tempted to strain the democratic ideal in order to avoid such contact. . . . These people were just as offensive to him as to the whites in the other end of the train. Surely if a classification of passengers on trains was at all desirable, it might be made of some more logical and considerate bias than a mere arbitrary, tactless, and by the very nature of things, brutal drawing of the color line.[43]

Here, Dr. Miller feels a greater kinship with "the whites in the other end of the train" than he does with "his people," bound as he and the white people are by their mutual distaste for these lowly folk. Through the politics of respectability, often some of the New Negroes trumpeted their difference within the race in an attempt to make the case that they should be treated differently from lower-class black people, whom they sometimes found embarrassing and with whom, they sometimes claimed, they had little in common.

Du Bois, recall, had argued that all races "are saved by [their] excep-tional men."[44] Nevertheless, it is shocking that in *The Souls of Black Folk*, which became instantly famous for its searching critique of Booker T. Washington's accommodationism, Du Bois himself says that he would have endorsed restrictions on the right to vote among the black poor. "The alternative thus offered the nation," he writes in *Souls*, "was not between full and restricted Negro suffrage; else every sensible man, black and white, would easily have chosen the latter."[45] In other words, even the radical Du Bois thought a case could be made that voting was a privilege—as long as the Talented Tenth were not excluded because of their race.

Du Bois had foreshadowed this belief in differentiating the treatment of black social classes in his classic of American sociology, *The Philadelphia Negro*: "The colored people are seldom judged by their best classes, and often the very existence of classes among them is ignored. . . . If the Negroes were by themselves[,] either a strong aristocratic system or a dictatorship would for the present prevail. With, however, democracy thus prematurely thrust upon them, the first impulse of the best, the wisest and the richest is to segregate themselves from the mass. . . . [I]t is just as natural for the well-educated and well-to-do Negroes to feel themselves far above the criminals and prostitutes of Seventh and Lombard streets, and even above the servant girls and porters of the middle class of workers. So far they are justified."[46]

David Levering Lewis argues that it was only the fact that the color curtain ultimately came down as hard on this black elite, these New Negroes, as it had on the black poor that forced the black elite to stop conceiving of itself as somehow separate. Lewis writes, "Not until the time when all hope of political rights and social equality had been definitively closed in the second decade of the twentieth century . . . did . . . leading black Americans think of themselves as Negroes first."[47]

Clearly, it was a class-blind form of black oppression more than anything else that cemented unity in the race. And that entailed responsibilities. As Du Bois concluded: "[T]hey make their mistake in failing to recognize that however laudable an ambition to rise may be, the first duty of an upper class is to serve the lowest classes. The aristocracies of all peoples have been slow in learning this and perhaps the Negro is no slower than the rest, but his peculiar situation demands that in his case this lesson be learned sooner."[48] The New Negro found himself in a precarious position, keenly aware of his need to remain distinct enough from the Old Negro to protect whatever standing he had gained in the eyes of the white world (sadly, very little), while at the same time honoring his obligation to lift that Old Negro up.

ENTER THE NEWER NEW NEGROES

The metaphor of the New Negro was a powerful construct, like an empty vessel or floating signifier that completely different—and even contradictory—ideologies could (and would) fill for their own political or propagandistic purposes. Among them were Washington's conservatism, William Monroe Trotter's political activism, Marcus Garvey's black nationalism, A. Philip Randolph's socialism, and Alain Locke's art for art's sake. It is important to note that these various New Negro movements between 1894 and 1925 occurred not only as a demonstration of black agency in the era of the imposition of Jim Crow, but also against the backdrop of the early phase of the Great Migration, when millions of poor, black, rural sharecroppers from the South—the Old Negroes—came flooding into the industrial centers in the North, further exacerbating class differences within the black community. We tend to forget that until 1910, 90 percent of the black community lived in the South; by 1930, that number had dropped to 79 percent.[49] Especially during the war years of 1916 to 1919 and then again from 1924 to 1925—at precisely the time Alain Locke was inventing *his* New Negro—the black population in urban centers exploded. Detroit saw an increase of 611 percent in its black population (36,200 people); Chicago's went up by 114 percent (65,000 people) and New York's by 66 percent (61,400 people).[50] Neither the Northern nor the Southern black community was monolithic, of course; both had upper middle, middle, and working classes, as Du Bois had noted in *The Philadelphia Negro* in 1899. The Great Migration, however, multiplied these class differentials, adding a layer of regional differentials to the race's traditional class structures. In fact, the size of the black population in the Northeast between 1910 and 1930 almost tripled, going from 484,176 in 1910 to 1,146,985 in 1930.

The racial and class complexion of Harlem visibly changed during this time. In 1910, this northern neighborhood of Manhattan was most certainly *not* a "Negro Mecca": it was 90.01 percent white and 9.89

percent black (with a total population of 181,949, 17,995 of whom were black). In 1920, Harlem was still predominantly white, but the percentage had dropped to 67.47 percent (with a total population of 216,026 people, 70,057 of whom were black). Between 1920 and 1930, during the Harlem Renaissance, the numbers of black and white residents almost completely flipped; Harlem became 70.18 percent black and only 29.43 percent white (with a total population of 209,663, of whom 147,141 people were black).[51] The new black population came primarily through migration of poor black people from the South, along with—to a much lesser extent—willing migrants from the Caribbean.

The arrival of their Southern brethren could be discomfiting to some of the New Negroes. These Southern blacks, simply put, weren't "their kind of people," as the black saying went. Black people whose families had lived in the North for generations, and whose ancestors had often been free since well before the Civil War, were not altogether welcoming of or excited by this (less-than-)great migration of black Southerners to their cities. They saw themselves as members of the black upper class, a cosmopolitan mobile elite that could be integrated into American society, even if "the slow moving black masses" (as the head of the Urban League Charles S. Johnson would actually call them) could not.[52] In the face of this influx of lower-class black folks from the rural South, some members of the black elite seized upon the concept of a New Negro to distinguish themselves from these new arrivals, the descendants of the Old Negroes, the freedpeople liberated by the Civil War and the Thirteenth Amendment.

But class differentials were not only marked economically among black people; they could also be observed *within* what we would ostensibly consider the same social class, as Alain Locke noted with brutal frankness in a letter to his mother about his African American Harvard classmates. Locke wrote:

> The colored fellow whom Dr. Flounders, Rowland's principal, asked me to meet called on me this afternoon. He took me to see the "boys." Of course they were colored. All together about 9 in one house. He took me right up into the filthy bedroom and there were 5 niggers, all Harvard men. Well, their pluck and their conceit were

wonderful. Some are ugly enough to frighten you but I guess they are bright. . . . They are not fit for company even if they are energetic and plodding fellows. I'm not used to that class and I don't intend to get used to them. . . . Most of them are waiters up here. . . . Mama, don't fear I am going to associate with such fellows. Its [*sic*] well enough for them to get an education but they are not gentlemen.[53]

This was a different setting, a different community, but the thrust of Locke's disdain had been felt by African Americans since slavery. (Frederick Douglass addressed it, as we've seen.) Social and class distinctions could be multiplied, as many scholars have long noted, by variables such as color, hair texture, place of origin (the North or the South), parents' profession, education, genetic admixture, even when one's black ancestors gained their freedom.

In many ways, the New Negro movement was about class differences within the black community. But it was also about politics, and the political aspect of the New Negro movements would assume radically different forms as they unfolded between the first decade of the century and the postwar period.

Then as now, politics and economics were inextricably intertwined, and in 1908, S. Laing Williams, the husband of Fannie Barrier Williams and an attorney allied with Booker T. Washington, shared his version of the New Negro in an address to the All Souls Church at the Abraham Lincoln Centre in Chicago. His focus, not surprisingly considering his affiliation with Washington, was largely on the economic progress African Americans had made since emancipation, and he acknowledged that the change in the status of the Negro could be jarring, particularly to whites. "The rise of a man from a low estate to a high estate, from dependence to independence, from ignorance to intelligence and self-sufficiency, is always interesting, always important and always more or less disturbing. . . . [W]e have in this country today what may be fittingly be called a 'New Negro,' and the race problem may be defined as the failure of the American people to recognize and know this

New Negro."[54] Williams's New Negro was literate, educated, civic-minded, and perhaps most important, a taxpayer:

> The Negro that most Americans picture as mendicant, shiftless and unenterprising, now pays taxes on over $300,000,000 worth of real estate. . . . [T]he man who forty-five years ago was a chattel has become in some instances a lawyer, a physician, a theologian, an artist, a poet, a journalist, a banker, a diplomat, a linguist, a soldier unafraid, an ardent patriot and a man who dares to have courage in the midst of discouragements. Who can afford not to respect men of this kind? . . . That chattel of the cotton field has become a gentleman in spirit and in fact. He is a self-made man and challenges the respect of all mankind. He asks to be respected for what he is and stands for in his new status and not for what the American people meanly think he is.
>
> The ignorant, uncivilized and empty-handed man of 1865 has become a man of culture, a man of force and a man of independence. We shall have to look at this new man to complete the great work of reconstruction.[55]

For Williams, Reconstruction wasn't over; it was merely suspended, and the New Negro's mission was to resurrect it. In other words, Williams's New Negro was self-sufficient, capable of his own upkeep and uplift. This New Negro flew in the face of white expectations, which that same year were described by the white journalist, historian, and, later, biographer of Woodrow Wilson, Ray Stannard Baker: "The old-fashioned Negro preferred to go to the white man for everything; he didn't trust his own people; the new Negro, with growing race consciousness, and feeling that the white man is against him, urges his friends to patronize Negro doctors and dentists, and to trade with Negro storekeepers." The South, Baker intimated, was baffled by this unfamiliar black man: "[T]he South has not yet decided how to deal with a Negro who owns property and demands rights. The South is suspicious of this new Negro: it dreads him; and the politicians in power are quick to play upon this sentiment in order that the South may remain solid and the present political leadership remain undisturbed. . . . [The South] loves the ignorant, submissive old Negroes, the 'mammies' and 'uncles'; . . . It wants Negroes who are really inferior and who *feel* inferior."[56]

Williams described a "self-made man" capable of "complet[ing] the great work of reconstruction." Baker pondered the presence in the South of African Americans not dependent on white Southerners for their livelihood. As the decade of the teens wore on, the New Negro lived alongside the continual perpetuation of the image of the Old Negro, nowhere more graphic, as we have seen, than in Griffith's *Birth of a Nation*, which debuted in 1915, the same year that Leslie Pinckney Hill, the African American president of the Cheyney Training School for Teachers in Pennsylvania, published the essay "Negro Ideals: Their Effect and Their Embarrassments" in the July issue of the *Journal of Race Development*. It was up to the New Negro, Hill asserted, to seize his own destiny, no matter how difficult the fight. The Old Negro was no longer; in fact, Hill's New Negro was born post-slavery, and was determined to fight for political rights:

> The clear, bare question presented to the young Negro of the twentieth century is, then, not whether the white man's Democracy and Christianity with respect to him have failed, but what his own attitude towards that failure shall be. What is to be his conscious ideal, his mind-picture of the development possible, under these embarrassed circumstances, to him? What definite program is he to project for himself? These questions will no longer be answered by dispirited or gentle Negroes of the "mammy" type. . . . The race problems of the future are to be confronted by Negroes who have known nothing of the slave regime, who have education, . . . who have learned to think and aspire. . . . Above all things, they are determined to spare neither their voices nor their energies in Zion until they achieved full, untrammeled American citizenship or gone down in the midst of a glorious warfare for it. . . .
>
> In the future the American Negro must work out more largely his own salvation in wholesome cooperation with white neighbors, if he *can*, but single-handed, if he must.[57]

William Pickens, a Phi Beta Kappa graduate of Yale in 1904, the dean of Morgan College in Baltimore, and a founding member and future field secretary of the NAACP, followed suit, in 1916 publishing a collection of essays called *The New Negro: His Political, Civil, and Mental Status.* Pickens focused on the commonality between the Old and the New Negroes: "The 'new Negro,'" he wrote, "is not really new: he is the same Negro under new conditions and subjected to new demands. Those who regret the passing of the 'old Negro' and picture the 'new' as something very different, must remember that there is no sharp line of demarcation between the old and the new in any growing organism like a germ, a plant or a race. The present generation of Negroes have received their chief heritage from the former and, in that, they are neither better nor worse, higher nor lower than the previous generation."[58] As Hill had done the previous year, Pickens rejected white notions of African Americans, and in presenting his own definition of the New Negro also stated outright that black people held their destiny in their own, able hands: "The new Negro is a sober, sensible creature, conscious of his environment, knowing that not all is right, but trying hard to become adjusted to this civilization in which he finds himself by no will or choice of his own. He is not the shallow, vain, showy creature which he is sometimes advertised to be. He still hopes that that unreasonable opposition to his forward and upward progress will relent. But, at any rate, he is resolved to fight, and live or die, on the side of God and the Eternal Verities."[59]

The language of Hill and Pickens, with their "glorious warfare" and "[resolve] to fight," reflected an increasingly militant strain in New Negro political thought. The scholar Adena Spingarn explains the shift: "Although [Booker T.] Washington and his supporters had described themselves as New Negroes, early in the new century, the rhetoric of a younger generation of leaders turned the Washingtonian New Negroes into Old Negroes whose Southern slave mentality was an active threat to the race's progress. A new New Negro movement emerged, charging the older generation with ineffective and even counterproductive leadership." Spingarn relates the evolving New Negro to the near-simultaneous change in the way many African Americans viewed "Uncle Tom": once a martyr, now a traitor. She writes, "As long as Uncle Tom was 'a historical factor of a time and period long since swallowed up by the sturdy advance of civilization and new customs,' as a 1903 account in *The* [Indianapolis] *Freeman* put it, he sparked limited antagonism. This would change, however, when instead of quietly passing away the Old Negro," embodied paradoxically now for a new and more politically active generation in Booker T. Washington himself, the original New Negro, "developed power both within the race and with whites, and then used it to support a racial order dangerously close to antebellum slavery." In other words, Uncle Tom—representing the Old Negro of slavery times—became conflated, because of his passivity, with Washington, who was then rechristened less than a decade after he delivered his Atlanta Exposition speech, now as an Old Negro himself. To these newer, more militant New Negroes, "Uncle Tom, the perpetual Old Negro, transformed from an unthreatening old slave to an old-fashioned leader who reproduced the dynamics of slavery. The New Negro now defined himself not by acquiring civilization but by self-assertion, and the importance of education was less as a marker of cultivation than as an experience that encouraged assertive resistance."

The *Chicago Defender* drove this point home in 1910 when reporting on a parade in which African Americans marched at the rear. The paper cemented the term "Uncle Tom" as a slur in no uncertain terms: "those who represent that young progressive class, that class that represent our colleges, that class that represent our business and professional side; but they are the class that the South is preparing to raise a monument to, the 'Good Nigger,' the Uncle Tom class, if you please, who by their lack of education they cannot ride beyond the scope of an errand boy to answer the bells or raps of a man and who would die for him because of the fact that they have no hopes, and if they had, their lack of training would prevent them from hoping."[60]

The St. Croix–born Hubert Harrison, who migrated to Harlem at age seventeen, would emerge as a prominent, albeit oft-forgotten, New Negro figure. A vocal opponent of both Booker T. Washington and W. E. B. Du Bois, he founded the Liberty League and the *Voice*, the first organization and newspaper, respectively, that provided a platform for those who took a more militant, indeed radical, black nationalist, and/or socialist stance in the New Negro movement. In the *Voice* he wrote that the league grew out of "the need for a more radical policy than that of the NAACP."[61] No more would black leadership "be chosen by whites (as in the era of

Washington's leadership)," Jeffrey B. Perry writes; "nor [would it] be based on the 'Talented Tenth' of the Negro race' (as advocated by Du Bois)."[62] In the *Voice*, Harrison backed various socialist causes, antilynching legislation, and armed self-defense against racial violence. He called his second newspaper, the *New Negro*, "an organ of the international consciousness of the darker races."[63] Both his newspapers were short-lived, as was his work with the far better-known activist and fellow Caribbean migrant, the Jamaican Pan-Africanist Marcus Mosiah Garvey, Jr.

As the rhetoric escalated in the late teens, the metaphor of the New Negro would be revised further still, triggered by horrific racist violence. On May 28, 1917, a powder keg of racial tensions exploded in East St. Louis, Illinois, after a rumor spread that a black man had shot a grocery store owner in a holdup. More than one hundred African Americans died as white people marauded their homes, businesses, and neighborhoods, the National Guard looking the other way. Two months later, the NAACP responded with a silent protest, with almost ten thousand African Americans marching in silence down Fifth Avenue in New York City. Their signs told the story: "Make America safe for democracy." "We march because we want our children to live in a better land."[64]

But the violence only grew worse, culminating in 1919 in what James Weldon Johnson called Red Summer. White-instigated violence tore through Chicago, Washington, DC, and Elaine, Arkansas, leaving dozens of African Americans dead, injured, or homeless. Across the country black veterans in particular were targeted for lynching, as white mobs feared that the end of the Great War would put them in competition for the same jobs that whites had previously held. In his powerful editorial "Returning Soldiers," W. E. B. Du Bois insisted on action: "We stand again to look America squarely in the face and call a spade a spade. We sing: This country of ours, despite all its better souls have done and dreamed, is yet a shameful land." America, Du Bois writes, "lynches . . . disfranchises its own citizens . . . encourages ignorance . . . steals from us . . . insults us." Democracy demanded a greater fight at home: "We return. We return from fighting. We return fighting. Make way for Democracy! We saved it in France, and by the Great Jehovah, we will save it in the United States of America, or know the reason why."[65]

The Jamaican-born poet Claude McKay turned to verse to protest Red Summer, penning the immortal "If We Must Die" (1919), a call to arms for black self-defense that helped to ignite the Harlem Renaissance. At this time, though, the call was literal, not literary.

> If we must die, let it not be like hogs
> Hunted and penned in an inglorious spot,
> While round us bark the mad and hungry dogs,
> Making their mock at our accursed lot.
> If we must die, O let us nobly die,
> So that our precious blood may not be shed
> In vain; then even the monsters we defy
> Shall be constrained to honor us though dead!
> O kinsmen! we must meet the common foe!
> Though far outnumbered let us show us brave,
> And for their thousand blows deal one death-blow!
> What though before us lies the open grave?
> Like men we'll face the murderous, cowardly pack,
> Pressed to the wall, dying, but fighting back![66]

James Weldon Johnson later said that McKay was one of the principal forces in bringing about the Negro literary awakening that would become the New Negro Renaissance.[67] "If We Must Die" was first published in the *Liberator* and soon republished in the *Messenger*, a paper founded in New York City by the African American activists A. Philip Randolph and Chandler Owen. The *Messenger* quickly became the most prominent socialist embodiment of the New Negro.[68]

By the end of World War I, the black socialist movement had seized upon the metaphor of the New Negro to declare a new day in American history, the birth of the day when black people fought their oppressors with guns, inspired by the fact that black men had served in the war and had been treated equally by white people in Europe. The socialist New Negro was nothing less than a warrior. Why should they return home after risking their lives and take Jim Crow racism lying down? In September 1919, the *Messenger* published contrasting cartoons. One was titled "Following the Advice of the 'Old Crowd' Negro." It lampooned Du Bois's argument that black citizens should "close ranks" around the war effort, that they should fight for the nation that held them in such low esteem in an effort to raise their standing (it didn't work). It mocked both Booker T. Washington's statement that they should "be modest and unassuming" as well as a minister's preaching of nonviolence: "When they smite thee on one cheek, turn the other." The other cartoon, "The 'New Crowd Negro': Making America Safe for Himself," featured an African American man firing back against his white oppressors and saying, "Since the government won't stop mob violence, I'll take a hand."

In August of the following year, 1920, Randolph and Owen would publish the radical manifesto "The New Negro—What Is He?" They defined the three aims of the New Negro as "political, economic, and social": political in that "the New Negro, unlike the Old Negro, cannot be lulled into a false sense of security with political spoils and patronage"; economic in that the New Negro's "immediate aim is more wages, shorter hours and better working conditions"; and social in that "he stands for absolute and unequivocal 'social equality.'" The editors also advocated self-defense: "[T]o fight back in self defense, should be accepted as a matter of course. . . . Yet the Old Crowd Negroes have counseled the doctrine of non-resistance."[69] Three months later, W. A. Domingo expanded on these ideas in even more explicitly socialist terms in his *Messenger* essay, "A New Negro and a New Day." Domingo defined a New Negro as a man or woman who recognized that "labor is the common denominator of the working class of the world. Exploitation . . . the common denominator of oppression everywhere." New Negroes had "grievances against those who profit from the present system which operates against the interests of all workers." And finally, a New Negro "speaks the language of the oppressed" to defy the "language of the oppressor."[70]

For the socialists, led by Randolph, even the militant black cultural nationalist Marcus Garvey somehow fell in line with the "Old Crowd Negroes." Yet Garvey, the father of the Back to Africa movement, presented himself as a New Negro, too. In a speech delivered in Newport News, Virginia, in the same year of the race riots, 1919, he defined what he meant by the term: "The New Negro," he says, "backed by the

Universal Negro Improvement Association, is determined to restore Africa to the world, and you scattered children of Africa in Newport News, you children of Ethiopia, I want you to understand that the call is now made to you. What are you going to do? . . . [A]re you going to link up your strength, morally and financially, with the other Negroes of the world and let us all fight one battle unto victory? . . . We new Negroes of America declare that we desire liberty or we will take death. . . . The war must go on; only that the war is not going on in France or Flanders, but the war will go on in the African plains, there to decide once and for all in the very near future whether black men are to be serfs and slaves or black men are to be free men."[71]

The vanguard of the race—think of them as the "black establishment," Du Bois's Talented Tenth—did not embrace the militancy of the black socialists or Marcus Garvey's "Back to Africa" form of black nationalism. These were not the New Negroes they had crafted. Rather, through key organizations like the NAACP and the National Urban League, they sought to defeat Jim Crow segregation through organized protests and a campaign to make lynching a federal offense, and eventually by challenging laws that were unconstitutional. In the 1920s, Alain Locke, the first black Rhodes Scholar and the first black person to earn a PhD in philosophy at Harvard, understanding the power of a good metaphor when he saw it, transformed the concept of the New Negro into an unprecedented artistic movement. Locke believed that the creation of great literature and art could achieve an implicit political effect by demonstrating that African Americans—the artistic elite—possessed as much intelligence and talent as great white writers and artists did. Indeed, Locke felt that a concentration of the efforts of this group under the umbrella of a New Negro Renaissance could forever bury Sambo stereotypes of black people as inherently inferior. In other words, Locke felt that he and his colleagues could strike the ultimate blow against Redemption and Jim Crow racism by creating a racial art that could have an *implicit* political effect without itself being overtly political. Locke sought nothing less than to give the reconstruction of the Negro a second life, a life in art and culture, without overtly trafficking in the kind of militant politics embraced by Garvey and Randolph and their comrades. Locke chose Harlem as the headquarters of this "renaissance" because Harlem, by 1925, as a result of migration, had become the undisputed "capital" of the Negro world, the place James Weldon Johnson would enshrine as "the Black Mecca" in his historical, literary, and social study *Black Manhattan* (1930). This would be the pinnacle, the culmination, of the New Negro movements that began in 1894. Locke would formulate his theory of the political efficacy of art and literature by returning (without attribution) to a sophisticated argument about the relation between the display of black genius in the arts and the fight against Jim Crow racism first postulated in 1895 by the feminist Victoria Earle Matthews.

A NEW RACE LITERATURE

During the New Negro Renaissance (later to be dubbed the Harlem Renaissance), the creation of literature and art became a vital part of African Americans' quest for civil rights. Du Bois's biographer David Levering Lewis would call it "civil rights by copyright."[72] In 1895, three decades before the Harlem Renaissance came to fruition, the pioneering black feminist and journalist Victoria Earle Matthews articulated the deep significance of literature in the struggle for black social and political rights in her essay "The Value of Race Literature." In July of that year, Matthews, who published under the name of Victoria Earle in major American newspapers, both in the mainstream (white) and black press, presented her groundbreaking essay at the first National Conference of Colored Women held in Boston. (Out of this conference was formed the National Federation of Afro-American Women, which merged with another group, the National League of Colored Women, to form the National Association of Colored Women in 1896.) Chair of the NACW's executive board, Matthews was an educator and an ardent activist, forming a Home for Colored Working Girls in New York City, which would become the White Rose Industrial Association. For Matthews, "race literature" was a form of activism, of protest and uplift. She commenced her seminal essay with an epigraph from Ralph Waldo Emerson, making the case that the Negro can be liberated only through intellectual achievements in general and, more specifically, through the creation of literary art. Quoting from Emerson, she wrote: "If the black man carries in his bosom an indispensable element of a new and coming civilization, for the sake of that element, no money, nor strength, nor circumstance can hurt him; he will survive and play his part. . . . If you have man, black or white is an insignificance. The intellect—that is miraculous!"[73]

Matthews recognized that black art forms—and black intellect—were undermined and undervalued. Spirituals and folklore, the purest form of expression of enslaved African Americans, were met with some ambivalence and even shame by a segment of the black middle class during Reconstruction and the harrowing years following. Ella Sheppard, a member of the Fisk University Jubilee Singers, the musical group that exposed the white public to African American oral traditions through national and international tours, recalled the reluctance with which the singers incorporated spirituals into their performance in their early years. "The slave songs were never used by us then in public," she said. "They were associated with slavery and the dark past, and represented the things to be forgotten. Then, too, they were sacred to our parents, who used them in their religious worship and shouted over them."[74] Of the first group of nine singers, seven were former slaves. The Fisk Jubilee Singers were the *sound* of Reconstruction, and the spirituals, as it turned out, would be the element of the Old Negroes' culture that the New Negro would most value—indeed, Du Bois would canonize the spirituals by devoting an entire chapter to their explication in *The Souls of Black Folk*, including his own list of the most sublime examples—with folklore a distant second.

Folklore, too, was met with both scorn and sentimentality by some African Americans as unpleasant reminders of pain and suffering and humiliations of the slave experience. Anna Julia Cooper, the renowned black feminist, who was born in slavery in North Carolina and went on to become the fourth African American woman to earn a PhD, staked out a clear position on the collection and cultivation of Negro folklore. To Cooper, it was an art form whose value lay in its organic growth out of the black experience. Unlike Sheppard, she was not ambivalent. This experience could not be expressed without heeding the impact of slavery, and she feared that "the so-called educated Negro" (precursor to the New Negro) was too willing to, or saw no choice other than to, negate his own past. "To my mind," she fumed, "the worst possibility yet is that the so-called educated Negro, under the shadow of this overpowering Anglo-Saxon civilization, may become ashamed of his own distinctive features and aspire only to be an imitator of that which can not but impress him as the climax of human greatness, and so all originality, all sincerity, all self-assertion would be lost to him."[75]

Matthews devoted a portion of her essay to the Czech Romantic composer Antonín Dvořák. He valorized Negro spirituals in a way that the black middle class—inheritors of this music—did not or would not. For Dvořák, she pointed out, Negro spirituals were not lowly. The greatest European classical composer of his day considered them inspiring, foundational. His most famous piece of music, Symphony no. 9, *From the New World*, regarded by some as the greatest original work in the history of American classical music, was based on the spirituals. Matthews found Dvořák's embrace of this music, on which the black middle class more often than not turned its back, inspiring itself, and instructional:

> Future investigations may lead to the discovery of what to-day seems lacking, what has deformed the manhood and womanhood in the Negro. What is bright, hopeful and encouraging is in reality the source of an original school of race literature, of racial psychology, of potent possibilities, an amalgam needed for this great American race of the future.
>
> Dr. Dvořák claims this for the original Negro melodies of the South, as every student of music is well aware. On this subject, he says, "I am now satisfied that the future music of this continent must be founded upon what are called the Negro melodies. . . .
>
> "In the Negro melodies of America I discover all that is needed for a great and noble school of music. They are pathetic, tender, passionate, and melancholy, solemn, religious, bold, merry, gay, gracious, or what you will. It is music that suits itself to any work or any purpose. There is nothing in the whole range of composition that cannot find a thematic source there."[76]

Matthews broadened Dvořák's claims about the originality of black American sacred music to underscore her call for a new race literature, one created by the very same African American people and out of the same wellspring of experience that had led to the creation of Negro art forms. "A Race Literature," she wrote, is "a necessity to dissipate the odium conjured by the term 'colored' persons."[77] It is interesting to note that Matthews presented her thoughts on the development of "a Race Literature" only two months before Booker T. Washington delivered his infamous "Atlanta Compromise" speech, desperately reminding us that "No race can prosper till it learns that there is as much dignity in tilling a field as in writing a poem." Matthews, with her expression of confidence in the literary abilities of black people, argued for dignity, for "elevation," through writing. Their experiences and their fight against racism, she insisted, were "the source of an original school of race literature, of race psychology, of potent possibilities" for the defeat of color prejudice and the progress of the race.

Matthews argued that this new, elevated race literature—"an outlet for the unnaturally suppressed inner lives which our people have been compelled to lead"—would "enlarge our scope, make us better known wherever real lasting culture exists, will undermine and utterly drive out the traditional Negro in dialect,—the subordinate, the servant as the type representing a race whose numbers are now far into the millions."[78] This subordinate Matthews described sounds strikingly similar to stereotypical depictions of the Old Negro, the typical "Darkey" stereotype that we have seen so frequently depicted in minstrelsy, in Sambo imagery, in plantation literature written by white authors—a "Darkey," Matthews says, that signifies "cowardice, self-negation and lack of responsibility."[79] In other words, Matthews here seems to be affirming, as Chesnutt's doctor did in *The Marrow of Tradition* and as Locke seemed to believe, that there was some truth in these stereotypes of the Old Negro, and hence, depictions of a New Negro were needed in the most urgent way if these images were to be used to further the cause of the black middle class in its battle to protect at least the rights of its citizens, even if protecting the rights of the black masses proved impossible.

The New Negroes emerging at the turn of the century took

Matthews's admonition seriously, a welcome contrast to Washington's embrace of what would be called accommodationism of the "separate but equal" doctrine of Jim Crow. One can think of the creation of literature emerging as a strategic weapon in the war against racist depictions of black people at the time, along with photography, which Frederick Douglass had effectively employed even before the Civil War and throughout Reconstruction and Redemption, and which Du Bois would embrace in Paris in 1900. Within a decade, painting, sculpture, classical music, and the spirituals would be added to the list of these "usable arts," as one might think of them.

Why literature among all of the arts? Writing as the visible sign of Reason had been valorized about the African's place in nature since the Enlightenment, and these arguments continued to play a key role in agitation to abolish slavery, right up through the abolitionist movement's discovery of the power of the testimony of former slaves such as Frederick Douglass in the genre of the slave narratives, as attested by the powerful speech of Emerson's that Victoria Matthews quoted (which Emerson, incidentally, delivered at an antislavery rally in Concord, Massachusetts, in 1844, with Douglass sitting on the stage behind him).

This stress on producing literature to display the intelligence and capabilities of "the race" would be widely repeated, becoming a veritable call to arms. As Daniel A. P. Murray put it at the time, "The true test of the progress of a people is to be found in their literature."[80] It was up to the New Negroes to publish literature that would display the intellect of the race through fiction and poetry.

Hence, the first New Negro literary renaissance movement was born, five years after Matthews published her essay, just about the same time that Du Bois turned to photography in the war to redefine the image of the New Negro in his exhibit at the Paris Exposition in 1900; and just about the same time that Booker T. Washington, already praised as the prototypical New Negro, published with Fannie Barrier Williams and Norman B. Wood what was effectively a manifesto for his concept of the New Negro, *A New Negro for a New Century: An Accurate and Up-to-Date Record of the Upward Struggles of the Negro Race* (1900). Williams was an African American feminist, activist, and educator, and Wood was a white minister and historian who had authored the book *The White Side of a Black Subject: A Vindication of the Afro American Race* (1897).[81] *A New Negro for a New Century* contained everything from slave narratives to war stories of blacks who served in the American Revolution and Civil War, to essays about the phenomenon of the New Negro by various black authors, including Du Bois. A year later, in 1901, the black Boston literary critic William Stanley Braithwaite declared, "We are at the commencement of a 'negroid' renaissance . . . that will have in time as much importance in literary history as the much spoken of and much praised Celtic and Canadian renaissance."[82]

Three years later, in the essay "The New Negro Literary Movement," published in the *African Methodist Episcopal Church Review*, W. H. A. Moore said that the works of three great black writers—the poetry of Paul Laurence Dunbar, W. E. B. Du Bois's *The Souls of Black Folk*, and the novels and short stories of Charles W. Chesnutt—were already of such high quality that they constituted the renaissance that Braithwaite had anticipated.[83]

In issuing her literary call to arms, Victoria Earle Matthews had prefigured an argument that James Weldon Johnson would pick up in 1922. In the preface to his *Book of American Negro Poetry*, Johnson, who was appointed the executive secretary of the NAACP in 1920 and who had no use for the social militancy of Randolph and his allies, issued his own "call to arts," a pronouncement about the role of literature in the civil rights movement.

A people may become great through many means, but there is only one measure by which its greatness is recognized and acknowledged. The final measure of the greatness of all peoples is the amount and standard of the literature and art they have produced. The world does not know that a people is great until that people produces great literature and art. No people that has produced great literature and art has ever been looked upon by the world as distinctly inferior.

The status of the Negro in the United States is more a question of national mental attitude toward the race than of actual condition. And nothing will do more to change that mental attitude and raise his status than a demonstration of intellectual parity by the Negro through the production of literature and art.[84]

This was the manifesto that led to the birth of the Harlem Renaissance, the most famous cultural movement in African American history. Braithwaite and Du Bois had spoken of a New Negro literary movement in 1901, but that never got off the ground, given the repression of Redemption racist politics. James Weldon Johnson's essay of 1922 would be a rallying cry: black leaders such as Charles S. Johnson of the National Urban League, Alain Locke, the distinguished Harvard graduate, and W. E. B. Du Bois, representing the NAACP, all decided to work together to wage the war against antiblack racism on an entirely different front than that advocated by the socialist and Garveyite New Negroes. They would fight through literature and the arts; they would use their creation as a weapon in the Negro's quest for civil rights. In this war, great artistic artifacts would stand as the demonstration of the Negro's intellectual equality, the implicit demonstration of the Negro's rights to the natural rights of man.

THE HARLEM RENAISSANCE: LET THE NEGRO SPEAK FOR HIMSELF

Called its dean by some, its father by others, and by Langston Hughes one of the three "midwives" (in addition to Charles S. Johnson and Jessie Fauset) who birthed the movement into existence, Alain Locke was the principal architect of the Harlem Renaissance. Aligned with the Du Boises of the time rather than with the Randolphs, Locke sought to harness the power of literature as a lightning rod for civil rights.[85] *The New Negro*, which grew out of the journal *Survey Graphic*'s special March 1925 issue, the "Harlem Number," was as carefully curated a collection as Du Bois's American Negro Exhibit in Paris in 1900 had been.

Broken into three sections—"The Negro Renaissance," "The New Negro in the New World," and a lengthy bibliography—the anthology was a vast compendium (more than four hundred pages, with color illustrations) of poetry, fiction, and essays presented by a veritable "Who's Who" among black artists, intellectuals, and scholars (with three white contributors as well, and black men outnumbering black women), according to Arnold Rampersad in his introduction to the 1992 edition.[86] To name but a few,

"Harlem, Mecca of the New Negro,"
Survey Graphic, cover, 1925.

Langston Hughes, Countee Cullen, and Angelina Grimké contributed poems; Jean Toomer and Zora Neale Hurston, fiction; Claude McKay, Gwendolyn B. Bennett, and Langston Hughes (again), essays on music; James Weldon Johnson, Kelly Miller, E. Franklin Frazier, and W. E. B. Du Bois, social sciences–oriented essays on black life in the postwar world; and Arthur A. Schomburg and Arthur Huff Fauset, essays on Negro folklore. Also included were two actual folktales, collected by Fauset as told to him by former slave Cugo (Cudjo) Lewis, the last living survivor among the men and women brought to the American South on the last slave ship—the *Clotilda*—to arrive on these shores (in a brazenly illegal move) in 1860.[87] "Uniting these men and women," Rampersad explained, "was their growing sense of certainty that black America was on the verge of something like a second Emancipation—this time not by government mandate but by the will and accomplishments of the people, especially the artists and intellectuals."[88] Perhaps a more fitting analogy would be a second Reconstruction.

In his "Notes to the Illustrations," Locke explained why he handpicked the German American artist Winold Reiss to illustrate the volume. To Locke's mind, Reiss's work enhanced the aesthetic that he believed defined the New Negro: "Concretely in his portrait sketches, abstractly in his symbolic designs, he has aimed to portray the soul and spirit of a people. By the simple but rare process of not forcing an alien idiom upon nature, or a foreign convention upon a racial tradition, he has succeeded in revealing some of the rich and promising resources of Negro types, which await only upon serious artistic recognition to become both for the Negro artist and American art at large, one of the rich sources of novel material both for decorative and representative art."[89]

The New Negro was, in a sense, a "generational declaration of independence," to use Jeffrey Stewart's term.[90] In his foreword to the anthology, Locke established the truths about the New Negro (the construct or the individual) that had not been previously self-evident to either black or white people:

> The Sociologist, the Philanthropist, the Race-leader are not unaware of the New Negro, but they are at a loss to account for him. He simply cannot be swathed in their formulæ. For the younger generation is vibrant with a new psychology; the new spirit is awake in the masses, and under the very eyes of the professional observers is transforming what has been a perennial problem into the progressive phases of contemporary Negro life.
>
> Could such a metamorphosis have taken place as suddenly as it has appeared to? The answer is no; not because the New Negro is not here, but because the Old Negro had long become more of a myth than a man. The Old Negro, we must remember, was a creature of moral debate and historical controversy. His has been a stock figure perpetuated as an historical fiction partly in innocent sentimentalism, partly in deliberate reactionism.[91]

Because African Americans had internalized commonly held white opinions of the so-called Negro Problem, had accepted the myth of the Old Negro, Locke argued, their own potential had been severely limited. "[T]he Negro has been more of a formula than a human being—a something to be argued about, condemned or defended, to be 'kept down,' or 'in his place,' or 'helped up,' to be worried with or worried over, harassed or patronized, a social bogey or a social burden. The thinking Negro even has been induced to share this same general attitude, to focus his attention on controversial issues, to see himself in the distorted perspective of a social problem. His shadow, so to speak, has been more real to him than his personality. . . . Little true social or self-understanding has or could come from such a situation."[92]

Locke dedicated the book to the "Younger Generation," addressing this cohort in his essay "Negro Youth Speaks." When Negro youth spoke, Locke said, they chose to do so in a very different voice from those who had gone before them. "The elder generation of Negro writers expressed itself in cautious moralism and guarded idealizations; . . . They felt art must fight social battles and compensate social wrongs; 'Be representative': put the better foot foremost, was the underlying mood."[93] Locke praised the new writers who instead "have now stopped speaking for the Negro—they speak as Negroes. Where formerly they spoke to others and tried to interpret, they now speak to their own and try to express. They have stopped posing, being nearer the attainment of poise."[94] In other words, Locke's New Negro poets would no longer see themselves as mediators between black people and the (white) reading public, but as speakers unto themselves and for themselves. Locke made an interesting point, as he himself—as part of the Talented Tenth—would be criticized for acting as a self-appointed go-between, his fine arts bridging the black masses, the "great unwashed" of the Great Migration, and the white elite.

African American artists, according to Locke, had trod the same road as their literary counterparts. In attempting to portray African or black subject matter in paintings, the "American Negro artists . . . have too long been the victims of the academy tradition and shared the conventional blindness of the Caucasian eye with respect to the racial material at their immediate disposal."[95]

According to Locke, however, the Caucasian eye had actually opened more quickly, and in his essay "The Legacy of the Ancestral Arts," Locke encouraged young African American visual artists to seek inspiration in African art, much as European artists had done. Picasso, the greatest artist of his age, used African masks not as subject matter but as a structuring principle for new ways of seeing and representing the human form, which led him to create an entirely new genre. Called cubism or modernism today, it first manifested itself in the form of the famous painting *Les Demoiselles d'Avignon* (1907).

With the "artistic discovery of African art," Locke wrote, "the African representation of form, previously regarded as ridiculously crude and inadequate, appeared cunningly sophisticated and masterful."[96] A little over a decade after the publication of *The New Negro*, Locke, in *Negro Art: Past and Present* (1936), suggested that in seeking and finding inspiration in the

Les Demoiselles d'Avignon, Pablo Picasso, oil on canvas, 1907.

art of their ancestors, young African Americans would find something akin to a new, authentic identity: "It is, thus, an African influence at second remove upon our younger Negro modernistic painters and sculptors," he wrote. "In being modernistic, they are indirectly being African."[97]

From the distance of that decade, Locke noted that even with the valorization of African art forms coming into vogue, African Americans had long had a strained relationship with the visual arts—creating them and, presumably, looking at them—because of the offensive attitudes and insulting images, with their concordant judgments, that were accepted as the norm in representation of black individuals. "The Negro artist . . . [came to] dread and avoid the Negro subject like the black plague itself."[98] This was an issue he had also tackled in the pages of *The New Negro*. Art, he said, must move beyond stereotype, and New Negro artists would do well to follow the example set by the Europeans, among them Matisse, Derain, Modigliani, and, of course, Picasso. "Art must discover and reveal the beauty which prejudice and caricature have overshadowed," he wrote. "While American art, including the work of our own Negro artists, has produced nothing above the level of the *genre* study or more penetrating than a Nordicized transcription, European art has gone on experimenting until the technique of the Negro subject has reached the dignity and style of virtuoso treatment and a distinctive style. No great art will impose alien canons upon its subject matter."[99]

Locke would always resist the idea of art being overtly political. "The newer motive, then, in being racial," he wrote in "Negro Youth Speaks," "is to be so purely for the sake of art."[100] But surely Locke's editing style was political, or at least hinted strongly at his politics. In what Arnold Rampersad considers a shocking omission, there is no mention of Marcus Garvey anywhere in *The New Negro*'s four hundred–plus pages, because "New Negroes did not go to jail"—but Garvey certainly did.[101] Jazz, too, got short shrift: "His moralizing analysis confined jazz—indeed music—to second-class status in the Harlem number," asserts Locke's biographer Jeffrey Stewart.[102] *The New Negro* contained only one essay on jazz, "Jazz at Home." Authored by the self-taught writer and historian Joel A. Rogers, whose *100 Amazing Facts about the Negro* came out in 1934, after the Harlem Renaissance had breathed its last, it said essentially that because jazz "vulgarizes," it needed what he called "more wholesome growth" to reach its full potential. Therefore, the piece concludes, it's necessary to "try to lift and divert it into nobler channels."[103] (Rogers later blamed Locke's editing for the essay's buttoned-up approach. "I am inclined to say in all good nature that there was injected into it a tinge of morality and 'uplift' alien to my innermost convictions."[104]) Locke's *New Negro* (and New Negro, sans italics) remained cloaked in the politics of respectability.

W. E. B. Du Bois balked at Locke's assertion that art and politics were two separate species. "[A]ll Art is propaganda and ever must be, despite the wailing of the purists. I stand in utter shamelessness and say that whatever art I have for writing has been used always for propaganda for gaining the right of black folk to love and enjoy. I do not care a damn for any art that is not used for propaganda."[105] Du Bois, in fact, assiduously used the pages of the *Crisis* to demonstrate the cultural genius of black people, even employing a literary editor, Jessie Fauset, between 1919 and 1926, and joined with *Opportunity* in sponsoring annual literary prizes to encourage younger writers to publish creative literature, a key component of the politics of the Harlem Renaissance.[106] But by 1926, he would become a critic, emphasizing that art and culture without politics could not ameliorate the plight of the race, a plight that was fundamentally political.

Yet Locke purported to seek purely intellectual and creative uplift through the arts. He "decided to use art . . . to transform the image of the Negro from a poor relation of the American family to that of the premier creator of American culture," Jeffrey Stewart writes. "Locke created a counter-image—that of a New Negro who was reinventing himself or herself in a new century often without the help of Whites. . . . Beauty, in other words, was a source of power, for it could transform the situation of Black people by transforming how they saw themselves. By focusing on Black cultural production, Locke sought to revitalize urban Black communities, elevate Black self-esteem, and create a role for himself as a leader of African-derived peoples."[107]

It was a heady goal, and these were heady times. Langston Hughes said that Negroes were creating art and literature as if their lives depended on it. But he would also later write that if there was a renaissance, the average Negro in Harlem never heard about it. Therein lay the problem. The Harlem Renaissance produced some of the greatest black writers and artists in our history, and the Renaissance would inspire a new generation of writers in the sixties in the Black Arts Movement, who looked back on them as founding mothers and fathers. The Renaissance, too, encouraged black artists to look to Africa as a source of artistic inspiration, precisely when even black people largely shared the stereotypes of Africa that white people did. That was a major achievement.

But whereas for Picasso, African art had been a structuring principle, a way of seeing so new and bold that European modernism in the visual arts was created by mimicking its forms and its modes of representation, for the writers of the Harlem Renaissance, African art never became a structuring principle, despite Locke's imploring. It remained on the surface, a theme, like putting palm trees and cowrie shells in the background of a landscape. Africa, for these Negroes, was a source of imagery, the home of the tom-tom. This is best illustrated in Countee Cullen's poem "Heritage":

> What is Africa to me:
> Copper sun or scarlet sea,
> Jungle star or jungle track,
> Strong bronzed men, or regal black
> Women from whose loins I sprang
> When the birds of Eden sang?
> One three centuries removed
> From the scenes his fathers loved,
> Spicy grove and cinnamon tree,
> What is Africa to me?[108]

This mode of representation is called primitivism. For many of these black artists, Africa was not a place or a source of formal inspiration; it was at best a theme, at worst a fad. No one indirectly or otherwise actually became African. Most African Americans, unfortunately, thought of Africa in the same terms as white Americans did. Duke Ellington's name for his original jazz band was the Jungle Band; there was the famous Jungle Alley in Harlem, a nightclub row on 133rd Street; and in her *Revue Nègre* in Paris, Josephine Baker played an African princess living in the jungle, dressed solely in a ring of very phallic bananas. For the Harlem Renaissance artists, few of whom ever visited the Mother Continent, Africa was something they were "of" or "from," but never "in."

It is important to remember the matter of audience: with the publication of *The New Negro* anthology by Locke in 1925, the Harlem Renaissance was officially launched for the *white* educated elite to see. Negro writers would liberate the race, at long last, from the demons of Redemption through art and culture, as Victoria Matthews had suggested some thirty years before. There was only one small problem with this: No people, in all of human history, has ever been liberated by the creation of art. None.

Yes, the Harlem Renaissance, consisting as it did of perhaps a hundred writers and artists, was a glorious awakening of creativity and self-consciousness in the life of the race. But given its grandiose, almost wistful ambitions for itself, it was doomed to fail. The Renaissance, as we see in the writings of Locke himself, was really an attempt to create a third term between white people and the broad black masses: a small, elite mediating body; a tiny class of intellectuals who could stand as interpreters—or middlemen or culture brokers—between the white elite and the black masses, the hundreds of thousands of poor, uneducated Old Negroes fleeing Jim Crow segregation and the racial terror of the long rollback to Reconstruction and flooding into Northern cities like a charcoal tidal wave, inundating the New Negro Northern elite.

There was, in fact, a genuine renaissance occurring during the Harlem literary renaissance, but it wasn't among the writers of the Harlem Renaissance, nor among its visual artists. The renaissance was occurring among those great geniuses of black vernacular culture, the musicians who created the world's greatest art form in the entire twentieth century—jazz. They were practitioners of an art with vital ties to both black folklore and the black vernacular traditions. This art emerged from the black underground, on the streets of lower-class black communities, in the cabarets and speakeasies, manifesting itself in the lyrical sublimity of the classic blues singers of the 1920s, and in its cousin, the new art form, the classical art form that we know today as jazz.

But Locke couldn't (or wouldn't) hear it, then or in later years. He would never come around on the subject of jazz, steadfastly remaining "[un]sympathetic to [it] on the level of taste."[109] Langston Hughes was one of the few Renaissance writers who understood jazz, its importance and its beauty. He was unperturbed by the fact that jazz and its companion blues were authentic and—yes—Old Negro art forms. James Weldon Johnson to his credit in 1922 praised key vernacular forms of black popular culture, forms originating with the freedmen or their descendants—including the spirituals (just as Du Bois had in 1903 in *The Souls of Black Folk*; Locke called them "a classic folk expression" in *The New Negro*); folktales, particularly "the Uncle Remus stories"; the cakewalk; and ragtime—as "the only things artistic that have yet sprung from American soil and been universally acknowledged as distinctive American products.[110] Nevertheless, the new and still emerging dynamic forms of jazz and blues, as Hughes would point out, evaded the older New Negro's purview, and that was a glaring omission.

As is apparent in this heated and often amusing exchange with the then-radical socialist journalist George S. Schuyler, Hughes presciently understood the significance of the birth of jazz in the 1920s and of its potential to serve as the foundation of a new aesthetic for black poetry and fiction. He expressed this quite eloquently—and controversially—in his essay "The Negro Artist and the Racial Mountain," his retort to George Schuyler's essay "The Negro Art Hokum," both of which were published in the *Nation* in 1926.

While Schuyler notes the creation of jazz, as well as other vernacular forms such as spirituals, the blues, and the Charleston, he argues that "these are contributions of a caste in a certain section of the country. They are foreign," he maintains, "to Northern Negroes, West Indian Negroes, and African Negroes." In other words, he continues, these are the artistic products of "the peasantry of the South," and are not in any way "expressive or characteristic of the Negro race." These are regional- and class-based artistic expressions, and not ethnic at all, or only incidentally. Indeed, he concludes, in the end, "the Aframerican is merely a lampblackened Anglo-Saxon," fundamentally the same in every significant way as his white neighbor. For Schuyler, who, ironically enough, had skewered Alain Locke as the "high priest of the intellectual snobbocracy,"[111] "environment," "nationality," and "education"—all keywords that he uses in his essay—trump race every time, since, as he puts it, "your American Negro is just plain American." And as for the so-called great renaissance of Negro art just around the corner waiting to be ushered on the scene in which "new art forms [would be developed] expressing the 'peculiar' psychology of the Negro," he says cuttingly, "[s]keptics patiently waited. They still wait."[112]

Hughes responded boldly. After pointing out what we might think of as a racial inferiority complex among the black upper and middle classes, and relating that members of this class frequently ask him, "What makes you do so many jazz poems?," he engages in his defense of jazz:

> [J]azz to me is one of the inherent expressions of Negro life in America: the eternal tom-tom beating in the Negro soul—the tom-tom of revolt against weariness in a white world, a world of subway trains, and work, work, work; the tom-tom of joy and laughter, and pain swallowed in a smile. Yet the Philadelphia clubwoman [a dig at the Philadelphia-born Alain Locke] is ashamed to say that her race created it and she does not like me to write about it. The old subconscious "white is best" runs through her mind. Years of study under white teachers, a lifetime of white books, pictures, and papers, and white manners, morals, and Puritan standards made her dislike the spirituals. And now she turns up her nose at jazz and all its manifestations—likewise almost everything else distinctly racial. . . . She wants . . . to make the white world believe that all Negroes are as smug and as near white in soul as she wants to be. But to my mind, it is the duty of the younger Negro artist, if he accepts any duties at all from outsiders, to change through the force of his art that old whisper "I want to be white," hidden in the aspirations of his people, to "Why should I want to be white? I am a Negro—and beautiful."[113]

But Hughes's was a lone voice—or at best a minority voice—that the leaders and shapers of taste and patronage in the Renaissance preferred to ignore.

As Hughes puts it at the conclusion of his essay, "Let the blare of Negro jazz bands and the bellowing voice of Bessie Smith singing Blues penetrate the closed ears of the colored near-intellectuals until they listen and perhaps understand." Let these sublime artists, he says, "cause the smug Negro middle class to turn from their white, respectable, ordinary books and papers to catch a glimmer of their own beauty."[114]

It wasn't only jazz. The debate that unfolded in the 1890s about the collection of the Old Negroes' folklore surfaced again in the 1920s (were Brer Rabbit and Brer Bear remnants of the ignorance and primitivism of illiterate slaves, or were they worthy of collection, study, and admiration?), and about the relation of the American Negro to Africa (was the black American an "African" American, or did the dreadful, deadly Middle Passage erase Africa from the enslaved person's memory?).

Ultimately, these questions were the most recent iteration of questions that arose during Reconstruction when the offensive against it began and continued through Redemption. In a sense, we might think of the first generation of the elite leaders of the freedmen and freedwomen, epitomized by Booker T. Washington and his followers emerging in the 1890s as Jim Crow became institutionalized, as the first New Negroes, defining themselves against the stereotyped former slaves and their descendants. But by the first decade of the twentieth century, even these supposedly New Negroes, like Washington, would be seen as distinctly "Old." As a result of their vulgar denigration within the various discourses of white supremacy, and their frustration about the lack of progress stemming from Washington's accommodationist tactics, a new generation of middle-class African Americans would construct a still "Newer Negro," once again at the expense of the Old, in a desperate process of collective self-fashioning as a form of racial survival. The point to remember as we deconstruct the successive figurations of the trope of the New Negro is that the guardians of the race felt cornered by the viciousness of the antiblack racism that had arisen against them and their people during the rise and fall of Reconstruction. In fact, we might think of the New Negro movement of the twenties as the tail end of "the long Reconstruction."[115] With great ingenuity and creativity, they improvised within the confines of the space for self-definition that they could seize as the powerful gains made under Reconstruction were being dissolved one by one. In that sense, the New Negro is one of the most important legacies of the Reconstruction era.

A common theme of these redefinitions of the New Negro is the importance of *class* as a way to draw distinctions within a group of people numbering between 8.8 and 10.4 million between 1900 and 1920, even if the law did not. As quoted in the epigraph to this chapter, Alain Locke put it baldly: "[W]ith the Negro rapidly in process of class differentiation, if it ever was warrantable to regard and treat the Negro en masse, it is becoming with every day less possible, more unjust and more ridiculous."[116] Moreover, Locke would argue, rather defensively in 1949, given the fact that the New Negro Renaissance didn't liberate the race through art, that each generation of black people needed to invent their own New Negro, in an endless chain of neologistic signifiers:

Far be it from me to disclaim or disparage a brain child. But in my view, if a "New Negro" is not born and reborn every half generation or so, something is radically wrong, not only with the society in which we live but with us also. According to this calendar, we should have had at least two "New Negroes" since 1925. Be that as it may, the one of 1925 that I am both proud and ashamed of having had something to do with, failed to accomplish all that it could and should have realized. This does not mean that it accomplished nothing. It does mean, however, that because of a false conception of culture it fell short of its potentialities. . . . Having signed that "New Negro's" birth certificate, I assume some right to participate in the post-mortem findings. In sum and substance, that generation of cultural effort and self-expression died of a fatal misconception of the true nature of culture.[117]

For liberal proponents of Negro equality during Reconstruction, for white supremacist Redeemers hell-bent on dismantling Reconstruction, and before the law at all times, there never was an Old Negro and a New Negro; there were only Negroes. Even some black writers, perhaps most famously Sterling A. Brown, who was considered a New Negro poet, railed against the distinction: Brown—rather like Bishop Henry McNeal Turner, as we shall see, and William Pickens, as we already saw—proudly declared himself to be, first and last, an Old Negro, legatee of a great people who not only survived the storm of antiblack racism, but who transcended the evils heaped upon them; who somehow, against the odds, managed to thrive, creating one of the world's most original and fecund cultures, despite the obstacles placed before them on that stoniest of roads.

REFRAMING RACE:
ENTER THE NEW NEGRO

A New Negro for a New Century, book cover featuring photograph of Booker T. Washington, 1900.

W. E. B. Du Bois at Paris International Exposition, photograph, 1900, W. E. B. Du Bois Papers (MS 312). Department of Special Collections and University Archives/W. E. B. Du Bois Library/ University of Massachusetts Amherst Libraries.

Half-length portrait
of a young woman in a
plumed shawl.

Daughter of Thomas Agnew,
photographer.

Full-length portrait
of a girl with blond tresses.

Half-length portrait of a young man.

Half-length portrait of a young
woman in a white dress.

Half-length portrait of a young man.

Portrait of a young man in
knee pants and boutonniere.

Half-length portrait of
a young woman.

Young man with pince-nez.

Three young women of varying skin tones.

Young woman in dress
with frilled collar.

Young middle-class
woman, seen in profile.

SIMILAR IN TONE TO THE PHOTOGRAPHS IN DU BOIS'S "AMERICAN NEGRO" EXHIBIT,
A COLLECTION OF SKETCHES OF THE "NEW NEGRO WOMAN" AND THE "NEW NEGRO MAN,"
PUBLISHED BY JOHN HENRY ADAMS, JR., IN *VOICE OF THE NEGRO*,
AUGUST AND OCTOBER 1904.

Here one catches a glimpse of rare beauty. But it is not buried there alone, Eva.

Eva: "Here one catches a glimpse
of rare beauty . . ."

We want more men who have the proper sense of appreciation of deserving women and who are deserving themselves. This is a death-knell to the dude and the well-dressed run-around. You ought to write a book on that, Eva.

Eva: " . . . deserving women . . .
who are deserving themselves . . ."

In this admirable face rises a happy response to the lofty impulses of her poetic soul. In the language of art this is Lacolia.

Lacolia: An "admirable
face . . . her poetic soul . . ."

Lena: "An uncommon sweep
of kindness . . . ., an industrious
turn of mind . . ."

In this face is an uncommon sweep of kindness and affection, linked with an industrious turn of mind, which have been the making of Lena.

An admirer of Fine Art, a performer on the violin and the piano, a sweet singer, a writer—mostly given to essays, a lover of good books, and a home making girl, is Gussie.

Gussie: "An admirer of Fine Art . . ."

This beautiful eyed girl is the result of careful home training and steady schooling. There is an unusual promise of intelligence and character rising out of her strong individuality. A model girl, a college president's daughter, is Lorainetta.

Lorainetta: " . . . the result of careful home
training and steady schooling . . ."

MR. GEO. WHITE, A. B.

Mr. White is a young man hardly 22 years old, but he has shown already that he has a work to do in helping to elevate the race. He is quiet and modest and has a strong personality.

Mr. Geo. White, A. B.: " . . . he has a work to do in helping to elevate the race."

Dr. J. D. HAMILTON.

Much has been added to the dental profession of Atlanta, in the person of Dr. Hamilton. He is rather socially inclined, but he knows the value of "sticking to business." His office shows the enterprise of the new Negro man.

Dr. J. D. Hamilton: "His office shows the enterprise of the new Negro man."

MR. R. T. WEATHERBY, B. D.

This is the strong hand underneath the succesful Y. M. C. A. of Atlanta. Mr. Weatherby has ability and character, which elements have raised him to the highest esteem and confidence of the people. He is a qualified Christian worker, and a faithful secretary of the Association.

Mr. R. T. Weatherby, B. D.: " . . . ability and character . . . have raised him to the highest esteem . . . of the people."

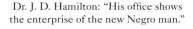

CHAS. L. HARPER, A. B.

Mr. Harper is one of the strong young men in the government service of Atlanta. He is paving the way for himself for higher things in life.

Chas. L. Harper, A. B.: "He is paving the way for himself for higher things in life."

MR. WM. J. DECATUR, A. B.

In this characteristic pose can be seen one of the new forces of the race. For years a successful teacher. Mr. Decatur is now partner to Mr. J. B. Long, the successful builder and contractor. Decatur and Long represent the spirit and demand of the times—thoroughly competent mechanics.

Mr. Wm. J. Decatur, A. B.: " . . . one of the new forces of the race."

PROF. JOHN HENRY ADAMS, Jr.,

of Morris Brown College. He is considered the rising negro Artist of the South. The Atlanta Constitution pronounces him "nothing short of a genius" and says that "he may some day startle the world with his paintings."

Prof. John Henry Adams, Jr.: " . . . the rising negro Artist of the South."

You cannot avoid the motion of this dignified countenance. College training makes her look so.

The college woman: "You cannot avoid the motion of this dignified countenance."

THE "NEGRO" IN JOURNALISM.

The above sketch shows Editor Jesse Max Barber in his characteristic attitude while engaged in study in what he calls his "Sanctum Sanctorum." Mr. Barber is a very close student of current, economic and sociological questions, as his narrations of current events in "Our Monthly Review" will show.

Editor Jesse Max Barber: "The 'Negro' in Journalism."

IMAGES OF ARTISTS, EDUCATORS, AND ACTIVISTS FROM *THE NEW NEGRO, AN INTERPRETATION*, ALAIN LEROY LOCKE, ILLUSTRATIONS BY WINOLD REISS, 1925. LOCKE CHOSE THE GERMAN AMERICAN ARTIST FOR WHAT LOCKE RECOGNIZED AS HIS ABILITY "TO PORTRAY THE SOUL AND SPIRIT OF A PEOPLE."

Charles S. Johnson

Jean Toomer

Jean Toomer (1894–1967), novelist, poet, and playwright.

Charles S. Johnson (1893–1956), sociologist, first black president of Fisk University.

Countee Cullen

Alain Locke

Alain Locke (1886–1954), editor, *The New Negro.*

Countee Cullen (1903–1946), poet, novelist, and playwright.

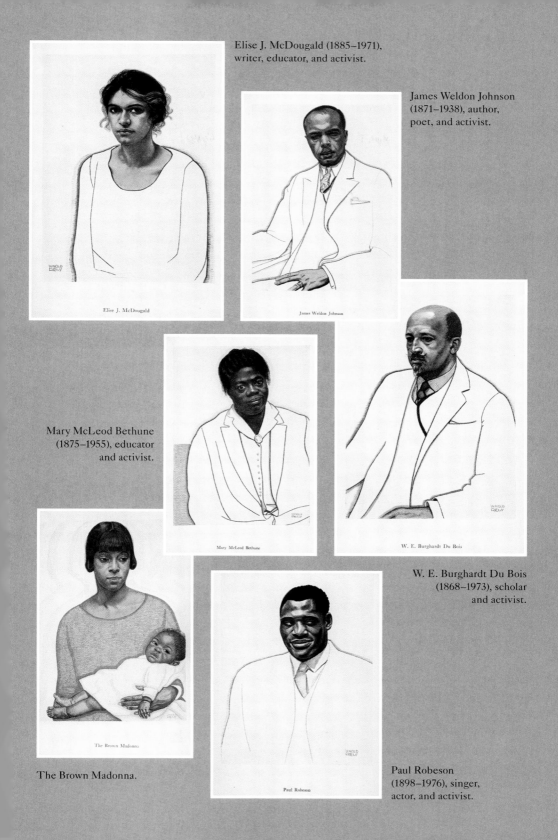

Elise J. McDougald (1885–1971), writer, educator, and activist.

James Weldon Johnson (1871–1938), author, poet, and activist.

Elise J. McDougald

James Weldon Johnson

Mary McLeod Bethune (1875–1955), educator and activist.

Mary McLeod Bethune

W. E. Burghardt Du Bois

W. E. Burghardt Du Bois (1868–1973), scholar and activist.

The Brown Madonna.

The Brown Madonna

Paul Robeson

Paul Robeson (1898–1976), singer, actor, and activist.

"Colored Man Is No Slacker," recruitment poster, 1918.

"Following the Advice of the 'Old Crowd' Negro," political cartoon, *Messenger*, 1919.

"The 'New Crowd Negro' Making America Safe for Himself," political cartoon, *Messenger*, 1919.

UNIA "First Great Convention" parade in Harlem, corner of 135th Street and Lenox Avenue, photograph, 1920.

EPILOGUE

Ever since the birth of our nation, white America has had a schizophrenic personality on the question of race. She has been torn between selves—a self in which she proudly professed the great principles of democracy and a self in which she sadly practiced the antithesis of democracy. This tragic duality has produced a strange indecisiveness and ambivalence toward the Negro, causing America to take a step backward simultaneously with every step forward on the question of racial justice, to be at once attracted to the Negro and repelled by him, to love and to hate him. There has never been a solid, unified and determined thrust to make justice a reality for Afro-Americans.

—MARTIN LUTHER KING, Jr., *Where Do We Go from Here?*, 1967

If the Redeemed South could magically transform itself into a "New South," despite looking suspiciously like the Old South of slavery times, then why shouldn't—or couldn't—the African American middle class reinvent itself as well? Hence, the Old Negro/New Negro divide. If white supremacy has long functioned as the "floating signifier" at the heart of American race relations, then it is also true that successive definitions of a purportedly "New Negro" became for three decades the floating signifier in African American discourse, emerging from the depths of the nadir in American race relations in the middle of the final decade of the nineteenth century, then recast in several different guises until the apex of the Harlem Renaissance in 1925. These redefinitions of the New Negro were one of the weapons that the thought leaders and culture brokers of the race used as they desperately fought back against the sickening stereotypes and racist claims marshaled against them. Indeed, as we saw in the previous chapter, the New Negro was a remarkably commodious concept, capable of standing for a variety of ideological positions, even some diametrically opposed to each other.

The ironies inherent in attempting to refashion the public image of a representative "vanguard" of a people—the face of the "exceptional" part rather than that of the "unexceptional" whole—were apparent to some black people from the beginning, when the concept of the New Negro was truly new. You might say that its own formulation embedded its own critique. That was certainly the belief of Bishop Henry McNeal Turner, who minced no words in telling a journalist identified only as "L. W. B." just that, in an article that was meant to be about the significance of Booker T. Washington's Atlanta Exposition speech, underscoring its role in elevating him to the summit of black leadership shortly after he delivered it, and in which Washington was named the very first New Negro.

The article, titled "Is He a New Negro?," was published on October 2, 1895, in the (Chicago) *Inter Ocean*, two weeks after Washington delivered the speech that redirected the course of black resistance to Redemption and Jim Crow segregation from the primacy of the political, as Frederick Douglass had championed, to the primacy of the economic, urging that the road to black citizenship and equal rights must commence slowly, essentially from the bottom up, with labor, and not in the ballot box or in state legislatures. Washington was declaring acceptance of the relegation of African Americans to the confines of a culture within a culture, a black private and semi-public sphere (perhaps best thought of as a sphere within a sphere, the black public sphere behind Du Bois's veil), one separate and decidedly not equal. In a ten-minute speech, Washington had repudiated, in the most public way possible, Frederick Douglass's lifelong commitment to black voting rights and his farewell message to the African American people to "Agitate! Agitate! Agitate!"[1] One of the most curious aspects of Washington's coronation effectively as Frederick Douglass's successor was the title conferred on him—a title, as it were, only a year old.

Strikingly, in the *Inter Ocean* essay, the writer L. W. B. recalled that almost as soon as Washington sat down on the podium following his remarks, "he was heralded as the new negro." Moreover, he continued, "talk with the people who were present at the opening of the exposition and you will get the impression that there was but one speech, and but one speaker there—Booker T. Washington, the new negro." It is unquestionably apparent that the organizers of "the negro exhibit" housed in "the negro building" at the Atlanta Exposition were keenly cognizant of the role of the image of the race at the height of Redemption. In fact, the very first volley of the counterattack in the battle of symbols and signs had been fired even before Washington rose to speak that day, in the design of the Negro Exhibit itself, before which Bowen had presented his "Appeal to the King": on "the pediment over the main entrance . . . representing the past and present condition of the negro. . . . The one side of the pediment represents the slave mammy, with the one-room log cabin, the rake, and the basket in 1865," the article read. "On the other side is the face of Frederick Douglass, a true representative of the growth and intelligence of the colored man. Near the relief of Douglass are the comfortable residences, the stone church, and symbols of the race's progress in science, art, and literature, all representative of the new negro in 1895."

Curiously, Frederick Douglass, who had died the previous February at age seventy-seven, stood as the representative Negro of the past but also effectively bridged the gap between the Old Negro and the New Negro. We can think of Douglass as a New Negro long before the concept was conceived. And no New Negro of the time would be more resplendently transcendent, more well spoken, more "properly Victorian" than Douglass, an Old Negro who dashed to freedom in 1838 at twenty years old and reinvented himself as "the representative colored man in the United States," as he sometimes presented himself and was often described.[2] But in moments of exhaustion, frustration, or extreme candor, even Frederick Douglass could admit to holding scornful attitudes about characteristics of some of the "Old Negro" community, attitudes that would be echoed at the turn of the century when the trope of the New Negro was conjured into being as the race's best chance against the New South's demonic white rule.

For Douglass, unlike Washington, politics trumped economics; black power resided in the power to vote. The vision of political engagement and the crucial importance of the ballot, which Douglass boldly and fearlessly articulated on the abolitionist circuit at least from 1847 literally to the end of his life, had now, on a national stage, been implicitly rejected by the New Negro himself, the young Booker T. Washington, age thirty-nine, in that damning second paragraph in which he lamented the pursuit of the franchise "by the ignorant and inexperienced," who had foolishly dreamed of "a seat in Congress or the state legislature" and participation in "the political convention" or the attraction of "stump speaking," that, unwisely and irresponsibly, "we began at the top instead of at the bottom."[3]

If Washington was mustering economics into battle with politics at this pivotal moment in the history of African Americans in 1895, what of the image of Africa and the age-old question of "the nature of the Negro"? Africa was indeed present in the Negro Exhibit, not as we might expect, in the form of Nubia's black pharaohs and queens of the Nile, but rather as marked contrast with the progress that the black descendants of Africans had made under slavery in the New World: Africa, L. W. B. explained, could be found "in one small corner of the negro building which represents the other extreme of the race. It is marked 'Uncivilized Africa,' and is an exhibit of some of the natural resources and some of the crude manufactures of the west coast of Africa." Bishop Henry McNeal Turner, "who has been for years urging the negroes to emigrate to Liberia," the reporter continued, "brought this exhibit home with him when he returned from Africa, a few weeks ago."[4]

Turner, age sixty-one, was one of the lions of the race, still roaring at the turn of the century. (He would live until 1915, the same year Washington died.) A contemporary of Douglass's, Turner couldn't have been further apart ideologically from Booker T. Washington.[5] Appointed the first black chaplain in the US Colored Troops (Company B) in 1863, he would be elected to the Georgia House of Representatives in 1868. In

1880, after several years in politics and civil service, he became the twelfth bishop of the African Methodist Episcopal Church. The first black Southerner to hold that post, Turner exemplified how the black church knit together so many important parts of black people's lives during and after Reconstruction. From his position of leadership in the church, Turner—like John Mercer Langston and Douglass—was bold and direct in his determination to fight the counterrevolution against Reconstruction, as expressed in his condemnation of the Supreme Court's ruling in 1883 that the Civil Rights Act of 1875 was unconstitutional: "The world has never witnessed such barbarous laws entailed upon a free people as have grown out of the decision of the United States Supreme Court, issued October 15, 1883," he railed. "It has made the ballot of the black man a parody, his citizenship a nullity and his freedom a burlesque. It has ingendered [sic] the bitterest feelings between the whites and blacks, and resulted in the deaths of thousands, who would have been living and enjoying life today."[6]

In the face of the rollback of Reconstruction, Turner would become a staunch Pan-Africanist and emigrationist, forming the International Migration Society in 1894 and organizing two shiploads of approximately five hundred emigrants who repatriated to Liberia in 1895 and 1896. Having recently returned from travel to Liberia, Turner found himself walking through the Atlanta exhibit—in a delightful bit of historical serendipity—at the same time as the journalist reviewing the speech of the original New Negro. Turner's intention, he told the reporter, was to demonstrate the untutored sophistication not "to represent civilized Africa, but the [ostensibly] uncivilized natives, the heathen of that country."[7]

Regarding the concept of a New Negro, L. W. B. noted, Turner was not amused:

Bishop Turner has little patience with those who talk about the new negro. He strolled through the negro building with me, but saw little that was new in the workmanship [of black craftspeople] that was evidenced by the exhibits. "There is nothing new in all this fine work," Turner commented. "The negroes always did the finest kind of work in the South. The slaves were skilled carpenters and wheel-wrights and blacksmiths. They did all the work in the old days of slavery. . . . No, this work is not the evidence of a new negro. It is the skill of the same old negro who was in slavery. The only thing new about it is the freedom of the negro to learn what trade he pleases and work out his own salvation in his own way."[8]

Turner and the journalist then left the Negro Building and headed over to the Dahomey Village, which supposedly housed "wild cannibals from the west coast of Africa." Turner faced his auditor and remarked sarcastically, "Here must be the new negro!" Confronting "a big-nosed white man" hawking the exoticism of the inhabitants of the ersatz village, Turner accused him of deliberately staging a hoax and perpetuating "some of the lies told by white men who went to Africa and had to lie about the country to magnify their own efforts and pose as heroes of great courage and endurance." Then he turned his wrath on the black actors posing as Dahomeans: "[A]nd these wild negro cannibals you have here, cavorting around like apes and baboons, never saw Africa. They are lazy, good-for-nothing negroes from New York, or some other town, where they have been taught to jump about like monkeys and yell like hyenas, while you tell these people that they are talking in their native tongue. Stop your lying about the negro!"[9]

As the bishop walked away, leaving a jeering crowd behind, he turned to the author of the piece and remarked with finality that "there was no new negro. He was simply the same old negro, showing his capacity as he was given opportunity by the new white man." Theoretically, Bishop Turner would have been correct, had a "new white man" materialized in the post-Reconstruction, Redeemed South. Unfortunately, as we have seen, the treatment of African Americans would only worsen and their rights erode, as black people faced the continuing decline in race relations in the new century. Over the next thirty years, various schools of black political thought would invent ever more iterations of a New Negro, in the vain attempt to confect positive images of noble black people powerful enough to brace against the maelstrom of excruciating images that the white supremacist imagination had spawned. And in the end, as Bishop Turner noted almost as soon as this contest of definitions began, the issue never really had been about who and what "a Negro" actually was; all along, the issue had been about the fabrication of hateful imagery in order to justify robbing black people of their constitutional rights and their economic potential, and then preventing them from marshaling, through the political system, the power to regain those rights. In the end, it would turn out, just as Bishop Turner seemed to have forecast, that Black America did not need a New Negro; it needed the legal and political means to curtail the institutionalization of antiblack racism perpetuated against the Old Negro at every level in post-Reconstruction American society through an ideology gone rogue, the ideology of white supremacy. One can say that to thrive, the Old and New Negroes needed a New White Man.

Eventually, politics would win out, in a process that began with the set of New Negroes at war with Booker T. Washington. W. E. B. Du Bois and his Harvard comrade, William Monroe Trotter, formed the Niagara Movement in 1905. Then, four years later, Du Bois, with white neo-abolitionist allies, launched the NAACP, recognizing that cultural constructions not built on or allied with political agency were destined to remain exactly what they'd started as: empty signifiers. In fact, Du Bois—though a participant himself—critiqued the premise of Locke's New Negro Renaissance in a famous speech he delivered at the NAACP's annual conference in 1926.[10]

W. E. B. Du Bois was born on February 23, 1868, mere months before the adoption of the Fourteenth Amendment. Though Du Bois was obviously an exceptional figure—like Douglass, to whom he was heir, one of the extraordinary figures of our nation's history, black or white—the arc of his life represents two interrelated arguments of this book. First is that resistance to white supremacy never ceased among African Americans, despite the unbearably hostile climate that white supremacy created, as it morphed from the justifications of slavery into ever more repulsive forms in response to slavery's abolition and the onset of Reconstruction. Second, black activists refused to grant that crucial events in the rise and fall of Reconstruction were endpoints to their drive for equitable race relations in America. In other words, we in hindsight cannot help but be dismayed at the reversals signified by the Compromise of 1877, the Supreme Court's overturning of the Civil Rights Act of 1875, the Wilson administration's reinstitution of segregation in government offices, and the caustic uses of mass media as propaganda tools against the African American populace. But black leaders didn't accept the fact that any of these reversals amounted to closing the chapter on black progress or on the struggle for equal rights in the United States, in the South or the North. For this hardheaded group, politics always mattered, first and foremost.

Through his position as a prolific writer and editor, Du Bois was at the center of political activism. Through the short-lived Niagara Movement, its long-lasting successor the NAACP, and the NAACP publication the *Crisis*, Du Bois often set the terms of the civil rights debate. Building on a position first advocated by Ida B. Wells, he beat the drum for antilynching legislation well before Congress took up the debate (and failed to pass an antilynching bill), and his critique of white supremacy was insistent. As he wrote in the *Crisis* in 1913: "Disfranchisement is undemocratic; 'Jim Crow' legislation adds insult to theft; 'color discrimination is barbarism—' When ten million voices say this they will, they must, be heard. And when their cause is once heard, its justice will be evident and its triumph sure. Agitate then, brother; protest, reveal the truth and refuse to be silenced." The NAACP, with such leaders as James Weldon Johnson, Walter White, his successor, and the legal genius Charles Hamilton Houston and his protégé Thurgood Marshall, and *his* protégé Constance Baker Motley, led the political and legal charge against racism and discrimination, at the local and national levels, until the "Second Reconstruction" saw the passage of the Civil Rights Act of 1964 and the Voting Rights Act of 1965.

Ever intrigued by the power of the written word, Du Bois understood that, even beyond the reality of politics, the romanticized, false Lost Cause narrative fabricated in the Redemption era threatened to rigidify a pernicious antiblack narrative in the annals of American history. In 1935 he published one of his most important works, *Black Reconstruction*, placing the struggles and triumphs of African Americans at the center of the Reconstruction story, a corrective to myriad Lost Cause advocates as well as to work such as that of the Dunning School, which, as we have seen, advanced the idea at the turn of the twentieth century that the failure of Reconstruction stemmed from black men—ignorant, incapable black men—getting the vote before they were equipped to use it responsibly. In addition, Du Bois, employing Marxian analysis, perceptively analyzed the economic underpinnings of white supremacy. Underappreciated then, *Black Reconstruction* in retrospect stands as a clarion call, evidence that African Americans refused to accept a history forced on them by white supremacists. Du Bois, the child of Reconstruction and one of the earliest of the New Negroes, rescued the Old Negro from the aspersions cast on their agency in Reconstruction. The symmetry was poetic.

Perhaps it's useful to think of the entire period of post–Civil War American history as a long Reconstruction locked in combat with an equally long Redemption, ebbing and flowing over decades. In a certain sense, if this is the case, then Du Bois lived through *two* reconstructions: first, the one that this book explores, and second, the civil rights movement that began in the 1950s. After fighting off accusations during the 1950s that he was a communist—and having his passport revoked—he finally joined the Communist Party in 1961. By then, with his passport restored in 1958, he moved to Ghana and became a citizen of that country.

With impeccable timing, Du Bois would die in Ghana on August 27, 1963, exactly one day before the March on Washington for Jobs and Freedom in Washington, DC. Though he did not live to see the phenomenal event for himself, it's clear that the march and the successful, in many ways revolutionary, legislation that came in its aftermath were the result in part because of (and in the spirit of) his long years of activism. But would Du Bois have said then, or even now, that Reconstruction had ended?

We can't know, of course. But we do know that eventually he saw clearly that the cultural constructions of the "New Negro," however laudable and impressive an act of self-defense and psychic resilience, were woefully inadequate without actual political agency. While all art, inevitably, is political, one cannot launch a political revolution through art alone. Without the political agency exemplified by the astonishing turnout of the freedmen in the local and national elections between 1867 and 1872, no firm ground could have been secured for the advancement of the race.

Nearly a half century after the US Constitution granted African American men the right to vote, the filmmaker D. W. Griffith lampooned black voters and those for whom they voted in his cinematic love letter to Redemption, *The Birth of a Nation*. Another half century would pass between the White House screening of the motion picture and the genuine progress epitomized by the passage of the Voting Rights Act, progress that is still, in some ways, incomplete, and frighteningly vulnerable to reversal. Yes, images on both sides of the color line were important, but they were not everything, and whatever power they held paled next to the power of the ballot. Frederick Douglass and Bishop Henry McNeal Turner recognized the significance of imagery and agency, as did W. E. B. Du Bois in picking up their mantle. They knew it then, and we know it now, as we hear ugly language spewed and see ugly images strewn, daily, across our ever-present screens, large and small: never has it been more important to heed Frederick Douglass's admonition to "Agitate! Agitate! Agitate!" than it is in these contemporary United States. That, finally, is the legacy of the cultural wars over the idea of a New Negro between 1894 and 1925 for our own struggles against the abhorrent face of antiblack racism and white supremacy today.

A Note about the Text

As I mentioned in the preface to this book, I've been fascinated with the subject of the New Negro since my sophomore year at Yale, when I wrote a research paper (quite speculative, I might add!) about the fact that declaring the birth of a "new" sort of black person implicitly entailed a rejection of something about the "old" sort of black person, and the curious idea that the fight for civil rights could be enhanced through the manipulation of the image of "the race." I have found this subject, and that of the Harlem Renaissance, endlessly intriguing and have circled back to it several times throughout my career, each time revising and, I hope, deepening my thinking about the concept and the larger movement.

Two important factors have forced me to reassess my understanding of the New Negro and the Harlem Renaissance in chapter 4 of this book. First, the digitization revolution that has made so many of our national, state, and local newspapers available to scholars and researchers helped lead to the discovery of sources on the New Negro that expanded, and enlivened, my understanding of its fascinating history. This included a review of Booker T. Washington's famous Atlanta Exposition speech in which he was named the first New Negro, which I address in the epilogue to this book. But just as important has been my work with the historian Eric Foner on a PBS documentary about Reconstruction and the counterrevolution that rose to undo it, the period known as

Redemption, when Jim Crow became the law of the land. Foner's thinking, especially in our many conversations about American race relations
after the Civil War and into the first quarter of the twentieth century,
allowed me to see the idea of the New Negro within a much longer historical frame, as both the tail end of the fight among black leaders to
refuse to allow Reconstruction to die, and as a key element in the fight
against Jim Crow, so dependent on manipulating images of black people
as inferior or subhuman.

Foner, in other words, helped me realize that the New Negro was a
direct response to the creation of the so-called New South in the 1880s,
and it was also part of the response of black intellectuals to the spate of
articles appearing at the time addressing the so-called Negro Problem.
For these reasons, I have significantly revised and expanded essays that I
published as "The Trope of the New Negro" in the journal *Representations* in 1988, and then as part of the introduction to the anthology of
essays on the New Negro that Gene Jarrett and I edited in 2007. Jeffrey
Stewart and I are in the process of editing an annotated edition of Alain
Locke's *The New Negro*, so I shall return to this subject once more.

In addition, this process of rethinking the origins of the Harlem Renaissance led me to understand more fully the key role that the pioneering black feminist and journalist Victoria Earle Matthews's 1895 essay,
"The Value of Race Literature," played as something of a blueprint or
precursor for the movement that Alain Locke defined in his anthology,
The New Negro, in 1925. To help explain how Matthews conceived of the
novel idea that black people could fight Jim Crow racism through literature, I have returned to the connection between the composer Antonín
Dvořák's praise for the spirituals and its influence on Matthews, a subject
I wrote about in 2013 in *The African Americans: Many Rivers to Cross*, with
Donald Yacovone. Finally, I have written several times previously about
racist depictions of black people in popular American culture, in a col-
umn for *The Root* published in 2013 and collected in *100 Amazing Facts
about the Negro*, published in 2017, and in an essay I published with Tanya
Sheehan in Volume 5 of *The Image of the Black in Western Art*, a series I
edit with David Bindman. Bindman and I hope to devote an entire

volume to this troubling subject. The sources for these earlier publications follow:

"The Trope of the New Negro and the Reconstruction of the Image of the Black," *Representations*, no. 24, Special Issue: America Reconstructed, 1840–1940 (Autumn 1988), 129–155.

The New Negro: Readings on Race, Representation, and African American Culture, 1892–1938, edited with Gene Andrew Jarrett (Princeton, NJ: Princeton University Press, 2007).

The African Americans: Many Rivers to Cross, written with Donald Yacovone (New York: Smiley Books, 2013).

"How did the Black Sambo memorabilia that is collected today come to be?," *100 Amazing Facts about the Negro* (New York: Knopf Doubleday Publishing Group, 2017), 117–120.

Tanya Sheehan and Henry Louis Gates, Jr., "Marketing Racism: Popular Imagery in the United States and Europe," in *The Image of the Black in Western Art, Volume V: The Twentieth Century*, Part 1: The Impact of Africa, eds. David Bindman and Henry Louis Gates, Jr. (Cambridge, MA: The Belknap Press of Harvard University Press, 2014).

Acknowledgments

When I first conceived of writing a book about Reconstruction, I envisioned it as a companion to the documentary series we were making for PBS, *Reconstruction: America after the Civil War*. As I began to write it, however, the book took on a life of its own. For their willingness to share their unmatched knowledge on the subject of Reconstruction, for their generosity of time and talent, I thank the following historians and advisers: Eric Foner, a key adviser on both the series and the book, whose impact on reshaping my interpretation of the history of the concept of Reconstruction, the rise of Jim Crow, and the concept of the "New Negro" as part of the African American response to the "New South" is profound; Kwame Anthony Appiah; Rhae Lynn Barnes; David Blight; Lawrence Douglass Bobo; Vincent Brown; Kimberlé Crenshaw; Gregory Downs; Allen Guelzo; Steven Hahn; Evelynn Hammonds; Evelyn Brooks Higginbotham; Thomas Holt; Tera Hunter; Gene A. Jarrett; Martha Jones; Kate Masur; Edna Greene Medford; Imani Perry; Jeffrey Stewart; and Cornel West. I would like to thank my professors at Yale, William F. McFeely and David Griffith, for introducing me to Reconstruction and Redemption, the Harlem Renaissance, and the concept of the New Negro in the 1969–1970 academic year at Yale. And though they are no longer with us, the late Ira Berlin, John W. Blassingame, Rayford W. Logan, and John Hope Franklin have had an immeasurable impact on my thinking.

Writing this book has been a dream of mine for some time now, and without the efforts of the following people, that dream would have remained unrealized. For the expertise they offered in curating images for the book, I am grateful to Rhae Lynn Barnes, David Bindman, Adrienne L. Childs, David Pilgrim, and Patty Terryn. My editor at Penguin Press, Scott Moyers, is an ideal combination of subtlety and sensitivity, and supported this project from start to finish, including coming to Martha's Vineyard this summer to work through hundreds of images for possible inclusion in the book. I would also like to acknowledge with appreciation the efforts of the rest of his team at Penguin: Mia Council, Christopher Richards, and Thea Traff.

I'd like to thank Kevin Burke for the pleasure of working alongside him on this project (both book and film) and so many other projects, and for his wisdom and advice, for his extraordinary knowledge of American history, his superlative research skills, and his capacity to keep others on track while understanding and contributing to every part of the project; Robert Heinrich for his outstanding research skills, the remarkable breadth of his knowledge, and his unbridled enthusiasm for this book's subject matter; Sheldon Cheek for his precision and care in compiling the images that comprise the visual essays between the chapters of the book; and Julie Wolf for her conscientiousness and compassion, her eagle eyes, and for her meticulous, tireless, and loving attention to the book's every detail. My debt to them is incalculable.

Our PBS documentary served as *Stony the Road*'s inspiration and foundation, and I want to express my gratitude to the production team of our documentary series, especially my brilliant production partner and loving friend, Dyllan McGee, and the following members of our production team: Mark Weigel, Jennifer Weigel, Julia Marchesi, Asako Gladsjo, Graham Smith, Rob Rapley, Cyndee Readdean, Stacey Holman, Robert Yacyshyn, Kevin Burke, Deborah Porfido, Veronica Leib, Christine Allen, Judson Wells, Ines Farag, Alexis Williams, Willy Fines, Yah-mari Cole, Judy Aley, Hampton Carey, Kelsi Lindus, Kate Gill, Jay Keuper, Jennifer McGarrity, Sonia Gonzalez-Martinez, Virginie Danglades, Katherine Swiatek, Reena Mangubat, Samantha Lerman, Caroline Bliss, Tony Rossi, and David Raphael.

Funding for the PBS series was generously provided by the following: Johnson and Johnson, CPB, PBS, Gilder Foundation, Dr. Georgette

Bennett and Dr. Leonard Polonsky CBE, Andrew W. Mellon Foundation, Ford Foundation, and Lloyd Carney Foundation. I would expressly like to thank Sharon Percy Rockefeller, president and CEO of WETA; Paula Kerger, president and CEO of PBS, along with Beth Hoppe, former chief programming executive and general manager of general audience programming, and Bill Gardner, vice president of programming and development; Patricia Harrison, president and CEO of the Corporation for Public Broadcasting; and Michael Levy, executive vice president and COO of CPB, for their support of this project and all of the projects that Dyllan McGee and I have the pleasure of producing for public broadcasting.

At the end of the day, it is my family and friends who keep me going, and I am eternally grateful to my wife, Marial Iglesias Utset; my daughters, Maggie and Liza Gates, my son-in-law, Aaron Hatley, and my beautiful granddaughter, Ellie; as well as my literary attorney, Bennett Ashley, and my literary agents David Kuhn and Lauren Sharp. And for their support of my work in so many ways, I would like to thank my friends Elizabeth Alexander, Lonnie Bunch, Larry Bobo and Marcyliena Morgan, Sarah Colamarino, Richard Gilder, Amy Gosdanian, Glenn H. Hutchins, Jamaica Kincaid, Earl Lewis, Howard and Abby Milstein, Louise Mirrer, Michael Sneed, Darren Walker, and Abby Wolf.

Notes

PREFACE

1. In *Freedom's Lawmakers: A Directory of Black Officeholders during Reconstruction* (New York: Oxford University Press, 1993), Eric Foner records 1,517 known officeholders, but he has since written that the actual number was closer to 2,000.
2. For a fascinating and in-depth study of Johnson's composition and the milieu in which it gathered its power, see Imani Perry, *May We Forever Stand: A History of the Black National Anthem* (Chapel Hill: University of North Carolina Press, 2018).

ONE: ANTISLAVERY/ANTISLAVE

1. Eric Foner, *Reconstruction: America's Unfinished Revolution, 1863–1877* (New York: Harper and Row, 1988), 281.
2. Charles Johnson, "The End of the Black American Narrative," *American Scholar* (Summer 2008), https://theamericanscholar.org/the-end-of-the-black-american-narrative/#.Wz-jO5JEoWo.
3. Charles Johnson, "The Meaning of Barack Obama," *Shambhala Sun*, November 2008.
4. Barack Obama, *The Audacity of Hope: Thoughts on Reclaiming the American Dream* (New York: Crown Publishers, 2006), 236.
5. Lawrence D. Bobo, "Somewhere between Jim Crow & Post-Racialism: Reflections on the Racial Divide in America Today," *Daedalus, The Journal of the American Academy of Arts and Sciences* 140, no. 2 (Spring 2011).
6. Johnson, "The Meaning of Barack Obama."
7. Ronald Williams, "The New Negro in African American Politics: Barack Obama and the Politics of Racial Representation," in *The Obama Phenomenon: Toward a Multiracial Democracy*, eds. Charles P. Henry, Robert L. Allen, and Robert Chrisman (Urbana: University of Illinois Press, 2011), 200–217.
8. Nathaniel Southgate Shaler, "The Nature of the Negro," *Arena* 3 (1890).
9. Alain Locke, "Frontiers of Culture," in *The Philosophy of Alain Locke: Harlem Renaissance and Beyond*, ed. Leonard Harris (Philadelphia: Temple University Press, 1991), 231–232.
10. Ta-Nehisi Coates, *We Were Eight Years in Power: An American Tragedy* (New York: Random House, 2017), xvi.
11. Eric Foner, email to author, June 26, 2018. On June 26, 2015, the US Supreme Court ruled in a 5–4 decision on the case *Obergefell v. Hodges* that states do not have the authority to ban same-sex marriages.
12. David Blight, *Race and Reunion: The Civil War in American Memory* (Cambridge, MA: Harvard University Press, 2001), 2.
13. Langston Hughes, *Montage of a Dream Deferred* (New York: Henry Holt and Company, 1951).
14. Rayford W. Logan, *The Betrayal of the Negro: From Rutherford B. Hayes to Woodrow Wilson* (New York: Collier Books, 1954; 1965), 62.
15. Logan, *The Betrayal of the Negro*, 52.
16. See, for example, Brook Thomas, *The Literature of Reconstruction* (Baltimore, MD: Johns Hopkins University Press, 2017); Gregory P. Downs, *After Appomattox: Military Occupation and the Ends of War* (Cambridge, MA: Harvard University Press, 2017); and Richard White, *The Republic for Which It*

Stands: The United States during Reconstruction and the Gilded Age, 1865–1896 (New York: Oxford University Press, 2017).

17. *Frederick Douglass' Paper*, April 5, 1856.

18. For a comprehensive discussion on Lincoln's use of the N-word, with examples, see Henry Louis Gates, Jr., and Donald Yacovone, eds., *Lincoln on Race and Slavery* (Princeton, NJ: Princeton University Press, 2009), xxi.

19. Abraham Lincoln, interview with John T. Mills, August 15, 1864, The American Presidency Project, http://www.presidency.ucsb.edu/ws/?pid=591.

20. *New York Times*, January 3, 1863; Foner, *Reconstruction: America's Unfinished Revolution*, 50.

21. Foner, *Reconstruction: America's Unfinished Revolution*, 103.

22. Foner, *Reconstruction: America's Unfinished Revolution*, 36.

23. Foner, *Reconstruction: America's Unfinished Revolution*, 31, 40–44, 76.

24. Eric Foner, *The Fiery Trial: Abraham Lincoln and American Slavery* (New York: W. W. Norton, 2010), 119; "Exclusion of Free Blacks," Slavery in the North, http://slavenorth.com/exclusion.htm.

25. David W. Blight, *Frederick Douglass: Prophet of Freedom* (New York: Simon & Schuster, 2018), 205.

26. Frederick Douglass, "Prejudice against Color," *North Star*, June 13, 1850, in *The Portable Frederick Douglass*, eds. John Stauffer and Henry Louis Gates, Jr. (New York: Penguin, 2016), 422.

27. Douglas A. Blackmon's *Slavery by Another Name: The Re-enslavement of Black Americans from the Civil War to World War II* (New York: Doubleday, 2008) offers an excellent analysis of what he calls "a nascent industrial slavery" in which black labor is controlled by such horrors as the convict-lease system. Black labor, and therefore black bodies, were trapped in a "cynical optimum of economic harmony, knitting together the interests of capitalists, white farmers, local sheriffs and judges, and advocates of the most cruel white supremacy—all joined and served by an unrelenting pyramid of intimidation."

28. Sven Beckert, *Empire of Cotton: A Global History* (New York: Vintage Books, 2014), 278, 282.

29. Gene Dattel, *Cotton and Race in the Making of America: The Human Costs of Economic Power* (Lanham, MD: Ivan R. Dee, 2009), 293, 331.

30. Pete Daniel, "Sharecropping and Tenantry," *Oxford Companion to United States History* (New York: Oxford University Press, 2004), http://www.oxfordreference.com.ezp-prod1.hul.harvard.edu/view /10.1093/acref/9780195082098.001.0001/acref-9780195082098-e-1393.

31. Dattel, *Cotton and Race in the Making of America*, 293, 331.

32. Edward A. Pollard, *The Lost Cause: A New Southern History of the War of the Confederates* (New York: E. B. Treat, 1866), 752.

33. Blight, *Race and Reunion*, 50–51.

34. Alan T. Nolan, "The Anatomy of a Myth," in *The Myth of the Lost Cause and Civil War History*, eds. Gary W. Gallagher and Alan T. Nolan (Bloomington: Indiana University Press, 2000), 13.

35. Foner, *Reconstruction: America's Unfinished Revolution*, 72.

36. History, Art & Archives, US House of Representatives, "Langston, John Mercer," https://history .house.gov/People/Detail/16682.

37. "First Annual National Equal Rights League Convention. Held in Cleveland, Ohio, October 19, 20, and 21, 1865," 4, 20, Colored Conventions: Bringing Nineteenth-Century Black Organizing to Digital Life, http://coloredconventions.org/items/show/562.

38. Quoted in Foner, *Reconstruction: America's Unfinished Revolution*, 288.

39. "The Freedmen," July 1867, in *A Just and Lasting Peace: A Documentary History of Reconstruction*, ed. John David Smith (New York: Signet Classics, 2013), Kindle locations 4410–4415.

40. Quoted in Edmund L. Drago, *Black Politicians and Reconstruction in Georgia: A Splendid Failure* (1982; reprint, Athens: University of Georgia Press, 1992), 33.

41. Quoted in Eric Foner, *Reconstruction: America's Unfinished Revolution*, 95.

42. Quoted in Foner, *Reconstruction: America's Unfinished Revolution*, 285.

43. Steven Hahn, *A Nation under Our Feet: Black Political Struggles in the Rural South from Slavery to the Great Migration* (Cambridge, MA: The Belknap Press of Harvard University Press, 2005), Kindle locations 2091–2095.

44. Michael W. Fitzgerald, *The Union League Movement in the Deep South: Politics and Agricultural Change during Reconstruction* (Baton Rouge: Louisiana State University Press, 2000), 161.

45. Foner, *Reconstruction: America's Unfinished Revolution*, 291.

46. Ira V. Brown, "An Antislavery Journey: Garrison and Douglass in Pennsylvania, 1847," *Pennsylvania History: A Journal of Mid-Atlantic Studies* 67, no. 4 (2000): 536, www.jstor.com/stable/27774292.

47. Foner, *Reconstruction: America's Unfinished Revolution*, 67; James M. McPherson, *The Struggle for Equality: Abolitionists and the Negro in the Civil War and Reconstruction* (1964; reprint, Princeton, NJ: Princeton University Press, 1992), 305.

48. Frederick Douglass, "What the Black Man Wants,"1865, Teaching American History, http://teachin gamericanhistory.org/library/document/what-the-black-man-wants/.

49. Frederick Douglass, "At Last, at Last, the Black Man Has a Future," in *A Just and Lasting Peace: A Documentary History of Reconstruction*, ed. John David Smith (New York: Signet Classics, 2013), Kindle locations 5920–5929.

50. Blight, *Race and Reunion*, 113–114.

51. White, *The Republic for Which It Stands*, 67, Kindle edition; Andrew Johnson, Veto of the First Reconstruction Act, March 2, 1867, America's Reconstruction: People and Politics after the Civil War, http://www.digitalhistory.uh.edu/exhibits/reconstruction/section4/section4_10veto.html.

52. Andrew Johnson, Third Annual Message, December 3, 1867, The American Presidency Project, http://www.presidency.ucsb.edu/ws/?pid=29508.

53. Malcolm X, "The Ballot or the Bullet," in *Malcolm X Speaks: Selected Speeches and Statements*, ed. George Breitman (1965; reprint, New York: Grove, 1990), 23–44.

54. Logan, *The Betrayal of the Negro*, 44.

55. Logan, *The Betrayal of the Negro*, 83.

56. *Williams v. Mississippi* (1898), *The Rise and Fall of Jim Crow*, PBS, https://www.thirteen.org/wnet /jimcrow/stories_events_williams.html.

57. "Booker T. Washington Delivers the 1895 Atlanta Compromise Speech," History Matters, http:// historymatters.gmu.edu/d/39/.

58. "What Shall Be Done with the Slaves?," *Weekly Anglo-African*, November 23, 1861.

59. Proceedings of National Convention of Colored Men Held in the City of Syracuse, NY (Boston: J. S. Rock and Geo. L. Ruffin, 1864), 34, Colored Conventions: Bringing Nineteenth-Century Black Organizing to Digital Life, http://coloredconventions.org/items/show/282.

60. Foner, *Reconstruction: America's Unfinished Revolution*, 108–109.

61. Foner, *Reconstruction: America's Unfinished Revolution*, 170.

62. General William T. Sherman's Special Field Order No. 15, Lowcountry Digital History Initiative, College of Charleston, http://ldhi.library.cofc.edu/exhibits/show/after_slavery_educator/unit_three _documents/document_five.

63. Foner, *Reconstruction: America's Unfinished Revolution*, 71.

64. Foner, *Reconstruction: America's Unfinished Revolution*, 105; Bayley Wyat, *A Freedman's Speech* (Philadelphia: Friends Association of Philadelphia and Its Vicinity for the Relief of Colored Freedmen, 1866), http://www.freedmen.umd.edu/wyatt.html.

65. John Mercer Langston, "Status of the Colored American, His Relationships and His Duties," reprinted in "The Civil Rights Law," *New York Globe*, October 27, 1883, 2; Marianne L. Engelman Lado, "A Question of Justice: African-American Legal Perspectives on the 1883 Civil Rights Cases," *Chicago-Kent Law Review* 70, no. 3 (April 1995): 1131.

66. Frederick Douglass, "The Civil Rights Case," Speech at the Civil Rights Mass-Meeting Held at Lincoln Hall, October 22, 1883, TeachingAmericanHistory.org, http://teachingamericanhistory .org/library/document/the-civil-rights-case/.

67. Mark Elliott, *Color-Blind Justice: Albion Tourgée and the Quest for Racial Equality from the Civil War to Plessy v. Ferguson* (New York: Oxford University Press, 2006), 284.

68. *Plessy v. Ferguson*, 163 US 537 (1896).

69. Allen Guelzo, email to author, July 2, 2018.

70. Noah Webster, *American Dictionary of the English Language*, 1828, online edition, http://webstersdic tionary1828.com/Dictionary/citizen.

71. Martha S. Jones, *Birthright Citizens: A History of Race and Rights in Antebellum America*, Studies in Legal History (Cambridge: Cambridge University Press, 2018).

72. Guelzo, email to author, July 2, 2018.

73. Guelzo, email to author, July 2, 2018.

74. Eric Foner, email to author, July 2, 2018; Foner, *Reconstruction: American's Unfinished Revolution*, Epilogue.

75. Eric Foner, "Why Reconstruction Matters," *New York Times*, March 28, 2015, https://www.nytimes .com/2015/03/29/opinion/sunday/why-reconstruction-matters.html.

76. Foner, email to author, July 2, 2018; Foner, *Reconstruction: America's Unfinished Revolution*, 232, 602–612.

TWO: THE OLD NEGRO

1. My thoughts on the free-floating signifier were influenced by Stuart Hall's elucidation of the concept in a brilliant lecture delivered at Harvard University in 1994. See Stuart Hall, "Race—The Sliding

Signifier," *The Fateful Triangle: Race, Ethnicity, Nation*; Volume 19 of *W. E. B. Du Bois Lectures*, ed. Kobena Mercer (Cambridge, MA: Harvard University Press, 2017), 31–79.

2. My thinking on scientific racism in the nineteenth century has benefited enormously from, and has been informed by, the pioneering work of my colleague Evelynn M. Hammonds. See especially her forthcoming *The Logic of Difference: A History of Race in Science and Medicine in the United States*, and Evelynn M. Hammonds and Rebecca M. Herzig, eds., *The Nature of Difference: Sciences of Race in the United States from Jefferson to Genomics* (Cambridge, MA: MIT Press, 2008).

3. Paul Finkelman and Matthew Wilhelm Kapell, "Race, Theories of," *Encyclopedia of African American History, 1619–1895: From the Colonial Period to the Age of Frederick Douglass*, Oxford African American Studies Center, http://www.oxfordaasc.com.ezp-prod1.hul.harvard.edu/article/opr/t0004/e0465; Lee D. Baker, *From Savage to Negro: Anthropology and the Construction of Race, 1896–1954* (Berkeley: University of California Press, 1998), 14.

4. Finkelman and Kapell, "Race, Theories of."

5. Ibram X. Kendi, *Stamped from the Beginning: The Definitive History of Racist Ideas in America* (New York: Nation Books, 2016), Kindle location 3022.

6. Kendi, *Stamped from the Beginning*, Kindle location 3023–3024.

7. Finkelman and Kapell, "Race, Theories of"; Kendi, *Stamped from the Beginning*, Kindle location 880.

8. Nancy Stepan, *Ideas of Race in Science: Great Britain, 1800-1960* (New York: Macmillan, 1982), ix.

9. Baker, *From Savage to Negro*, 14.

10. Finkelman and Kapell, "Race, Theories of."

11. Molly Rogers, "Louis Agassiz: Full Face and Profile," Mirror of Race, January 18, 2012, http://mirrorofrace.org/louis-agassiz-full-face-and-profile/.

12. Baker, *From Savage to Negro*, 14.

13. Quoted in Michael Zimmerman, "Glenn Beck Wrong on Darwin: How Evolution Affirms the Oneness of Humankind," *Huffington Post*, August 24, 2010, https://www.huffingtonpost.com/michael-zimmerman/glenn-beck-attacks-charle_b_690250.html.

14. Thomas V. DiBacco, "The Frenzy over Phrenology," *Washington Post*, March 8, 1994, https://www.washingtonpost.com/archive/lifestyle/wellness/1994/03/08/the-frenzy-over-phrenology/c7f08143-c219-45fc-b93e-5c85317b3e1a/?noredirect=on&utm_term=.276ab56b35e0; David Bindman, email to author, September 23, 2018.

15. Samuel George Morton, *Crania Americana; or, A Comparative View of the Skulls of Various Aboriginal Nations of North and South America* (Philadelphia: John Pennington, 1839), 5–7; Finkelman and Kapell, "Race, Theories of."

16. Finkelman and Kapell, "Race, Theories of."

17. Samuel Cartwright, "Diseases and Peculiarities of the Negro Race," *Africans in America*, PBS/WGBH, http://www.pbs.org/wgbh/aia/part4/4h3106t.html.

18. Cartwright, "Diseases and Peculiarities of the Negro Race."

19. Cartwright, "Diseases and Peculiarities of the Negro Race."

20. Cartwright, "Diseases and Peculiarities of the Negro Race."

21. Baker, *From Savage to Negro*, 15.

22. J. C. Nott and George R. Gliddon, *Types of Mankind: or, Ethnological Researches, Based upon the Ancient Monuments, Paintings, Sculptures, and Crania of Races* (1854; reprint, Philadelphia: J. B. Lippincott, 1860), 11.

23. Kendi, *Stamped from the Beginning*, Kindle locations 3162–3165.

24. Donald Yacovone, "A Covenant with Death and an Agreement with Hell," Massachusetts Historical Society, July 2005, https://www.masshist.org/object-of-the-month/objects/a-covenant-with-death-and-an-agreement-with-hell-2005-07-01.

25. Kendi, *Stamped from the Beginning*, Kindle locations 3191–3193.

26. Reprinted in "The True Foundation of Slavery," *The National Era*, January 27, 1853, 14.

27. Thomas Holt, *Black over White: Negro Political Leadership in South Carolina during Reconstruction* (Urbana: University of Illinois Press, 1977), 25; Douglas R. Egerton, *The Wars of Reconstruction: The Brief, Violent History of America's Most Progressive Era* (New York: Bloomsbury, 2014), Kindle location 3055–3027.

28. Reprinted in "Affairs at the South: Ex-Gov. Perry Reiterates His Views—Denunciation of Negro Suffrage and the Disenfranchisement of Southern States," *New York Times*, June 3, 1867, 2.

29. Ronnie W. Faulkner, "Hinton Rowan Helper (1829–1909)," North Carolina History Project, https://northcarolinahistory.org/encyclopedia/hinton-rowan-helper-1829-1909/.

30. Hinton Rowan Helper, *Nojoque: A Question for a Continent* (New York: George W. Carleton, 1867), 69–70; Forrest G. Wood, *Black Scare: The Racist Response to Emancipation and Reconstruction* (Berkeley: University of California Press, 1970), 12.

31. Baker, *From Savage to Negro*, 43–45; Finkelman and Kapell, "Race, Theories of."

32. Lewis H. Morgan, *Ancient Society, or Researches in the Lines of Human Progress from Savagery through Barbarism to Civilization* (New York: Henry Holt, 1877), 553.

33. Finkelman and Kapell, "Race, Theories of."

34. Randall Fuller, *The Book That Changed America: How Darwin's Theory of Evolution Ignited a Nation* (New York: Penguin, 2017), ix, 227.

35. Frederick L. Hoffman, *Race Traits and Tendencies of the American Negro* (New York: Published for the American Economic Association by the MacMillan Company, 1896), 328–329.

36. Kelly Miller, "A Review of Hoffman's *Race Traits and Tendencies of the American Negro*," The American Negro Academy, Occasional Papers, No. 1 (Washington, DC: American Negro Academy, 1897), 35, https://babel.hathitrust.org/cgi/pt?id=emu.010000154223;view=1up;seq=3.

37. W. E. B. Du Bois, "Review of *Race Traits and Tendencies of the American Negro*, by Frederick L. Hoffman," *Annals of the American Academy of Political and Social Science* 9 (January 1897), 133.

38. W. E. B. Du Bois, "The Conservation of Races," Teaching American History, http://teachingamericanhistory.org/library/document/the-conservation-of-races/.

39. Du Bois, "The Conservation of Races."

40. Rudolph Matas, *The Surgical Peculiarities of the American Negro: A Statistical Inquiry Based upon the Records of the Charity Hospital of New Orleans.* Reprinted from *Transactions of the American Surgical Association* 14 (1896), 6, https://archive.org/details/b28717983.

41. Melville J. Herskovits, "The Negro's Americanism," in *The New Negro*, ed. Alain Locke (1925; reprint, New York: Touchstone, 1997), 353–360. For more on the debates between Herskovits and Frazier, see Jonathan Scott Holloway, *Confronting the Veil: Abram Harris Jr., E. Franklin Frazier, and Ralph Bunche, 1919–1941* (Chapel Hill: University of North Carolina Press, 2002), 126–134.

42. Matas, *The Surgical Peculiarities of the American Negro*, 124, 126.

43. William A. Dunning, "The Undoing of Reconstruction," *Atlantic*, October 1901, https://www.theatlantic.com/magazine/archive/1901/10/the-undoing-of-reconstruction/429219/.

44. Charles Carroll, *The Negro, a Beast; or, "In the Image of God"* (St. Louis, MO: American Book and Bible House, 1900), 45.

45. Carroll, *The Negro, a Beast*, title page.

46. Carroll, *The Negro, a Beast*, 87.

47. Carroll, *The Negro, a Beast*, 234.

48. Carroll, *The Negro, a Beast*, 161.

49. Carroll, *The Negro, a Beast*, 114.

50. Carroll, *The Negro, a Beast*, 161.

51. Daniel J. Kevles, *In the Name of Eugenics: Genetics and the Uses of Human Heredity* (New York: Alfred A. Knopf, 1985), Kindle location 87.

52. Adam S. Cohen, "Harvard's Eugenics Era," *Harvard Magazine*, March–April 2016, https://harvardmagazine.com/2016/03/harvards-eugenics-era.

53. Quoted in Siddhartha Mukherjee, *The Gene: An Intimate History* (New York: Scribner, 2016), Kindle location 1325.

54. Cohen, "Harvard's Eugenics Era."

55. Peter Hudson, "Eugenics," *Africana: The Encyclopedia of the African and African American Experience, Second Edition*, Oxford African American Studies Center, http://www.oxfordaasc.com.ezp-prod1.hul.harvard.edu/article/opr/t0002/e1405.

56. "Indiana Eugenics: History and Legacy, 1907–2007," Indiana University–Purdue University, Indianapolis, http://www.iupui.edu/~eugenics/.

57. Cohen, "Harvard's Eugenics Era."

58. Congressional Record: Proceedings and Debates of the Sixteenth Congress, Second Session (Washington, DC: Government Printing Office, 1909), 3482; Logan, *The Betrayal of the Negro*, 363.

59. Cohen, "Harvard's Eugenics Era."

60. Cohen, "Harvard's Eugenics Era."

61. Hudson, "Eugenics."

62. Kevles, *In the Name of Eugenics*, Kindle location 1174.

63. Cohen, "Harvard's Eugenics Era."

64. Charles Benedict Davenport, *Heredity in Relation to Eugenics* (New York: Henry Holt, 1911), 1, 4.

65. Kendi, *Stamped from the Beginning*, Kindle locations 4804–4809.

66. Stephen Jay Gould, *The Mismeasure of Man* (New York: W. W. Norton, 1981), 226–227.
67. Kathy J. Cooke, "Grant, Madison," *American National Biography Online*, https://doi-org/10.1093/anb/9780198606697.article.1300642.
68. Madison Grant, *The Passing of the Great Race; or, The Racial Bias of European History* (1916; reprint, New York: Charles Scribner's Sons, 1921), xix–xxi.
69. Henry Fairfield Osborn, preface to Madison Grant, *The Passing of the Great Race*, vii–xi.
70. Cohen, "Harvard's Eugenics Era."
71. Lothrop Stoddard, *The Rising Tide of Color against White World-Supremacy* (New York: Charles Scribner's Sons, 1921), vi, 4–5, 7–8, 298, 300.
72. *Buck v. Bell*, 274 US 200 (1927), https://www.law.cornell.edu/supremecourt/text/274/200; Cohen, "Harvard's Eugenics Era."
73. Brooks D. Simpson, ed., *Reconstruction: Voices from America's First Great Struggle for Racial Equality* (Washington, DC: Library of America, 2018), 89.
74. George Fitzhugh, "Camp Lee and the Freedmen's Bureau," *De Bow's Review* 2, no. 3 (October 1866), 347; White, *The Republic for Which It Stands*, 78, Kindle edition.
75. Cullen Murphy, "The Atlantic: A History," *Atlantic*, November 1994, https://www.theatlantic.com/magazine/archive/1994/11/the-atlantic-a-history/308366/.
76. Bill Hardwig, *Upon Provincialism: Southern Literature and National Periodical Culture* (Charlottesville: University of Virginia Press, 2013).
77. Jonathan Baxter Harrison, "Studies in the South," *Atlantic* 49, February 1882, 183; Logan, *The Betrayal of the Negro*, 244.
78. N. S. Shaler, "The Negro Problem," *Atlantic*, November 1884, https://www.theatlantic.com/magazine/archive/1884/11/the-negro-problem/531366/.
79. Shaler, "The Negro Problem."
80. Shaler, "The Negro Problem"; Ta-Nehisi Coates has similarly observed how Shaler absolved white Americans from the responsibility of slavery: "At the very moment that Shaler was disowning American responsibility for enslavement, there were thousands, perhaps millions, of freedmen alive as well as their enslavers. It had barely been 20 years since enslavement was abolished. It had not been ten years since the rout of Reconstruction. In that time, sensible claims for reparations were being made. The black activist Callie House argued that pensions should be paid to freedmen and freedwomen for unpaid toil. The movement garnered congressional support. But it failed, largely because the country believed, as Shaler did, that 'none of the men of this century' were 'responsible.'" Ta-Nehisi Coates, "The Radical Practicality of Reparations: A Reply to David Frum," *Atlantic*, June 4, 2014, https://www.theatlantic.com/business/archive/2014/06/the-radical-practicality-of-reparations/372114/.
81. Shaler, "The Negro Problem."
82. Shaler, "The Negro Problem."
83. Alexander Crummell studied at Cambridge's Queens College between 1849 and 1853. William J. Moses, "Introduction," Alexander Crummell, *Destiny and Race: Selected Writings, 1840–1898* (Amherst: University of Massachusetts Press, 1992), 4.
84. Egerton, *The Wars of Reconstruction*, Kindle location 2723–2724; Elizabeth Hyde Botume, *First Days amongst the Contrabands* (Boston: Lee and Shepard, 1893), 4, https://archive.org/details/firstdaysamongst00botu.
85. Joel Williamson, *Crucible of Race: Black-White Relations in the American South since Emancipation* (New York: Oxford University Press, 1984), 119, 406–407.
86. Henry Grady, "New South Speech," December 21, 1886, GeorgiaInfo: An Online Georgia Almanac, http://georgiainfo.galileo.usg.edu/topics/history/article/late-nineteenth-century-1878-1900/henry-gradys-new-south-speech-dec.-22-1886.
87. Grady, "New South Speech."
88. A firm believer in white supremacy and a racial order that would find peace and harmony in black people being on the bottom and white people paternalistically looking after their best interests, Grady was not deluded, as many Lost Cause apologists were, about the fact that slavery was central to the sectional conflict that resulted in the Civil War. In 1882 he said: "There have been elaborate efforts made by so-called statesmen to cover up the real cause of the war, but there is not a man of common sense in the south to-day who is not aware of the fact that there would have been no war if there had been no slavery." Ethan J. Kytle and Blain Roberts, *Denmark Vesey's Garden: Slavery and Memory in the Cradle of the Confederacy* (New York: The New Press, 2018), Kindle locations 2157–2163.
89. Henry W. Grady, "The South and Her Problems," in *The Complete Orations and Speeches of Henry W. Grady*, ed. Edwin DuBois Shurter (New York: Hinds, Noble & Eldredge, 1910), 28.
90. Grady, "The South and Her Problems," 30.

91. Grady, "The South and Her Problems," 31–35.
92. Harold E. Davis, *Henry Grady's New South: Atlanta, a Brave and Beautiful City* (Tuscaloosa: University of Alabama Press, 1990), 2.
93. Black Americans in Congress: Legislative Interests, US House of Representatives, http://history .house.gov/Exhibitions-and-Publications/BAIC/Historical-Essays/Temporary-Farewell/Legislative -Interests/.
94. James Bryce, "Thoughts on the Negro Problem," *North American Review* 153, no. 421 (December 1891): 641–643.
95. Bryce, "Thoughts on the Negro Problem," 643.
96. Bryce, "Thoughts on the Negro Problem," 657; Elliott, *Color-Blind Justice: Albion Tourgée and the Quest for Racial Equality from the Civil War to* Plessy v. Ferguson, 248.
97. Thomas Nelson Page, "The Negro Question," in *The Old South: Essays Social and Political* (1892; reprint, Chautauqua, NY: The Chautauqua Press, 1919), 314–315; Theodore L. Gross, "The Negro in the Literature of Reconstruction," *Phylon* 22, no. 1 (1961): 8.
98. George Washington Williams, "The Negro as a Political Problem," Asbury Church, Washington, DC, April 19, 1884 (Boston: Alfred Mudge and Son, 1884), 2–3, https://ia800201.us.archive.org /18/items/1862emancipatio00will/1862emancipatio00will_bw.pdf.
99. Williams, "The Negro as a Political Problem," 35–36.
100. Williams, "The Negro as a Political Problem," 39–40.
101. Frederick Douglass, "Lessons of the Hour (Excerpt)," January 9, 1894, TeachingAmericanHistory.org, http://teachingamericanhistory.org/library/document/lessons-of-the-hour-excerpt/; "Address . . . January 9th, 1894, on the Lessons of the Hour," Library of Congress, https://www.loc.gov/item /mfd.26001/.
102. Richard T. Greener, "The White Problem," *Cleveland Gazette*, September 22, 1894; Katherine Reynolds Chaddock, *Uncompromising Activist: Richard Greener, First Black Graduate of Harvard College* (Baltimore, MD: Johns Hopkins University Press, 2017), 121–22.
103. Kendi, *Stamped from the Beginning*, Kindle locations 4813–4817; Franz Boas, *The Mind of Primitive Man* (New York: Macmillan, 1921), 273.
104. In 1890, at the First Mohonk Conference on the Negro Question, Albion Tourgée boldly stated that there is a white problem, not a Negro problem. See Foner, *Reconstruction: America's Unfinished Revolution*, 605–606.
105. Emory Finding Aids, Joel Chandler Harris Papers, Stuart A. Rose Manuscript, Archives, and Rare Book Library, Emory University, https://findingaids.library.emory.edu/documents/harrisjoel5/; Jeremy Wells, *Romances of the White Man's Burden: Race, Empire, and the Plantation in American Literature, 1880–1936* (Nashville, TN: Vanderbilt University Press, 2011), 73.
106. Wells, *Romances of the White Man's Burden*, 41.
107. Wells, *Romances of the White Man's Burden*, 40.
108. Kevin Polowy, "Whoopi Goldberg Wants Disney to Bring Back 'Song of the South' to Start Conversation about Controversial 1946 Film," Yahoo Entertainment, July 15, 2017, https://www.yahoo.com /entertainment/whoopi-goldberg-wants-disney-bring-back-song-south-start-conversation -controversial-1946-film-154030256.html.
109. Sterling A. Brown, "Negro Character as Seen by White Authors," *Journal of Negro Education* 2, no. 2 (April 1933): 179.
110. Brown, "Negro Character as Seen by White Authors," 180.
111. Lexi Browning and Lindsey Bever, "'Ape in Heels': W. Va. Mayor Resigns amid Controversy over Racist Comments about Michelle Obama," *Washington Post*, November 16, 2016, https://www.wash ingtonpost.com/news/post-nation/wp/2016/11/14/ape-in-heels-w-va-officials-under-fire-after -comments-about-michelle-obama/?utm_term=.3a4bfdb837d1. For other recent examples, see Rebecca Wanzo, "The Racist Serena Cartoon Is Straight Out of 1910," CNN, September 12, 2018, https:// www.cnn.com/2018/09/11/opinions/racist-serena-cartoon-mark-knight-rebecca-wanzo/index.html; "Editorial: Mark Knight's Cartoon Rightly Mocks Serena Williams's US Open Finals Dummy-Spit," *Herald Sun*, September 11, 2018, https://www.heraldsun.com.au/news/opinion/editorial-mark -knights-cartoon-rightly-mocks-serena-williams-us-open-finals-dummyspit/news-story/bff 3c329c6c706b966636620bcb21be7; John Koblin, "After Racist Tweet, Roseanne Barr's Show Is Canceled by ABC," *New York Times*, May 28, 2018, https://www.nytimes.com/2018/05/29/business /media/roseanne-barr-offensive-tweets.html.
112. Sterling A. Brown, *The Negro in American Fiction* (1937; reprint, Port Washington, NY: Kennikat Press, 1968), 49.
113. Brown, *The Negro in American Fiction*, 50.
114. Brown, *The Negro in American Fiction*, 62–63.

115. Brown, *The Negro in American Fiction*, 54; Joel Chandler Harris, *Uncle Remus: His Songs and His Sayings, The Folklore of the Old Plantation* (New York: D. Appleton and Company, 1881), 223, Documenting the American South, https://docsouth.unc.edu/southlit/harris/harris.html.

116. Joel Chandler Harris, "Mom Bi," in Joel Chandler Harris, *Balaam and His Master, and Other Sketches and Stories* (New York: McKinlay, Stone and McKenzie, 1919), 191; see also Brown, *The Negro in American Fiction*, 56.

117. For a broad overview of regional Southern literature and local color, see Anne F. Rowe, "Regionalism and Local Color," in *The New Encyclopedia of Southern Culture: Volume 9: Literature*, ed. Thomas Inge (Chapel Hill: University of North Carolina Press, 2008), 137–140.

118. William K. Bottorff, "Smith, Francis Hopkinson," *American National Biography Online*, https://doi-org.ezp-prod1.hul.harvard.edu/10.1093/anb/9780198606697.article.1601524.

119. Paul M. Gaston, *The New South Creed: A Study in Southern Mythmaking* (1970; reprint, Montgomery, AL: NewSouth Books, 2002), 189; Francis Hopkinson Smith, *Colonel Carter of Cartersville* (Boston: Houghton Mifflin, 1891), 61–63, Documenting the American South, https://docsouth.unc.edu/southlit/smith1/smith.html.

120. Joan Wylie Hall, "King, Grace Elizabeth," *American National Biography Online*, https://doi-org.ezp-prod1.hul.harvard.edu/10.1093/anb/9780198606697.article.1600914.

121. Grace Elizabeth King, *Balcony Stories* (New Orleans: Ingraham, 1914), 103, 116–118, 121–122, Documenting the American South, http://docsouth.unc.edu/southlit/kingbalc/king.html.

122. James Lane Allen, *Two Gentlemen of Kentucky* (New York: Harper & Brothers, 1899), 16, 22–23, 42, 68–69.

123. Mary Alice Kirkpatrick, summary of *In Ole Virginia; Or, Marse Chan and Other Stories*, Documenting the American South, http://docsouth.unc.edu/southlit/pageolevir/summary.html.

124. Thomas Nelson Page, *In Ole Virginia; Or, Marse Chan and Other Stories* (1887; reprint, New York: Charles Scribner's Sons, 1895), 10, Documenting the American South, http://docsouth.unc.edu/southlit/pageolevir/page.html.

125. Joel Chandler Harris, *Gabriel Tolliver: A Story of Reconstruction* (New York: McClure, Phillips, 1902), 291–292.

126. Thomas, *The Literature of Reconstruction*, Kindle locations 2344–2349; Harris, *Gabriel Tolliver*, 242–243.

127. Thomas, *The Literature of Reconstruction*, Kindle location 2358; Harris, *Gabriel Tolliver*, 244.

128. Thomas Nelson Page, *Red Rock: A Chronicle of Reconstruction* (New York: Charles Scribner's Sons, 1904), 266–267.

129. Thomas, *The Literature of Reconstruction*, Kindle locations 5850–5852.

130. Matthew R. Martin, "The Two-Faced New South: The Plantation Tales of Thomas Nelson Page and Charles Chesnutt," *Southern Literary Journal* 30, no. 2 (Spring 1998): 20.

131. Kytle and Roberts, *Denmark Vesey's Garden*, Kindle location 2158–2159.

132. Jennifer L. Larson and Mary Alice Kirkpatrick, summary of *The Leopard's Spots*, Documenting the American South, http://docsouth.unc.edu/southlit/dixonleopard/summary.html.

133. Blight, *Race and Reunion*, 111.

134. Thomas Dixon, Jr., *The Clansman: An Historical Romance of the Ku Klux Klan* (New York: Doubleday, Page, 1905; electronic edition, 2007), 244, 320–321, Documenting the American South, http://docsouth.unc.edu/southlit/dixonclan/dixon.html.

135. Thomas Dixon, Jr., *The Leopard's Spots: A Romance of the White Man's Burden, 1865–1900* (reprint, New York: A. Wessels, 1908), 98.

136. Dixon, *The Leopard's Spots*, 196.

THREE: FRAMING BLACKNESS

1. Frederick Douglass, *Narrative of the Life of Frederick Douglass, an American Slave* (Boston: Anti-Slavery Office, 1845), 65–66, Documenting the American South, https://docsouth.unc.edu/neh/douglass/douglass.html.

2. Homi K. Bhabha, *The Location of Culture* (New York: Routledge, 1994), 112.

3. Bhabha, *The Location of Culture*, 118.

4. Kobena Mercer, "Carnivalesque and Grotesque: What Bakhtin's Laughter Tells Us about Art and Culture," in *No Laughing Matter: Visual Humor in Ideas of Race, Nationality, and Ethnicity*, ed. Angela Rosenthal with David Bindman and Adrian W. B. Randolph (Lebanon, NH: Dartmouth College Press, 2016), 12.

5. Bhabha, *The Location of Culture*, 111.

6. Walter Benjamin, "The Work of Art in the Age of Its Technological Reproducibility," in *The Work of Art in the Age of Its Technological Reproducibility, and Other Writings on Media*, eds. Michael W.

Jennings, Brigid Doherty, and Thomas Y. Levin (Cambridge, MA: Harvard University Press, 2008), 24–25, 27.

7. Tanya Sheehan, "Comical Conflations: Racial Identity in the Science of Photography," in *No Laughing Matter*, eds. Rosenthal with Bindman and Randolph, 224.

8. W. E. B. Du Bois, *Black Reconstruction in America* (New York: The Free Press, 1935; reprint 1992), 30, 678, 707–708.

9. *Williams v. Mississippi*, 170 US 213 (1898).

10. David Hume, "Of National Characters," in *David Hume: Select Essays*, edited with an introduction by Stephen Copley and Andrew Edgar (Oxford: Oxford University Press, 1998), 119n, 360.

11. Justin E. H. Smith, "The Enlightenment's 'Race' Problem, and Ours," *New York Times* Opinionator Blog, February 10, 2013, https://opinionator.blogs.nytimes.com/2013/02/10/why-has-race-survived/.

12. For more on the significance of advertising in spreading Sambo images around the country and the world, see Karen L. Cox, *Dreaming of Dixie: How the South Was Created in American Popular Culture* (Chapel Hill: University of North Carolina Press, 2011); and Jason Chambers, *Madison Avenue and the Color Line: African Americans in the Advertising Industry* (Urbana: University of Illinois Press, 2008).

13. Barbara Johnson, "The Critical Difference," *Diacritics* 8, no. 2 (Summer 1978): 2; Barbara Johnson, *A World of Difference* (Baltimore, MD: The Johns Hopkins University Press, 1987).

14. Chimamanda Ngozi Adichie, *The Danger of a Single Story*, online video clip, YouTube, July 2009. Retrieved July 21, 2018.

15. Bhabha, *The Location of Culture*, 94–95.

16. Carter G. Woodson, *The Mis-Education of the Negro* (1933; San Diego, CA: The Book Tree, 2006).

17. Thomas C. Holt, "Marking: Race, Race-Making, and the Writing of History," *American Historical Review* 100, no. 1 (February 1995): 2, 14, 16–17.

18. John H. Van Evrie, *Subgenation: The Theory of the Normal Relation of the Races; An Answer to "Miscegenation"* (New York: John Bradburn, 1864), 29–30, 45; Wood, *Black Scare: The Racist Response to Emancipation and Reconstruction*, 53–54, 58–62.

19. Wood, *Black Scare*, 29; S. S. Nicholas, *Conservative Essays: Legal and Political* (Philadelphia: J. B. Lippincott, 1865), 30–31.

20. Quoted in Wood, *Black Scare*, 72; Elise Lemire, *"Miscegenation": Making Race in America* (Philadelphia: University of Pennsylvania Press, 2002), 122–123.

21. Brooks D. Simpson, ed., *Reconstruction: Voices from America's First Great Struggle for Racial Equality* (Washington, DC: The Library of America, 2018), 62.

22. *Evening Telegraph*, November 15, 1867, Chronicling America, https://chroniclingamerica.loc.gov/lccn/sn83025925/1867-11-15/ed-1/seq-2/.

23. Simpson, ed., *Reconstruction: Voices from America's First Great Struggle for Racial Equality*, 343.

24. Edward L. Ayers, *The Promise of the New South: Life after Reconstruction—15th Anniversary Edition* (Oxford; New York: Oxford University Press, 2007), 139–140.

25. Quoted in Ida B. Wells, "Southern Horrors," in *Southern Horrors and Other Writings: The Anti-Lynching Campaign of Ida B. Wells, 1892–1900*, ed. Jacqueline Jones Royster (Boston: Bedford Books, 1997), 62–63.

26. "White Women in Danger," *Charlotte News*, reprinted in *Salisbury (NC) Post*, December 21, 1909.

27. "The Absurdity of Disfranchisement," *Wilmington Messenger*, December 2, 1888.

28. Ayers, *The Promise of the New South*, 301.

29. Charles Joyner, "Styron's Choice: A Meditation on History, Literature, and Moral Imperatives," in *Nat Turner: A Slave Rebellion in History* (New York: Oxford University Press, 2003), 196–197.

30. "Minutes of the Fourth Annual Convention for the Improvement of the Free People of Colour" (New York: 1834).

31. Sigmund Freud, *Moses and Monotheism* (New York: Vintage Books, 1939), 94, 127; Jean-François Rabain, "Return of the Repressed," *International Dictionary of Psychoanalysis*, ed. Alain de Mijolla (Detroit, MI: Thomson Gale, 2005), 1491.

32. Wells, "Southern Horrors," in *Southern Horrors and Other Writings: The Anti-Lynching Campaign of Ida B. Wells, 1892–1900*, 63–64.

33. Frantz Fanon, *Black Skin, White Masks*, trans. Richard Philcox (New York: Grove Press, 1967), 137, 142.

34. Fanon, *Black Skin, White Masks*, 143. Fanon also writes, "France is a racist country, for the myth of the bad nigger is part of the collective unconscious," 72.

35. Scholars, building on resources such as the NAACP report on lynchings, the work of Ida B. Wells, and records kept by the *Chicago Tribune*, have tried to break down what percentage of lynchings resulted from claims of black men raping white women. Stewart E. Tolnay and E. M. Beck estimate that 29.2 percent of lynchings across the South cited rape as a justification. See Stewart E. Tolnay and E. M.

Beck, *A Festival of Violence: An Analysis of Southern Lynchings, 1882–1930* (Urbana: University of Illinois Press, 1992), 92. A more recent report by the Equal Justice Initiative, which also cites Tolnay and Beck, focuses on a broader time period (1877–1950) and states, "Of the 4084 African American lynching victims EJI documented, nearly 25 percent were accused of sexual assault and nearly 30 percent were accused of murder." See Equal Justice Initiative, "Lynching in America: Confronting the Legacy of Racial Terror," 3d edition, https://lynchinginamerica.eji.org/report/ ida b.

36. Brian Roberts, *Blackface Nation: Race, Reform, and Identity in Popular Music, 1812–1925* (Chicago: University of Chicago Press, 2017), 18–21. For additional information on the intersection between racial ideologies, the black body, and performance, see Daphne A. Brooks, *Bodies in Dissent: Spectacular Performances of Race and Freedom, 1850–1910* (Durham, NC: Duke University Press, 2006); and Douglas A. Jones, *The Captive Stage: Performance and the Proslavery Imagination of the Antebellum North* (Ann Arbor: University of Michigan Press, 2014).

37. Bhabha, *The Location of Culture*, 116–117.

38. Carolyn Wedin, "Birth of a Nation, The," *Encyclopedia of African American History, 1896 to the Present: From the Age of Segregation to the Twenty-first Century*, Oxford African American Studies Center, http://www.oxfordaasc.com.ezp-prod1.hul.harvard.edu/article/opr/t0005/e0130.

39. Leon F. Litwack, *"The Birth of a Nation,"* in *Past Imperfect: History according to the Movies*, ed. Mark C. Carnes (New York: Henry Holt, 1995), 139.

40. Ron Chernow, *Grant* (New York: Penguin Press, 2017), 784.

41. James S. Pike, *The Prostrate State: South Carolina under Negro Government* (New York: D. Appleton, 1874), 5–6, 12, 15.

42. Foner, *Reconstruction: America's Unfinished Revolution*, images; Thomas Nast, "Colored Rule in a Reconstructed (?) State," Library of Congress, https://www.loc.gov/resource/cph.3c02256/; "Colored Rule in a Reconstructed (?) State," History Matters, http://historymatters.gmu.edu/d/6754/.

43. In his biography *Wilson*, A. Scott Berg disputes Wilson's hearty endorsement of the film. Dixon claimed in a letter to Wilson's secretary, Joseph Tumulty, that he did not inform the president of his real motivation for offering a private screening: "Of course," Dixon later wrote Tumulty, "I didn't dare allow the President to know the real big purpose back of my film—which was to revolutionize Northern sentiments by a presentation of history that would transform every man in my audience into a good Democrat! . . . [or] that I would show him the birth of a new art—the launching of the mightiest engine for moulding public opinion in the history of the world." Berg could find only one confirmed remark from Wilson on the film, from a 1918 letter: "I have always felt that this was a very unfortunate production and I wish most sincerely that its production might be avoided, particularly in communities where there are so many colored people." Berg notes that it was more than two decades before the "lightning" quotation appeared in print. See A. Scott Berg, *Wilson* (New York: Penguin, 2013), 348–349.

44. Erin Blakemore, "*The Birth of a Nation*: 100 Years Later," February 4, 2015, *JStor Daily*, https://daily.jstor.org/the-birth-of-a-nation/; Carolyn Wedin, "Birth of a Nation, The"; Andrea Shea, "Documentary Resurrects Civil Rights Crusader's Battle to Ban 'Birth of a Nation' in 1915 Boston," WBUR, January 30, 2017, http://www.wbur.org/artery/2017/01/30/birth-movement-boston; Blight, *Race and Reunion*, 395–396. For an excellent documentary on Trotter's leadership of protests against *The Birth of a Nation*, see *Birth of a Movement*, directed by Susan Gray and Bestor Cram (Boston: Northern Light Productions, 2017).

45. Blight, *Race and Reunion*, 395–396.

46. See also these outstanding books: Dick Lehr, *The Birth of a Nation: How a Legendary Filmmaker and a Crusading Editor Reignited America's Civil War* (New York: PublicAffairs, 2014); Patricia Sullivan, *Lift Every Voice: The NAACP and the Making of the Civil Rights Movement* (New York: The New Press, 2009); Linda Gordon, *The Second Coming of the KKK: The Ku Klux Klan of the 1920s and the American Political Tradition* (New York: Liveright, 2017), 11–12; and this essay: Joshua Rothman, "When Bigotry Paraded through the Streets," *Atlantic*, December 4, 2016.

FOUR: THE NEW NEGRO

1. Trevon D. Logan, "Health, Human Capital, and African American Migration before 1910," *Explorations in Economic History* 46, no. 2 (April 2009): 171.

2. History, Art & Archives, US House of Representatives, Office of the Historian, "Elections," Black Americans in Congress, 1870–2007, https://history.house.gov/Exhibitions-and-Publications/BAIC/Historical-Essays/Temporary-Farewell/Elections/.

3. Henry Bibb, *Narrative of the Life and Adventures of Henry Bibb, an American Slave* (New York: self-published, 1849), 33.

4. Foner, *Reconstruction: America's Unfinished Revolution*, 101.

5. "Minutes of the Fourth Annual Convention for the Improvement of the Free People of Colour," July 2–13, 1834 (New York: Published by Order of the Convention, 1834), 3.

6. Henry Highland Garnet, "An Address to the Slaves of the United States of America, Buffalo, NY, 1843," https://digitalcommons.unl.edu/etas/8/.

7. Frederick Douglass, "An Address to the Colored People of the United States," in *Frederick Douglass: Selected Speeches and Writings*, ed. Philip S. Foner, abridged and adapted by Yuval Taylor (Chicago: Lawrence Hill Books, 1999), 119.

8. *Frederick Douglass' Paper*, September 15, 1854; Blight, *Frederick Douglass: Prophet of Freedom*, 275.

9. Frederick Douglass, "These Questions Cannot Be Answered by the White Race," address in New York City, May 11, 1855, Frederick Douglass Papers, series 1: 3:86–89; Blight, *Frederick Douglass: Prophet of Freedom*, 290.

10. *Frederick Douglass' Paper*, April 13, 1855.

11. Frederick Douglass, "Citizenship and the Spirit of Caste," May 11, 1858, Frederick Douglass Papers, series 1, 3: 209–212; Blight, *Frederick Douglass: Prophet of Freedom*, 290.

12. Foner, *Reconstruction; America's Unfinished Revolution*, 100–101.

13. W. E. C. Wright, "The New Negro," *American Missionary* 48, no 1 (January 1894): 9–10.

14. "New York and Civil Rights," *Richmond Planet*, June 29, 1895, 2.

15. Henry Lyman Morehouse, "The Talented Tenth," *The Independent*, April 23, 1896; Evelyn Brooks Higginbotham, *Righteous Discontent: The Women's Movement in the Black Baptist Church, 1880–1920* (Cambridge, MA: Harvard University Press, 1993), 25. See also Henry Louis Gates, Jr., "Who Really Invented 'The Talented Tenth'?," *The Root*, February 18, 2013, https://www.theroot.com/who-really-invented-the-talented-tenth-1790895289.

16. W. E. B. Du Bois, "The Talented Tenth," September 1903, TeachingAmericanHistory.org, http://teachingamericanhistory.org/library/document/the-talented-tenth/.

17. "Booker T. Washington Delivers the 1895 Atlanta Compromise Speech," History Matters, http://historymatters.gmu.edu/d/39/.

18. L. W. B., "Is He a New Negro?," (Chicago) *Inter Ocean*, October 2, 1895.

19. Ralph E. Luker, "Bowen, John Wesley Edward," *African American National Biography*, eds. Henry Louis Gates, Jr., and Evelyn Brooks Higginbotham, Oxford African American Studies Center, http://www.oxfordaasc.com/article/opr/t0001/e1014.

20. J. W. E. Bowen, "An Appeal to the King: The Address Delivered on Negro Day in the Atlanta Exposition," October 21, 1895, 7–8, https://babel.hathitrust.org/cgi/pt?id=emu.010002406372;view=1up;seq=1.

21. Higginbotham, *Righteous Discontent*.

22. On the pitfalls of the politics of respectability, see Coates, *We Were Eight Years in Power*, xvi.

23. Fannie Barrier Williams, "The Intellectual Progress of Colored Women of the United States since the Emancipation Proclamation (1894)," in *The New Negro: Readings on Race, Representation, and African American Culture, 1892–1938*, eds. Henry Louis Gates, Jr., and Gene Andrew Jarrett (Princeton, NJ: Princeton University Press, 2007), 63.

24. Bowen, "An Appeal to the King," 8.

25. Du Bois, "The Conservation of Races"; Kendi, *Stamped from the Beginning*, Kindle locations 4488–4490.

26. Du Bois, "The Conservation of Races."

27. Linda Barrett Osborn, introduction to *A Small Nation of People: W. E. B. Du Bois and African American Portraits of Progress* (New York: HarperCollins, 2003), 16.

28. David Levering Lewis, "A Small Nation of People: W. E. B. Du Bois and Black Americans at the Turn of the Twentieth Century," in *A Small Nation of People: W. E. B. Du Bois and African American Portraits of Progress*, 26.

29. Osborn, introduction, *A Small Nation of People*, 18.

30. W. E. B. Du Bois, "The American Negro at Paris," *American Monthly Review of Reviews* 22, no. 5 (November 1900): 575–577, http://www.webdubois.org/dbANParis.html.

31. *The Colored American*, November 3, 1900, quoted in Lewis, "A Small Nation of People: W. E. B. Du Bois and Black Americans at the Turn of the Twentieth Century," 46–47.

32. From October 2016 to January 2017, the Musée du Quai Branly Jacques Chiraq in Paris featured an exhibit called *The Color Line: African American Artists and Segregation*, curated by Daniel Soutif, which included photos from Du Bois's exhibition. See http://www.quaibranly.fr/en/exhibitions-and-events/at-the-museum/exhibitions/event-details/e/the-color-line-36687/.

33. Deborah Willis, "The Sociologist's Eye: W. E. B. Du Bois and the Paris Exposition," in *A Small Nation of People: W. E. B. Du Bois and African American Portraits of Progress*, 77.

34. W. E. B. Du Bois, *The Souls of Black Folk: Essays and Sketches* (Chicago: A. C. McClurg, 1903), 3, Documenting the American South, https://docsouth.unc.edu/church/duboissouls/dubois.html; Kendi, *Stamped from the Beginning*, Kindle locations 4647–4691.

35. W. E. B. Du Bois, *The Philadelphia Negro: A Social Study* (Philadelphia: University of Pennsylvania Press, 1899), 310–311.

36. David Levering Lewis, "Harlem Renaissance: The Vogue of the New Negro," *Africana: The Encyclopedia of the African and African American Experience, Second Edition*, Oxford African American Studies Center, http://www.oxfordaasc.com.ezp-prod1.hul.harvard.edu/article/opr/t0002/e1807.

37. Martha H. Patterson, *The American New Woman Revisited: A Reader, 1894–1930* (New Brunswick, NJ: Rutgers University Press, 2008), 168–169.

38. John H. Adams, Jr., "Rough Sketches: A Study of the Features of the New Negro Woman," *Voice of the Negro* 1, no. 8 (August 1904): 325–326; Patterson, *The American New Woman Revisited*, 171.

39. John H. Adams, Jr., "Rough Sketches: 'The New Negro Man,'" *Voice of the Negro* 1, no. 10 (October 1904): 447.

40. W. E. B. Du Bois, "A Negro Student at Harvard at the End of the 19th Century," *Massachusetts Review* 1, no. 3 (Spring 1960): 442.

41. Booker T. Washington, *Up from Slavery: An Autobiography* (Garden City, NY: Doubleday & Company, 1901), 174–176, https://docsouth.unc.edu/fpn/washington/washing.html.

42. Advertisement for Madam C. J. Walker Products, Smithsonian Museum of African American History and Culture, https://www.si.edu/object/nmaahc_2013.153.11.1.

43. Charles W. Chesnutt, *The Marrow of Tradition* (Boston: Houghton, Mifflin, 1901), 60–61, Documenting the American South, http://docsouth.unc.edu/southlit/chesnuttmarrow/chesmarrow.html.

44. W. E. B. Du Bois, "The Talented Tenth," September 1903, TeachingAmericanHistory.org, http://teachingamericanhistory.org/library/document/the-talented-tenth/.

45. Du Bois, *The Souls of Black Folk*, Documenting the American South, 38.

46. Du Bois, *The Philadelphia Negro*, 316–317.

47. Lewis, "A Small Nation of People: W. E. B. Du Bois and Black Americans at the Turn of the Twentieth Century," in *A Small Nation of People*, 25–26.

48. Du Bois, *The Philadelphia Negro*, 317.

49. Stewart E. Tolnay and E. M. Beck, "Black Flight: Lethal Violence and the Great Migration, 1900–1930," *Social Science History* 14, no. 3 (1990): 347–370. doi:10.2307/1171355.

50. L. Diane Barnes, "Great Migration," *Encyclopedia of African American History, 1896 to the Present: From the Age of Segregation to the Twenty-first Century*, ed. Paul Finkelman (New York: Oxford University Press, 2009), 326–329.

51. Andrew A. Beveridge, David Halle, Edward Telles, and Beth Leavenworth DuFault, "Residential Diversity and Division: Separation and Segregation among Whites, Blacks, Hispanics, Asians, Affluent, and Poor," in *New York and Los Angeles: The Uncertain Future*, eds. David Halle and Andrew A. Beveridge (New York: Oxford University Press, 2013), 320.

52. Charles S. Johnson, "The New Frontage on American Life," in *The New Negro*, ed. Alain Locke (1925; reprint, New York: Touchstone, 1997), 291.

53. Jeffrey C. Stewart, *The New Negro: The Life of Alain Locke* (New York: Oxford University Press, 2018), Kindle locations 1240–1248.

54. "The New Negro: An Address Delivered by the Hon. S. Laing Williams at the Morning Service Held at All Souls Church in the Abraham Lincoln Centre, Chicago, Sunday, July 26, 1908," *Unity*, August 13, 1908, 375.

55. "The New Negro: An Address Delivered by the Hon. S. Laing Williams," 376.

56. Ray Stannard Baker, *Following the Color Line: An Account of Negro Citizenship in the American Democracy* (New York: Doubleday, Page, 1908), 39, 241.

57. Leslie Pinckney Hill, "Negro Ideals: Their Effect and Their Embarrassments," *Journal of Race Development* 6, no. 1 (July 1915), 97–98.

58. William Pickens, *The New Negro: His Political, Civil, and Mental Status, and Related Essays* (New York: Neale, 1916), 224.

59. Pickens, *The New Negro*, 239.

60. Adena Spingarn, *Uncle Tom: From Martyr to Traitor* (Palo Alto, CA: Stanford University Press, 2018), Kindle locations 2734–2738, 2755–2760, 2877–2880.

61. Published in *Voice* (November 7, 1917); Jeffrey B. Perry, "Harrison, Hubert Henry," *American National Biography*, https://doi-org.ezp-prod1.hul.harvard.edu/10.1093/anb/9780198606697.article.1500307. See also Perry's biography of Harrison, *Hubert Harrison: The Voice of Harlem Radicalism, 1883–1918* (New York: Columbia University Press, 2009).

62. Perry, "Harrison, Hubert Henry."

63. Perry, "Harrison, Hubert Henry."

64. Alonford James Robinson, "East St. Louis Riot of 1917," *Africana: The Encyclopedia of the African and African American Experience, Second Edition* (New York: Oxford University Press, 2005), 488–489; "Silent Protest Parade Centennial," NAACP website, https://www.naacp.org/silent-protest-parade-centennial/.

65. W. E. B. Du Bois, "Returning Soldiers," *Crisis* 18 (May 1919): 13, https://glc.yale.edu/returning-soldiers.

66. Claude McKay, "If We Must Die," Poetry Foundation, https://www.poetryfoundation.org/poems/44694/if-we-must-die.

67. William J. Maxwell, introduction to *Claude McKay: Complete Poems*, ed. William J. Maxwell (Urbana: University of Illinois Press, 2004), xxi.

68. Jervis Anderson, *A. Philip Randolph: A Biographical Portrait* (Berkeley: University of California Press, 1972), 113.

69. A. Philip Randolph and Chandler Owen, "The New Negro—What Is He?," *Messenger*, August 1920, in Jeffrey B. Ferguson, ed., *The Harlem Renaissance: A Brief History with Documents* (Boston: Bedford/St. Martin's, 2008), 39–42.

70. W. A. Domingo, "A New Negro and New Day," *Messenger*, November 1920, 144–145.

71. Marcus Garvey, "The New Negro and the U.N.I.A. (1919)," in *The New Negro: Readings on Race, Representation and African American Culture*, eds. Henry Louis Gates, Jr., and Gene Andrew Jarrett (Princeton, NJ: Princeton University Press, 2007), 94.

72. David Levering Lewis, *W. E. B. Du Bois: A Biography* (New York: Macmillan, 2009). 469–492; David Levering Lewis, "Dr. Johnson's Friends: Civil Rights by Copyright during Harlem's Mid-Twenties," *Massachusetts Review* 20, no. 3 (Autumn 1979): 501–519.

73. Victoria Earle Matthews, "The Value of Race Literature (1895)," in *The New Negro: Readings on Race, Representation and African American Culture*, eds. Gates, Jr., and Jarrett, 287.

74. Ella Sheppard, "Slave Songs Not in Repertoire," in "Historical Sketch of the Jubilee Singers" (1911), in *The Portable Nineteenth-Century African American Women Writers*, eds. Hollis Robbins and Henry Louis Gates, Jr. (New York: Penguin, 2017), 230.

75. Anna Julia Cooper, Letter to the Editor, *Southern Workman* 22, no. 1 (January 1894): 5.

76. Matthews, "The Value of Race Literature," 288.

77. Matthews, "The Value of Race Literature," 288.

78. Matthews, "The Value of Race Literature," 289.

79. Matthews, "The Value of Race Literature," 290.

80. "Daniel A. P. Murray," *African American Perspectives: Materials Selected from the Rare Book Collection*, Library of Congress, https://www.loc.gov/collections/african-american-perspectives-rare-books/articles-and-essays/the-progress-of-a-people/daniel-a-p-murray/.

81. Norman B. Wood, *The White Side of a Black Subject: A Vindication of the Afro American Race* (Chicago: American Publication House, 1897), front matter; Angela D. Sims, *Ethical Complications of Lynching: Ida B. Wells's Interrogation of American Terror* (New York: Palgrave Macmillan, 2010), 43.

82. Quoted in Henry Louis Gates, Jr., and Gene Andrew Jarrett, introduction to *The New Negro: Readings on Race, Representation and African American Culture*, eds. Gates, Jr., and Jarrett, 1.

83. W. H. A. Moore, "The New Negro Literary Movement," *AME Church Review* 21 (1904): 49–54.

84. James Weldon Johnson, preface to *The Book of American Negro Poetry* (1922), in *The New Negro: Readings on Race, Representation and African American Culture*, eds. Gates, Jr., and Jarrett, 427.

85. Arnold Rampersad, introduction to *The New Negro*, ed. Alain Locke (1925; reprint, New York: Touchstone, 1997), xi.

86. Rampersad, introduction, xiii.

87. In 1927 Zora Neale Hurston interviewed Cudjo Lewis at his home in Alabama. The stories he told of his experiences making the Middle Passage aboard the *Clotilda*, which in 1860 transported captured Africans from their homeland to America five decades after the transatlantic slave trade had been outlawed, and of his life in slavery and in freedom formed the narrative that Hurston would call *Barracoon*. She completed writing it in 1931; it would not be published until 2018: Zora Neale Hurston, *Barracoon: The Story of the Last "Black Cargo"* (New York: Amistad, 2018).

88. Rampersad, introduction, xiv.

89. Alain Locke, "Notes to the Illustrations," *The New Negro*, ed. Alain Locke (1925; reprint, New York: Touchstone, 1997), 419.

90. Stewart, *The New Negro: The Life of Alain Locke*, Kindle location 9741.

91. Alain Locke, "The New Negro," in *The New Negro*, ed. Alain Locke, 3.

92. Locke, "The New Negro," 3–4.

93. Alain Locke, "Negro Youth Speaks," in *The New Negro*, ed. Alain Locke, 50.

94. Locke, "Negro Youth Speaks," 48.

95. Alain Locke, "The Legacy of the Ancestral Arts," in *The New Negro*, ed. Alain Locke, 264.

96. Alain Locke, ed., "The Legacy of the Ancestral Arts," 258.

97. Alain Locke, *Negro Art: Past and Present* (Washington, DC: Associates in Negro Folk Education, 1936), 70.

98. Locke, *Negro Art: Past and Present*, 10.

99. Locke, "The Legacy of the Ancestral Arts," 264.

100. Locke, "Negro Youth Speaks," 51.

101. Rampersad, introduction to *The New Negro*, ed. Alain Locke (1955; reprint: Touchstone, 1997), Kindle locations 287–301.

102. Stewart, *The New Negro: The Life of Alain Locke*, Kindle location 10998–11002.

103. J. A. Rogers, "Jazz at Home," in *The New Negro*, ed. Alain Locke (1925; reprint, New York: Touchstone, 1997), 224.

104. Stewart, *The New Negro: The Life of Alain Locke*, Kindle locations 11003–11004.

105. Quoted in Adam Kirsch, "Art and Activism: Rediscovering Alain Locke and the Project of Black Self-Realization," *Harvard Magazine*, March–April 2018, https://harvardmagazine.com/2018/03/alain-locke-the-new-negro.

106. Brent Edwards, "Harlem Renaissance: 1919–1940," in *The Norton Anthology of African American Literature*, 3rd ed., eds. Henry Louis Gates, Jr., and Valerie A. Smith (New York: W. W. Norton, 2014), 934.

107. Stewart, *The New Negro: The Life of Alain Locke*, Kindle locations 216–238.

108. Quoted in Wallace Thurman, "Negro Poets and Their Poetry (1928)," in *The New Negro: Readings on Race, Representation and African American Culture*, eds. Gates, Jr., and Jarrett, 420; W. E. B. Du Bois, *Dusk of Dawn: An Essay toward an Autobiography of a Race Concept* (New York: Oxford University Press, 2014).

109. Stewart, *The New Negro: The Life of Alain Locke*, Kindle locations 20445–20455.

110. Edwards, "Harlem Renaissance: 1919–1940," in *The Norton Anthology of African American Literature*, eds. Gates and Smith, 937; James Weldon Johnson, preface, *The Book of American Negro Poetry* (New York: Harcourt, Brace and Company, 1922), viii.

111. Rampersad, introduction to *The New Negro*, Kindle locations 272–287.

112. "The Harlem Renaissance: George Schuyler Argues against 'Black Art,' History Matters, http://historymatters.gmu.edu/d/5129/.

113. Langston Hughes, "The Negro Artist and the Racial Mountain," *Nation* 122 (June 23, 1926), https://www.thenation.com/article/negro-artist-and-racial-mountain/.

114. Hughes, "The Negro Artist and the Racial Mountain."

115. Numerous scholars have begun to consider the notion of "the long Reconstruction." See especially Gregory P. Downs, *Declarations of Dependence: The Long Reconstruction of Popular Politics in the South, 1861–1908* (Chapel Hill: University of North Carolina Press, 2011); and the essays in Gregory P. Downs and Kate Masur, eds., *The War the Civil War Made* (Chapel Hill: University of North Carolina Press, 2015).

116. Alain Locke, "Enter the New Negro," *Survey Graphic* (March 1925), http://nationalhumanitiescenter.org/pds/maai3/migrations/text8/lockenewnegro.pdf.

117. Alain Locke, "Frontiers of Culture," in *The Philosophy of Alain Locke: Harlem Renaissance and Beyond*, ed. Leonard Harris (Philadelphia: Temple University Press, 1991), 231–232.

EPILOGUE

1. Quoted in James A. Colaiaco, *Frederick Douglass and the Fourth of July* (New York: Palgrave Macmillan, 2006), 202. Ironically, Douglass, like Washington, was an early advocate of industrial education for black people, as he forcefully argued in an 1853 letter to Harriet Beecher Stowe seeking her financial support for such programs. "What I propose," he wrote, "is intended simply to prepare men for the work of getting an honest living—not out of dishonest men—but out of an honest earth. . . . The argument in favor of an Industrial College—a college to be conducted by the best men—and the best workmen which the mechanical arts can afford; a college where colored youth can be instructed to use their hands, as well as their heads; where they can be put into possession of the means of getting a living whether their lot in after life may be cast among civilized or uncivilized men; whether they choose to stay here, or prefer to return to the land of their fathers—is briefly this: Prejudice against the free colored people in the United States has shown itself nowhere so invincible as among mechanics. The farmer and the professional man cherish no feeling so bitter as that cherished by these. The latter would starve us out of the country entirely. At this moment I can more easily get my son into a

lawyer's office to learn law than I can into a blacksmith's shop to blow the bellows and to wield the sledge-hammer. . . . The fact is—every day begins with the lesson, and ends with the lesson—the colored men must learn trades; and must find new employment; new modes of usefulness to society, or that they must decay under the pressing wants to which their condition is rapidly bringing them." Frederick Douglass to Harriet Beecher Stowe, March 8, 1853, http://teachingamericanhistory.org /library/document/letter-to-harriet-beecher-stowe/.

2. For contemporary and historical allusions to Frederick Douglass as representative of African Americans, see John Stauffer, "Frederick Douglass's Self-Fashioning and the Making of a Representative American Man," in *The Cambridge Companion to the African American Slave Narrative*, ed. Audrey Fisch (Cambridge: Cambridge University Press, 2007), 201–217; Robert S. Levine, *Martin Delany, Frederick Douglass, and the Politics of Representative Identity* (Chapel Hill: University of North Carolina Press, 1997); James McCune Smith, introduction to Frederick Douglass, *My Bondage and My Freedom* (New York: Miller, Orton & Mulligan, 1855), xxv, https://docsouth.unc.edu/neh/douglass55 /douglass55.html. See also comments from Senator John Hoar (Republican from Massachusetts), who called Douglass a "representative colored man" on August 3, 1886: *Congressional Record: Containing the Proceedings and Debates of the Forty-Ninth Congress, First Session; Also, Special Session of the Senate* (Washington, DC: Government Printing Office, 1886), 7881.

3. "Booker T. Washington Delivers the 1895 Atlanta Compromise Speech," History Matters, http:// historymatters.gmu.edu/d/39/.

4. L. W. B., "Is He a New Negro?"

5. For an excellent biography of Turner, see Andre E. Johnson, *The Forgotten Prophet: Bishop Henry McNeal Turner and the African American Prophetic Tradition* (Lanham, MD: Lexington Books, 2012), especially his disagreements with Washington on p. 95.

6. Henry McNeal Turner, *The Barbarous Decision of the United States Supreme Court Declaring the Civil Rights Act Unconstitutional and Disrobing the Colored Race of All Civil Protection* (Atlanta: self-published, 1893), 3, Documenting the American South, https://docsouth.unc.edu/church/turnerbd/turner .html.

7. L. W. B., "Is He a New Negro?"

8. L. W. B., "Is He a New Negro?"

9. L. W. B., "Is He a New Negro?"

10. W. E. B. Du Bois, "Criteria of Negro Art," *Crisis* 32 (October 1926): 290–297, http://www.webdubois .org/dbCriteriaNArt.html.

Index

Illustration Credits

ONE: ANTISLAVERY/ANTISLAVE

p. 9 Currier & Ives/Library of Congress
p. 12 Hutchins Center for African & African American Research/Harvard University

BACKLASH

p. 41 top, Edward Williams Clay/Library of Congress; bottom, Library of Congress
p. 42 top, Library of Congress; bottom, Division of Political and Military History, National Museum of American History, Smithsonian Institution
p. 43 top, Peter Righteous/Alamy; bottom, American Antiquarian Society
p. 44 top and bottom right, Library of Congress; bottom left, Broadside Collection/Library of Congress
p. 45 top and bottom, Thomas Nast/Library of Congress
p. 46 top, Broadside Collection/Library of Congress; bottom, Library of Congress
p. 47 top, Thomas Nast/Library of Congress; bottom, Art and Picture Collection/The New York Public Library
p. 48 bottom, Thomas Nast/Library of Congress
p. 49 top, Special Collections/The Newberry; bottom right, Thomas Nast/Library of Congress; bottom left, Arthur Burdett Frost/Wikimedia Commons
p. 50 top and bottom, Currier & Ives/Library of Congress
p. 51 top, Collection of Professor Rhae Lynn Barnes
p. 52 top, Library of Congress; bottom, Hutchins Center for African & African American Research/Harvard University
p. 53 top, National Park Service (FRDO 3912); bottom, Old Politicals Auctions

TWO: THE OLD NEGRO

p. 66 Broadside Collection/Library of Congress
p. 97 Documenting the American South/UNC–Chapel Hill Library

CHAINS OF BEING

p. 111 bottom left, Library of Congress; bottom right, Transcendental Graphics/Getty
pp. 114–117 Hutchins Center for African & African American Research/Harvard University
p. 118 top, AF Fotografie/Alamy; center, Special Collections/The Newberry; bottom, Library of Congress
p. 119 top, David M. Rubenstein Rare Book & Manuscript Library/Duke University; bottom, Jim Crow Museum
p. 120 Courier Company/Library of Congress
p. 122 Fred Gildersleeve/Library of Congress
p. 123 bottom, Lawrence Beitler/Bettmann/Getty

THREE: FRAMING BLACKNESS

p. 134 bottom, Courtesy CardCow
p. 135 Granger

p. 136 Library of Congress
p. 137 Division of Rare and Manuscript Collections/Cornell University Library
p. 149 Collection of Henry Louis Gates, Jr.
p. 150 U.S. Lithograph Co./Library of Congress
p. 154 Thomas Nast/Library of Congress

THE UNITED STATES OF RACE

p. 161 top, Boston Public Library; center, Warshaw Collection of Business Americana/Soap, Archives Center/National Museum of American History, Smithsonian Institution; bottom left, Wellcome Collection
p. 162 top right, Pictures From History; center left, Transcendental Graphics/Getty; bottom right, Jim Crow Museum; bottom left, authentichistory.com
p. 163 top and left, The Advertising Archives/Alamy
pp. 164–165 top and bottom, Jim Crow Museum
p. 166 top, Heidi Kellner/Z and K Antiques; bottom, AntiqueAdvertising.com
p. 167 top, San Francisco History Center/San Francisco Public Library; bottom, Jim Crow Museum
p. 168 bottom, collection of Henry Louis Gates, Jr.
p. 169 top left, Heidi Kellner/Z and K Antiques; bottom, Library of Congress
p. 170 top, Baldwin Library of Historical Children's Literature in the Department of Special Collections and Area Studies/George A. Smathers Libraries/University of Florida
p. 171 top left and bottom right, collection of Professor Rhae Lynn Barnes; top right, Library of Congress
p. 172 top and bottom, collection of Professor Rhae Lynn Barnes
p. 173 top, courtesy CardCow; bottom left, Jim Crow Museum
p. 174 top, courtesy CardCow; bottom left, Jim Crow Museum
p. 175 top, Hutchins Center for African & African American Research/Harvard University; center left, courtesy CardCow
pp. 176–177 top, Currier & Ives/Library of Congress
p. 178 bottom, collection of Professor Rhae Lynn Barnes
p. 179 top, Music Division/The New York Public Library; bottom, Harry I. Robinson and Will J. Harris/Library of Congress
p. 180 top, Library of Virginia
p. 180 bottom and p. 181, Pictorial Press Ltd/Alamy

FOUR: THE NEW NEGRO

p. 221 Schomburg Center for Research in Black Culture, Manuscripts, Archives and Rare Books Division/The New York Public Library

REFRAMING RACE

p. 236 top, Givens Collection/University of Minnesota; bottom, Department of Special Collections and University Archives/W. E. B. Du Bois Library/University of Massachusetts Amherst
pp. 237–239 Library of Congress
pp. 240–243 Hutchins Center for African & African American Research/Harvard University
pp. 244–245 and p. 246 bottom, Schomburg Center for Research in Black Culture, Manuscripts, Archives and Rare Books Division, The New York Public Library